CARNEGIE

EX LIBRIS

**Mary
Lamo-Putnam**

BECOMING LOS ANGELES

MYTH, MEMORY, AND A SENSE OF PLACE

BECOMING LOS ANGELES

MYTH, MEMORY, AND A SENSE OF PLACE

D.J. WALDIE

Thank you
for your support
of libraries!

D.J. Waldie

ANGEL CITY PRESS

Everything I've written has been for my neighbors in Lakewood
and for my goddaughters
Anne, Becky, Catherine, Emma, and (if not officially) Maureen.
I hope they'll not fault me for my part
in making the California they're inheriting.

CONTENTS

The ordinary, that strangest and most elusive of enigmas.
—JOHN BANVILLE, *Time Pieces: A Dublin Memoir*, 2018

[T]here is still a lot you'll come to learn
if you study the Insignificant in depth.
—ODYSSEUS ELYTIS, *The Axion Esti* (***Το Άξιον Εστί***), 1959

Before. Now. After.

WHILE WE WAITED—for the big one, for the long drought, for the fires every autumn, for any of the apocalyptic fates we're heir to—this happened. Before this, we made out to be the country's great exception, more magical and footloose than other American places. The implications of our history didn't matter to us (we told ourselves), nor what we'd been. Before this happened, we could be whatever we believed ourselves to be or seemed to be in our glamour, insularity, and the assumed transcendence of being an Angeleno. Until comfortable Angelenos realized that the furnace of COVID-19 burned unequally, preferentially consuming the homeless, the working poor, the asylum seeker, people of color, their old and sick, and those of my mid-century generation who had been born to extravagant hopes and racial assumptions we left unquestioned. We were amazed to see the empty streets our absence disembodied. We were appalled to see the fires of 1965 and 1992 burning again, the glitter of glass shards in the street, the clouds of tear gas, and soldiers in battle dress. We saw—if such a revelation was still needed—that Black, Latinx, Asian, and Native American lives are daily constrained by inequality and the denial of justice. The killing of George Floyd and others before him, the pandemic's racial disparities, and police violence in reply to protest have shown us an intolerable future.[1]

Now isn't yet after this. The shape of after is still formless, ironically so like the boundless Los Angeles of its dreams. Aside from a cataclysmic end to democracy (not so improbable) or a terminal natural disaster (always one heartbeat away), now is a passage of uncertain transition, like the moment when we, newly arrived, stepped into the light of Los Angeles, breathed its risky air for the first time, and nothing would be the same.

Los Angeles—famously a city of second chances—is being invented again, sometimes grossly like a gutted storefront, sometimes subtly like an extra degree of physical distance, and sometimes dramatically like a toppled monument to white privilege. At last and awfully, Angelenos have a common past, and it's of suffering. There have been deaths, some not yet mourned. There are the jobless, the homeless, the undocumented, the discarded, and the scapegoated from whom the shiny promise of Los Angeles has been stolen. But there also is a growing realization of why and how some Angelenos contrived to make many lives matter less. Temperamentally, geographically, and demographically, communal resistance to systematic racism and abusive law enforcement is different now.

A Sense of Place

It's June 2020 as I write this. The gray of the season has been wrung out of the day, as it always is, and the sun is glowing through a slit in the western horizon. The scent of dust and jasmine will come in the twilight, as it always does. The Los Angeles we thought we knew persists, mostly in memory. *Becoming Los Angeles* asks if our memories of the city's touch, the feel of it getting under the skin, can be of any use when now becomes after. Forgetting and misremembering are what too many Angelenos, with mingled self-deception and hope, are best at.

These pieces were written between 2008 and the end of 2018. They were assembled and revised in 2019. The manuscript was finished in the last weeks of December. This is a book about a place Angelenos no longer live in. Proximity to the general tragedy has displaced us. So has the unnatural stillness of the quarantined and curfewed city, perhaps for the better. An intensified awareness of the sorrows that plague Los Angeles—of the things right under our feet—is changing us. Another Los Angeles—potentially better than the twentieth-century city—is being invented that may critically question and democratically reform the city's distorted power relationships. After will require an intense effort of attention which is, the French philosopher Simone Weil wrote, "the same thing as prayer." To be authentic, she said, prayer "presupposes faith and love."[2]

Before no longer exists. Now is a season of change. After is almost on us. Pray for Los Angeles.

Dreams So Heartbreaking

A FEW DAYS AFTER MY BIRTH in 1948, on a smoggy, mid-September Wednesday, I was brought home to the tract house in Lakewood my parents had bought in 1946. To be born into that kind of house in that kind of neighborhood hadn't yet become a suburban cliché. The torrent of newcomers to post-war Los Angeles, propelled by defense spending and dreams, hadn't yet reached flood stage. I lived a boy's life there, among white, working-class kids whose accents were colored by the border south from which their parents had migrated to assemble planes at the nearby Douglas Aircraft plant. I absorbed old habits that assumed white privilege and others that were so new that my parents and their friends hardly had the language to name them. They would have to read the ads in the *Los Angeles Times* to know what they wanted.

This was not a better time, nor was Lakewood a perfect place. Still, I wish I could hand on, with no inheritance of exclusion, the charmed life that had been given me, with such thoughtless abundance, as a child of suburban Los Angeles. I grew up to write about it. I've tried again in this book to understand what it has made of me.

Everything Missing

When we talk about Los Angeles, we mostly dwell on what has been made of its original elements—its earth, air, and water—and much less on how the city shaped those of us who live here. The form of Los Angeles, critics told us, is grotesque or it's contemptible, and its incoherence ought to be considered a warning and not a model. Angelenos have heard so often that Los Angeles is counterfeit, and the unreality has rubbed off on us. When faced with the homelessness we've found in ourselves, we prefer to talk about the climate.

Except for the sunshine, the Anglo possessors of the city after 1850 found little here they recognized as the basis for a home. Mid-nineteenth-century Los Angeles was a collection of things Anglo immigrants missed—year-round rainfall, regular seasons, coal, a canopy of trees, and the fellowship of like-minded, white Americans. Los Angeles was a semi-tropical semi-desert and only semi-familiar. Everything ordinary, in immigrant memory, was subtly estranged. The landscape itself was unnerving. It didn't face the Atlantic and the European shore from which Victorian culture arrived. Instead, it was the alien Pacific and the end of optimistic American wandering westward. Glamour and dread were born from the city's terminal landscape and relentless climate—geography turned into psychology.

Boosters pasted myths over everything that they missed in Los Angeles. A desirable Los Angeles was written into existence before it was sold off. More guides, pamphlets, broadsides, and magazines ballyhooed Los Angeles between 1850 and 1900 than there were Los Angeles residents. By 1920, the Chamber of Commerce had circulated millions of copies along the East Coast and throughout the Midwest. Words were the scrim on which the hoped-for Los Angeles of the boosters was projected. It would be The Wonder City, Our Italy, The Mediterranean Shores of America, or a Southern California Paradise, never the indifferent piece of occupied Mexico that stubbornly persisted behind the scrim. To Latinx Angelenos, written out of the Anglo sales pitch, climate mattered less than work, access to housing, and the support of communal networks.

The city of Anglo desire didn't have a past, and so the boosters supplied it. It was a Spanish Fantasy Past, what historian Eric Avila calls an "ethnic masquerade,"[1] in which the fictional Zorro and Ramona dance the fandango and mission bells call lordly *Californios* to prayer while shiftless *mestizos* doze beneath their sombreros. In flattening the city's history of class antagonism and racial conflict into a Days of the Dons pageant, the fantasy past wrung difference and complexity out of the city's story. Most accounts of Los Angeles still do, generalizing the city's particulars into sprawl and spectacle or enumerating a few of its social ecologies or hovering speculatively overhead at an altitude of five thousand feet. From there, Los Angeles could be made to look like America's dead-end.

These misreadings are embedded in the narratives of Anglo encounters with the city. From its Catholic past, its racial hybridity, and its cycles of boom and bust was fashioned the sinister double that haunts twentieth-century Los Angeles—a city of terrible allure and perverse enigmas. As Eve Babitz quipped in *Slow Days, Fast Company* (1974), "In Los Angeles, it's hard to tell if you're dealing with the real true illusion or the false one."

Sacred Ordinariness

Despite the attention of interpreters as diverse as Carey McWilliams, Reyner Banham, Esther McCoy, Mike Davis, Joan Didion, and Kevin Starr, the boundaries of Los Angeles remain uncertain. Is Los Angeles a municipal corporation of some 503 square miles? An amalgam of the eighty-eight cities in Los Angeles County, along with the county's unincorporated districts? Or all of Southern California from San Clemente to Ventura? Not just *where* Los Angeles is but *when* is unresolved. "No other city," former Mayor James Hahn said in 2005, "embodies the future quite like Los Angeles."[2] Mayor Eric Garcetti in 2014 thought of Los Angeles as "the cutting edge . . . the promised land . . . the future."[3] Hahn and Garcetti were echoing nineteenth- and twentieth-century citymakers who insisted that the only authentic Los Angeles was the city of tomorrow. Having displaced the present and in flight from its yesterdays, the always future Los Angeles hangs suspended between the commonplace and a place that exists only in dreams. This ambiguity has implications for what Angelenos expect Los Angeles can do.

As one example of future mindedness leading to historical amnesia, historian Greg Hise cites the erasure of blue-collar Los Angeles:

[F]or all the talk of futurity, modernity, and progress, most Los Angeles stories ignore, obscure, or misinterpret a preeminent aspect of the modern city: manufacturing and industrialism. Recovering that history is critical for understanding economies and ecologies as well as immigration and demographics in the twentieth- and twenty-first-century metropolis.[4]

What's left out of the picture of a post-industrial economy isn't just contrary evidence that blue-collar Los Angeles persists. Also missing is the space in the imagination that's made when we get word of actual conditions from those who have lived them. In that space of the imagination, Angelenos could see themselves standing together for economic and social justice, accountable law enforcement, affordable housing, access to healthcare, and protection of workers' rights. Similarly, disputes about gentrification could pause to absorb the local knowledges that supply circumstance and nuance to situations where there has been only slogans. Planning for a denser, more connected city could begin by acknowledging the durability of prior choices that still shape the built environment. And by recognizing the informal civic structures their neighbors make and manipulate, Angelenos could see themselves as actors in their own history, armed with strategies to confront the pitiless mask of official authority. In clinging to outdated images of Los Angeles, too many Angelenos avoid encountering the city as a real place. The results are often tragic.

Denied access to the sacred ordinariness in our stories and barred from cherished locales mapped on a skin of memories, talk about Los Angeles turns to exceptionalism. Author and architect Michael Maltzan wondered if Los Angeles has "reached a point where past vocabularies of the city and of urbanism are no longer adequate, and at this moment, the very word *city* no longer applies . . . . Perhaps it is not a city—perhaps it can only be described as Los Angeles."[5] If not a city, what have we made? And if Los Angeles is beyond words, what unspeakable thing is being made of us? A *sui generis* Los Angeles, having muted our ability to imagine it, can be described only in terms of wonder or dismay. We ought to heed other stories of Los Angeles—stories to make the indecipherable city a little harder to see.

Los Angeles, whose geographic, psychological, and perceptual limits have been reached, is at an inflection point. Tomorrow has arrived for a city that saw its true self in the future, but tomorrow has come with unexpected company: the working poor, discarded homeless Angelenos, a shrinking middle class, and the callous hyper-rich. Conditions—environmental, economic, and demographic—that Angelenos thought were fixed are rapidly transforming. How are

we to be Angelenos when Los Angeles isn't exactly "Los Angeles" anymore—
not the sum of its clichés, without the option to escape to another suburban
utopia and now poised to be reconfigured by climate change, economic dislocation, popular resistance to injustice, and the passing of an Anglo hegemony?

Building Intimacy

To paraphrase urbanist Benjamin Schneider, Los Angeles may be a dream
world to the rest of America—an extravagance of "pools and palm trees, of
music videos and reality TV, the garages where nerds create the future, the
freeways and subdivisions coursing with Tarantino's kinks and Didion's neu-
roses"[6]—but to its residents, Los Angeles is simply the place where they are,
as beautiful as it is infuriating. Historian Eric Monkkonen insisted that Los
Angeles is permeated with localism, with patterns of living, working, and re-
membering characteristic of beloved places.[7] These enfold the specifics of
landmarks, memorials, and lore and have the capacity to be what geographer
Doreen Massey calls a locality: a site experienced within "networks of social
relations and understandings."[8] Localities, argues sociologist Kathleen Stewart, draw their intensity from the resonances that linger in familiar scenes,
commonplace relationships, and ordinary manifestations, steadily picking up
texture and inference over time, until everything at hand becomes "tentative,
charged, overwhelming, and alive." These qualities emerge where "sensations,
expectations, daydreams, encounters, and habits of relating . . . catch people up
in something that feels like something."[9]

Despite the expanse of Los Angeles and the distracting effect of freeway
travel, wayfinding is possible when coordinated by sites where something that
felt like something is remembered. But as author Lynell George cautions, our
journey through this city's contested landscape needs the intervention of indigenous guides and the traveler's wary trust in them, along with a measure of
humility, deference to local customs, a tolerance for puzzlement, and a suspension of assumptions.

Even the myths of Los Angeles should be part of our traveling kit. (Erase
the myths of Los Angeles in service to the myth of objectivity and our reality
is made less real.[10]) We're lost in the city—and the city is lost to us—if we prefer
a generic Los Angeles that (at best) is an archipelago of lifestyle islands connected by the nowhere of gridlocked freeways. That isn't the Los Angeles of

our dreams, not because the presence of other Angelenos has stalled the fluid motion that was this city's trade-off for a life in a regime of speed, but because, lately, dreams of Los Angeles have become so heartbreaking.

Inhabiting Los Angeles

This book is a remapping of Los Angeles to know where I am, but it's a peculiar sort of cartography, not an abstract model but a cloud of associations and projections, apprehensions and guesses, minor knowledges and family legends, as well as lived places both actual and virtual, some unchanging over my lifetime, others evanescent or only provisionally fixed. For author and critic David Ulin, "the very act of living in L.A. requires an ongoing process of reconceptualization, of rethinking not just the place but also our relationship to it, our sense of what it means."[11] Ulin rethinks on his feet, spanning Los Angeles step by step until the city is felt as a presence. In the immediate and tangible materials of the local, Los Angeles discloses itself, renders traces of its past in aspects of the present, and constructs inheritable traditions. Pedestrian Angelenos—slowed down amid the overlooked and the lowly, "placing memories alongside the lived experiences of being"[12]—are able to interrogate the local "in an effort to drag things into view"[13] and furnish the city with what's needed to make it inhabitable. Author and environmentalist Barry Lopez, writing about his boyhood home in the San Fernando Valley, took even more from his localism. He found "the ground that propels me past the great temptation of our time, to put one's faith in despair."[14] The key, he thought, "is to become vulnerable to a place. If you open yourself up, you can build intimacy. Out of such intimacy may come a sense of belonging, a sense of not being isolated in the universe."[15] With intimacy as the mediator between self and city, we are grounded on the street grid of Los Angeles, implicated in its history, and present in the localities where our individual and communal memories are sheltered. Those memories can be harrowing; they should belong to all of us.

David Ulin has taken note of places where history, memory, and the imagination have recently pooled in Los Angeles. He cites the Los Angeles River and Chris Burden's sculptural assemblage *Urban Light* (202 vintage Los Angeles street lamps) as places that are recentering Los Angeles. Places like these touch us and in that contact reveal themselves as the outcome of our lives

Becoming Los Angeles

together and not merely as a backdrop. Fear of contaminating encounters defeated Anglo migrants in the past and still defeats those for whom Los Angeles perpetually shimmers under its too bright sun in uncanny otherness. A critical sense of place is the only antidote, as well as a mode of resistance and a means to repatriate our history.

People of color will bring to our sense of place their grief for communities erased, lives excluded, and narratives dismissed. Their demand for justice will be part of it. Writer and critic Ismail Muhammad grew up in middle-class, African American Windsor Hills, "sandwiched between Inglewood to the south, Culver City to the west, and the Crenshaw district to the north."[16] Windsor Hills is above South Central but, by its blackness, is deemed part of it, since South Central is "a catchall term for anywhere black bodies [are] found." Windsor Hills exists as a beloved place of Black lives because, Muhammad writes, white people did not want it. Native American, Asian, and Latinx Angelenos have comparable knowledges to bring to our sense of place. Sorrow is always a part of it, as is resistance, but so are the small triumphs of the local and the everyday.

Deeply flawed and insistently human, tragic and joyful, burdened and liberated by its self-invention, Los Angeles is becoming us, and we who are Angelenos are becoming Los Angeles. In our becoming is the potential for the intimacy that moved architect and urban philosopher Juhani Pallasmaa to declare, "I experience myself in the city, and the city exists through my embodied experience. The city and my body supplement and define each other. I dwell in the city, and the city dwells in me."[17] To inhabit and be inhabited allows me to experience Los Angeles in relation to who I am, the reciprocal touch of the city and its dweller reinforcing an awakened sympathy.

— D.J. WALDIE
June 11, 2020

Fandangos of the Mythmakers

MYTHIC LOS ANGELES seems as primal as the sunshine, but myth has a past. The exceptionalism of Los Angeles was woven by contending mythmakers (*Mythmakers Fandango*), by crooks and rock stars (*Laurel Canyon Suite*), and by our hunger for a usable history (*A Table and Historical Uncertainty*). The most durable of the myths bound the landscape of Los Angeles to an invented Anglo identity (*Climates of Opinion*). The mythmakers made something irresistible from the elemental qualities of Los Angeles and sold their desire to the world (*Los Angeles Sells Itself*).

Liberating for some (*Architecture of Dreams*), myths distorted who we had been (*Eugene Plummer: The Last Californio*) and fed us fake hopes (*The Hoard of the Lizard Men*) and birthed nightmares rather than dreams (*Shelter. Fallout.*).

A Table and Historical Uncertainty

It's a perfectly ordinary table, big enough for two to sit across from each other. The grain in the wood shows through the worn finish in places. The panels of the top are uneven but not enough to make the table unusable. It's a piece of homely furniture that could have been found in any kitchen anywhere in Los Angeles until the middle of the twentieth century. A table like it might be in someone's garage today—a place to set a clothes hamper or lay garden tools. Except this table isn't in a garage. It's in the Natural History Museum of Los Angeles County. It stands, elevated and highlighted in a tall, glass box, as a witness to history (although both the witness and the history are ambiguous). The museum's *Becoming Los Angeles* exhibition regards the table as so significant that it's one of the "touchdown" points visually linked to other focal point objects by a swooping ribbon of bright metal overhead that symbolizes the flow of time.

If we imagine time that way, as a flow that condenses in a particular place to make history, then a single hour gave this table significance. History is supposed to have touched down on its well-used top on the morning of January13, 1847, while the table stood on the porch of an adobe house in a pasture called Campo de Cahuenga (or Cauenga) about twelve miles northwest of the Los Angeles plaza. The United States and Mexico (of which California was then a fractious part) had been at war since April 1846. Los Angeles, the sometime capital of Mexico's Department of California, had been occupied by American forces in August and then retaken by the city's militia in September. Beginning in December 1846, Angeleno and Sandieguino cavalry attempted to stop the American forces dispatched to retake the city. The Californians and the Americans fought three small but occasionally bloody engagements: the Battle of San Pasqual (December 6–7), the Battle of Rio San Gabriel (January 8) and the Battle of La Mesa (January 9). The Battle of San Pasqual was dominated by the Californians. The engagements at Rio San Gabriel and La Mesa were skirmishes the Americans dominated, although the Californians had shown that they could fight. But they couldn't win. On January 10, American troops re-occupied Los Angeles without resistance.

The Table

The Mexican War, the county museum says, ended in California on this tabletop. Given the realities of Southern California in the 1840s, the well-made table would probably have been the best available in a house that, according to many accounts, belonged to Tomás Féliz. The table was positioned (ceremoniously? anxiously? thoughtlessly?) on the long porch in front of the house in anticipation of a meeting between the commanders of the approaching American forces and the embattled Californian militia. (In a tinted photo postcard sold fifty years later, a shingled roof shades the porch. The Los Angeles Public Library identifies the house in the photograph as the location of the meeting.[1])

January 13, 1847, was a Wednesday. The day was said to be overcast and rainy. The houses of colonial California, with few windows, were notoriously dark. The porch would have been the best location for any business that required, for example, writing out a formal document.

The table on the porch is in the foreground of the events on that Wednesday morning. In Hugo Ballin's 1931 mural (still mounted in the lobby of the Guarantee Trust Building at 5th and Hill streets in Los Angeles), General Andrés Pico, commanding the Mexican forces in California and de facto head of government, is shown seated at the table. Standing behind him are members of his staff. Facing Pico, who is shown in Californio costume, stands Major John C. Frémont. Frémont wears a U.S. Army uniform. Frémont wasn't the most senior American officer in California in 1847. General Stephen Watts Kearny and Commodore Robert Stockton of the Navy jointly commanded the American forces. But Frémont was the most impetuous. In Ballin's mural, Frémont (helpfully? insistently? arrogantly?) is pointing out something on the sheet of paper on the table. The paper Pico is about to sign is the capitulation of the Mexican forces in California.

Remembering

Days before he met with Frémont, Pico was prepared to end hostilities and hand over California to the invading Americans. He expected that treating with Frémont—not Kearny or Stockton—could serve both his and Frémont's interests. Sitting across from each other (if they did sit together), Frémont and Pico, for different but complementary reasons, wanted the war in California to end on that Wednesday morning. Pico wanted peace on terms that weren't punitive. (He expected to be imprisoned, perhaps shot, if captured by Stockton or Kearny.) Frémont wanted publicity. (He intended to have a political career and perhaps be president one day.) Frémont's decision to sit down (or not) with Pico, between them a generously worded surrender agreement waiting to be signed, meant that Frémont should be remembered as the man who ended the war in California and gave America a Pacific gateway. (Kearny, as Frémont's superior, bitterly complained later that he had led the Americans to victory, not Frémont.)

Other memories of January 1847 are equally contentious. In illustrations of the scene around the small, wooden table (that most sources say belonged to Tomás Féliz), Frémont is always in uniform. Sometimes Pico is in uniform, sometimes not. The house itself, substantial in Ballin's mural, is cruder, even rundown, in some illustrations. It's never raining in any of them. Perhaps it wasn't raining. Edwin Bryant, a lieutenant in Frémont's battalion, didn't mention rain in his account of the meeting between Pico and Frémont, published a year later. Bryant wrote that it rained heavily the day after when Frémont and his troops entered Los Angeles. Maybe the two days have been conflated.

It isn't only the rain that appears and disappears from the morning of January 13. The house where Pico and Frémont met probably didn't belong to Tomás Féliz, who had died in 1830. (And Féliz, whose table this may or may not have been, is sometimes Félix or Felez in published accounts, or not mentioned at all.) According to archival research done in 2000, the house in 1847 was the property of Eulogio de Célis, who had purchased the Campo de Cahuenga and the surrounding Rancho Ex-Mission San Fernando from Pío Pico, Andrés Pico's older brother, less than a year before the meeting on the porch.

According to some accounts (but neither Bryant's nor Frémont's), Andrés Pico, who never grew proficient in English, directed Captain José Antonio Carrillo to write out, in both Spanish and English, the terms for the cessation of hostilities. In the illustrations, you never see the bilingual Carrillo, acting as a peace commissioner for Mexico and at work on the agreement.

Frémont, needing something grander than the surrender of a provincial militia, called the agreement a treaty in his report to Kearny and Stockton. Historians call it the Capitulation of Cahuenga. Perhaps in the illustrations, "capitulation" is rendered by the image of Pico dressed in the everyday clothes of a Californio and "treaty" when Pico is dressed in the uniform of a Mexican general. (Bryant noted that both the officers and men of Frémont's "small army" wore buckskins "smeared with mud and dust" on their way from the Campo de Cahuenga the following day, although Frémont might have dressed more formally for the Wednesday-morning meeting.)[2]

Pico signed the treaty/capitulation as militia commander and "head of all the national forces in California." Pio Pico, the governor of California, had left for Mexico the previous August to raise support for the province's defense. And José María Flores, the nominal commander of the "national forces," had turned them over to Andrés Pico on January 11 before Flores fled California for Sonora. Andrés Pico, both politically and militarily, had been left with the necessity of sitting at a small, wooden table on the porch of an empty house to surrender California to a junior officer of the US Army.

It's unlikely that Eulogio de Célis or Pio Pico (or Andrés Pico, who had leased the rancho for a time) ever lived there. The house with the table was probably built for the Mission San Fernando Rey de España around 1811. But it might have been built in either 1783 or 1795 for Mariano de la Luz Verdugo, who had been granted grazing rights to the Campo de Cahuenga before the property, at the insistence of the mission fathers, was transferred to the mission.

The house has been described as abandoned on that January Wednesday. Bryant wrote that it was deserted, which isn't exactly the same thing, particularly when armies are expected. The presence of one small table can't resolve the ambiguity. It seems unlikely, though, that a well-made table, like the one in the museum exhibition, with its planed top, turned legs and drawer (which has gone missing), would have been left behind in an abandoned house. Perhaps Bryant mistook the typically sparse arrangements of a rancho household as evidence that the house had been discarded. Perhaps the abandoned/deserted/unoccupied house had been left untenanted when Los Angeles was first captured by the Americans in August 1846. Deserted out of fear or abandoned by an indifferent owner or temporarily unoccupied, the house may have held a table and chairs that could have been brought out beneath the overhanging porch roof that may not have been dripping rain.

The house was demolished around 1900, but much of its foundation and flooring was excavated between 1995 and 1998 during the construction of the Red Line subway. An archeological survey found both European and Native American artifacts at the site suggestive of daily life in the first half of the nineteenth century. Reburied to preserve them, the ruins of the house were overlaid by replica ruins with interpretive signage.

Another ambiguity is submerged in the often-repeated story of the rainy/not so rainy Wednesday on the porch of the house where General Andrés Pico in uniform/in nondescript attire did or didn't sit together with Lieutenant Colonel John C. Frémont (presumably in uniform) to read and sign, along with members of his military staff and Frémont's, the formal agreement that ended the war in California and made California suddenly American. The ambiguity includes a half-remembered name mentioned in Frémont's memoirs (published in 1887). It may have been Bernarda or, because Frémont isn't clear, perhaps it was Maria Bernarda. The rest of the name was supplied by a telegram to Frémont from José de Jésus Pico, a cousin of Pio and Andrés Pico. The name Frémont couldn't fully recall, the name José de Jésus Pico provided, was Doña Maria Bernarda Ruiz de Rodriguez.

José de Jésus Pico had a good reason to remember Bernarda Ruiz's name (apart from her status as a respected widow and businesswomen whose mail service from Santa Barbara to Mexico, conducted by her four sons, José de Jésus Pico may have used). Pico had been arrested in San Luis Obispo on December 14, summarily tried by Frémont two days later, and convicted of violating a parole that required him not to rejoin the Californian forces opposing the Americans. Sentenced to be shot—the soldiers were already in formation to carry out Frémont's order—José de Jésus Pico pleaded for clemency, aided, Frémont later wrote, by the tears of his wife and his children. Apparently moved, Frémont suspended the execution. Frémont's compassion went only so far, however. An indigenous Californian (one account calls him Pico's servant), taken prisoner on December 13 and accused of spying, was summarily executed in front of the families living in a Native village not far from Paso Robles.

Set free, José de Jésus Pico attached himself to Frémont's staff and followed him south to Santa Barbara, out of gratitude, Frémont believed. But perhaps, as an ardent Californian who had violated his parole and twice risked his life in defense of his home, Pico intended to influence what would happen next. He might be able to warn his cousin Andrés if Frémont intended to be as belligerent as the Californians feared.

José de Jésus Pico brought Bernarda Ruiz to meet with Frémont while he rested his troops at Santa Barbara in the week after Christmas. Frémont's memoir glosses over the details of their meeting, only complimenting Ruiz on her "sound reasoning" in wanting the fighting in California to end and encouraging her to be an advocate of peace among the Californians she knew.[3] Some accounts have her appeals to Frémont motivated by concern for her four sons, then among the Californians opposing the Americans. Some have Ruiz eager to retrieve horses that Frémont had commandeered from her corrals. (Frémont apparently sent them back.) Jessie Frémont, who described the meeting in a memoir written years later, suggests that Ruiz also offered to get word of Frémont's conciliatory attitude to Andrés Pico, but Jesse Frémont provides no details, and her husband's memoir makes no further mention of Ruiz after their meeting in Santa Barbara.

Some later accounts credit Ruiz with brokering the treaty/capitulation that Andrés Pico and Frémont signed on January 13. Some accounts have her delivering a well-rehearsed outline of peace terms to Frémont during a two-hour conference in Santa Barbara. (Frémont doesn't record the time in his memoir.) A few accounts (plausible?) have Ruiz riding with José de Jésus Pico and Frémont to the Campo de Cahuenga to witness the signing of a document she had seemingly dictated to Frémont, the terms of which she had already secretly communicated to Andrés Pico.

On Tuesday morning, January 12, Frémont met with Francisco Rico and Francisco de la Guerra, representatives of Andrés Pico. The meeting continued into the afternoon. Neither Bernarda Ruiz nor José Antonio Carrillo is present in Frémont's and Bryant's accounts of the preliminary meeting. When Rico and de la Guerra left Frémont's camp, the final terms weren't yet concluded, according to Bryant. Other accounts have the entire document being written out that evening. Perhaps some terms were still to be decided when Frémont rode from his camp the following morning to meet with Andrés Pico at the house in the Campo de Cahuenga. But were there any negotiations at all, apart from technical details, the agreement having been concluded in principle three weeks before in Santa Barbara and accepted by Andrés Pico, his agreement reaching Frémont through the network of related Californians who seem, in all these accounts, to be always at hand? Was the agreement already written out in English, ready for Carrillo's translation as he sat at the table under the sloping roof of a house that some say belonged to the long-dead Tomás Féliz, some to his widow, others to Eulogio de Célis, and some say was abandoned?

Frémont, perhaps to magnify his own role, said that he arrived at the house on the morning of January 13 alone (except for the vigilant, helpful José de Jésus Pico.) No place at the table is assigned to Bernarda Ruiz in Frémont's memoir (even her full name was missing until José de Jésus Pico supplied it almost forty years later). In illustrations of the events on the porch, she's never depicted (although a mural of the scene painted in 1951 for the Campo de Cahuenga Memorial Association shows a crowd of onlookers that includes the figure of a woman). Bernarda Ruiz seems to be everywhere and then nowhere.

What if the operatic qualities of these events—armies marching, noble women pleading, lonely rides to fateful meetings in the rain, solemn officers standing around in colorful uniforms—were something else, something designed to be a usable history and not what the meeting on the porch had been?

At some point on the morning of January 13, 1847, American and Californian signatories (who also seem to appear out of nowhere) stepped up to the table to make the treaty/capitulation official. The American signers were P.B. Reading, major; William H. Russell, ordnance officer; and Louis McLane Jr., commanding officer of the Artillery from Frémont's California Battalion. The Californian signers were José Antonio Carrillo, *commandante de escuadrón*, and Agustin Olvera, *diputado* (deputy of the Californian Assembly). Both Frémont and Andrés Pico signed their approvals below the signatures of the peace commissioners.

Plausible History

Like much of history, the accounts of the meeting between Pico and Frémont are either unreliable or romanticized. They only seem authentic because the account includes details like the rain or Carrillo writing out the agreement. (The copy that Frémont forwarded to Stockton that night, according to one scholarly analysis, bears the handwriting of Theodore Talbot, an artillery lieutenant in Frémont's brigade. Talbot, in his letters home, doesn't place himself around the increasingly crowded table at the Campo de Cahuenga that Frémont said he went to alone, except for José de Jésus Pico, who seems to have gone from enemy combatant to Frémont's retainer.)

The figures around the table are blurry. Who they are shifts from account to account, illustration to illustration. Fresh memories of January 13, 1847, (Bryant and Talbot's) and memories nearly forty years old (Frémont's and a few others) align only partially with the details in secondary narratives, which begin mythologizing these events as soon as the Mexican War ends. Something happened that morning at the Campo de Cahuenga. A war (widely considered unjust then and now) ended, in California at least, on honorable terms, something worth holding on to even though we can't assign a definite role to every person who may have caused history to touch down at a deserted/unoccupied/abandoned house that also happened to hold a well-made wooden table at which a document essential to the history of California and the West could be negotiated (perhaps), written out (by someone), and signed.

And although the table in the case at the museum might be one of the few things that bear witness to the few facts we can accept, we can't be sure that this table—the one in the Natural History Museum—is the witness to history we want it to be. The museum believes that its table (a loan from the Charles J. Prudhomme collection in the museum's Seaver Center for Western History Research) was made in 1844 by Charles Burroughs and used for the signing of the Capitulation of Cahuenga on January 13, 1847, at the home of María Jesús Lopez de Féliz, the widow of Tomás Féliz (and married since 1835, another source says, to Jordan Pacheco). John M. Foster (archeologist), Leonard Pitt (historian), and Edna E. Kimbro (architectural conservator and historian), who researched the Campo de Cahuenga site for the Red Line subway, discounted the table's connections to the treaty/capitulation. They wrote:

> In 1916 . . . Zaragosa Lopez de Briton presented to the Los Angeles County Museum of Natural History a table that she asserted was made in 1844 by Carlos Barros (also known as Charles Burroughs) and used for the signing of the treaty. There is no corroborating proof of this and since the rancho was said to be in deserted condition, it seems implausible, especially since the same claim has been made for another table in the possession of the Campo de Cahuenga Historical Memorial Association.[4]

Aftermath

After signing the agreement, Pico turned over to Frémont the two cannons the Californians had captured from Kearny at the Battle of San Pasqual (Bryant said only one was returned). In some later accounts, when Frémont and his troops entered Los Angeles the following day, the recently demobilized Californians threw a grand ball at the home of Alexander Bell that Frémont, Kearny, and Stockton attended as honored guests (although the three men were constantly at odds, a conflict that would lead to Frémont's conviction for insubordination at his court-martial in 1848). The Californians and the American officers may have danced that night with the wives of the Californians they had lately been fighting, but Bryant, writing a year after the signing of the treaty/capitulation, found Los Angeles deserted on January 14. None of the pretty Angeleno girls he'd been told were there could be found.

Aging and somewhat forlorn, Frémont returned to the Campo de Cahuenga in 1877 to identify the site of his meeting with Andrés Pico. He found the house in ruins, despite a much later postcard photograph that shows it standing with roses blooming at the edge of the porch.

Perhaps history isn't a ribbon unrolling overhead that touches down on a tabletop, turning a silent, overlooked thing into a relic of time. Perhaps history is only the stories we want to hear.

Mythmakers' Fandango

Helen Hunt Jackson—misunderstood novelist and nearly forgotten activist—sojourned in Los Angeles between December 1881 and the end of January 1882 on assignment for *The Century Magazine* to write about Southern California. Los Angeles had only recently been connected, via San Francisco, to the transcontinental rail system, and interest in Southern California was growing. Jackson arrived with a larger purpose than tourism. She was already known for writing *A Century of Dishonor* (1881), her account of the crimes committed in the name of Manifest Destiny against Native Americans in the Midwest and East. Jackson had heard the Californian version of that bitter story and wanted it to reach a national audience.

Jackson wrote the magazine articles and submitted a report on the condition of the Mission Indians to the Bureau of Indian Affairs. Then she began a novel with, she hoped, the power of *Uncle Tom's Cabin* to stir a nation's conscience. But the seductive power of a mythic past made her plan a failure and Helen Hunt Jackson famous as the author of *Ramona*.

Substitutions

In the fall of 1881, following what would become a well-worn tourist route from Santa Barbara to San Diego, Jackson researched four pieces for *The Century Magazine*. The first was an uncritical account of the life of mission founder Fray Junípero Serra (published in May 1883), followed by Jackson's bleak observations on the Mission Indians (August) and a boosterish account of the riches of Southern California's agriculture and industry (October). The series ended with a lyrical and intimate evocation of Los Angeles (November). Jackson described Los Angeles as an uncanny place suspended between a languid Spanish past and the American present.

Even as Jackson researched Serra's life in Santa Barbara and visited Native villages around Temecula, she was arranging to be appointed a special agent of the Bureau of Indian Affairs with authority to investigate the condition of Southern California's indigenous communities. Since Jackson didn't know much Spanish, her appointment from Commissioner of Indian Affairs Hiram Price in July 1882 included the services of real estate developer Abbot

Kinney as translator and guide. (Jackson had recruited Kinney, whose interest in Native American ethnography she knew from previous visits to Los Angeles.) Jackson and Kinney visited *rancherias* (Native villages) in San Diego County and in the desert valleys around Riverside and San Bernardino. Conditions there appalled them.

Jackson's time in Southern California united three aspects of her professional life—as a journalist, social critic, and novelist. Her travel pieces enlarge on the booster narrative already marketing Southern California. Her outrage at the desperate condition of Native communities fires the "Report on the Condition and Needs of the Mission Indians" that Jackson and Kinney submitted to the Bureau of Indian Affairs in 1883. Her experiences in Los Angeles color the stories of the Native and *mestizo* (mixed-race) characters in *Ramona*, a melodramatic novel of Southern California under American domination that Jackson completed in early 1884.[5] Jackson wrote her travel articles to introduce the exoticism of Southern California to genteel, middle-class America. She hoped her essay on the Mission Indians and her report to the Bureau of Indian Affairs would bring justice to indigenous communities. She wrote *Ramona* to change the hearts of her readers. But instead of inciting protest, *Ramona* enthralled Anglo readers, furnishing a theater of sentiment in which they learned to identify a place they hardly knew with a newly-made sensibility.

The affective landscape of Jackson's Southern California—elegiac and contemplative—was under construction before *Ramona*, but to it, Jackson now added indigenous, mestizo and *Californio*[6] (native Californian) characters whose stories she told with piercing sweetness. Jackson didn't create the image of an idyllic land of ease and hospitality under a vaguely Spanish sun, but Jackson's novel, as the instigator of nearly a century of false Ramona memories, expanded Anglos' daydreams of a substitute Southern California that, although already gone, was still present in the qualities of its light, atmosphere, landscapes, and rhythms of daily life. The unease that still confounds an Angeleno sense of place is the paradoxical capacity to possess a paradise and regret that it lies just out of reach.

As a sentimental novel about doomed love, *Ramona* was wildly successful. As social criticism, it was a failure. Jackson's goal was igniting support among progressive Christians for California's Native communities, but her narrative strategy sabotaged her intention. Readers sighed over the sad fates of Ramona and her murdered husband Alessandro, but they longed to be in the romantic landscapes Jackson described so vividly and from which Jackson's characters emerged as if they had been formed from the shaded valleys and golden hills she placed them in.

Jackson died in mid-1885, fearing that *Ramona* hadn't achieved the effect she sought. The novel had failed to be another *Uncle Tom's Cabin* (1852), Chelsea Leah Pearson argues in "'Call me a Californio,'"[7] because Jackson was unable to manage the substitutions underway in the Americanization of Southern California. The substitutions included fixed categories of ethnic and racial identity in place of the more fluid identities possible in pre-American California. Anglo readers of *Ramona* regrouped Jackson's non-Anglo characters—indigenous, mestizo, and Californio—into a single historical category. Whatever their race or ethnicity, they were the former Californians, soon to be superseded by a dynamic Anglo civilization, a secessionist view that Jackson shared. She regretted that a simpler way of life had fallen before a relentless Gilded Age of capital and speed, but the substitution was inevitable.

The Coronels

Although Jackson had been an occasional tourist in Southern California before 1881, her travel pieces needed additional sources for the local color that readers expected. To encounter the historic California, Bishop Francisco Mora y Borrell, head of the Diocese of Monterey-Los Angeles, urged Jackson to visit the Los Angeles home of Antonio Coronel and his wife. What Jackson found there was far more than she expected:

> In the western suburbs of Los Angeles is a low adobe house, built after the ancient style, on three sides of a square, surrounded by orchards, vineyards, and orange groves, and looking out on an old-fashioned garden, in which southernwood, rue, lavender, mint, marigolds, and gillyflowers hold their own bravely, growing in straight and angular beds among the newer splendors of verbenas, roses, carnations, and geraniums. On two sides of the house runs a broad porch, where stand rows of geraniums and chrysanthemums growing in odd earthen pots. Here may often be seen a beautiful young Mexican woman, flitting about among the plants, or sporting with a superb Saint Bernard dog. Her clear olive skin, soft brown eyes, delicate sensitive nostrils, and

broad smiling mouth, are all of the Spanish madonna type; and when her low brow is bound, as is often her wont, by turban folds of soft brown or green gauze, her face becomes a picture indeed. She is the young wife of a gray-headed Mexican señor, of whom—by his own most gracious permission—I shall speak by his familiar name, Don Antonio. Whoever has the fortune to pass as a friend across the threshold of this house finds himself transported, as by a miracle, into the life of a half-century ago.[8]

"I went for but a few moments call," Jackson marveled, "I stayed three hours and left carrying with me bewildering treasures of pictures of the olden time." She returned in the following days, sitting with the Coronels in the shade of their veranda, marveling at the winter profusion of flowers and listening to stories of *las días pasados*, of days long ago.

Antonio F. Coronel was a vigorous sixty-five when Jackson met him and his much younger wife, Mariana. But Mariana, who so captivated Jackson as a "Spanish madonna type," wasn't Spanish or exclusively Mexican. Her Latinx heritage was mestizo-ized in a characteristically borderlands way. Mariana had been born in San Antonio, Texas, in 1851, the eldest daughter of Nels (or Nelson) Williamson of Augusta, Maine, and Gertrudes Romana, born, some sources say, in Mexico. In 1859, the Williamsons came to Los Angeles, where Mariana began her education in the city's newly formed school system. She married Antonio Coronel in 1873, when she was twenty-two. Mariana arrived too late to have experienced the pre-American Los Angeles in which Jackson situated the Coronel adobe, although when costumed as a *doña* of an indeterminate Hispano-Mexicano past, Mariana was Jackson's model of pre-conquest Californio womanhood, just as Mariana's husband was Jackson's icon of the Californio way of life that Americanization had supplanted.

Antonio Coronel was born in Mexico City in 1817, studied to be a physician, and immigrated with his family to Los Angeles in the early 1830s. He witnessed the end of the mission system and the further immiseration of the Native communities that were the source of exploited labor. Coronel participated in the Californio defense of the city during the Mexican War of 1846 to 1848. He watched the ruin of Californio landowners, bankrupted by American moneylenders and displaced by sharp real estate operators in the collapse of the cattle economy after the killing drought of 1862 to 1865. Coronel also was a key figure in the political transition from Mexican to American Los Angeles. He was the first Los Angeles County Tax Assessor in 1850, mayor of Los Angeles in 1853, a city councilman (serving nine terms between 1854 and 1867), a County Supervisor in 1863, and California State Treasurer from 1867 to 1871. He was an appointed member of city and county advisory committees in the 1870s and a founder of the Historical Society of Southern California in 1883. Courtly, amusing, and gracious—the best waltzer in Los Angeles, Jackson wrote (although she doesn't say how she knew)—Coronel had years of experience harmonizing the American and Californio dualisms of mid-nineteenth century Los Angeles. Coronel persisted in this challenging program through the 1860s, a time when racially motivated violence by Anglo vigilantes against Latinx and indigenous communities peaked.

But when Jackson arrived, with Bishop Mora's letter of introduction, to call on Coronel in late 1881, it wasn't the seasoned politician she met. It was quaint, antique Don Antonio who, in the midst of his reminiscences, "would take up his guitar, and in a voice still sympathetic and full of melody, sing an old Spanish love-song, brought to his mind by . . . living over the events of his youth." Coronel, so full of stories, "speaks little English," Jackson explained to her readers. "It is an entrancing sight to watch his dark weather-beaten face, full of lightning changes as he pours out torrents of his nervous, eloquent Spanish speech." Fortunately, Doña Mariana "knows just enough of the [English] language to make her use of it delicious, as she translates for her husband." And yet Coronel corrects his wife's choice of English expressions, "watching his wife intently, hearkening to each word she uses, sometimes interrupting her urgently with, 'No, no; that is not it'—for he well understands the tongue he cannot or will not use for himself."[9]

"Cannot use" is a possibility (an obituary in 1894 will mention his limited English). "Will not use" might have been a gesture of protest, except for the elaborateness of the Coronels' linguistic performance,[10] apparently designed to convince Jackson of the authenticity of Don Antonio's sentiments and the accuracy of his memories of an arcadian Los Angeles before the Americans came. The Coronels' performance and their curio-laden home were arranged to project a way of life and to mask Coronel's biography as a civic leader, a businessman, and a significant figure in the state's Democratic Party through the 1870s.

"Full of sentiment, of an intense and poetic nature, [Coronel] looks back to the lost empire of his race and people on the California shore with a sorrow far too proud for any antagonisms or complaints,"[11] Jackson wrote. In part because of Coronel, Californios would now be remembered as too noble to protest their displacement and too humble to nurse any grudges, although many of them had in fact protested and some still remained bitter. In yet another substitution, Californios wouldn't be remembered as agents in their own history or as fighters who had driven occupying American troops from Los Angeles during the Mexican War or as political allies of secessionist southerners in Los Angeles during the Civil War. They would instead be remembered for the unthreatening sensibility the Coronels so deftly presented.

Jackson's sketch of her stay in Los Angeles for *The Century Magazine* presents a wistful tableau animated by the presence of the Coronels, who sing the old songs and dance the old steps of the fandango at the margin between the American present and a supposed Californio past. Jackson's charming hosts performed a superbly crafted evocation of an idealized way of life that Jackson eagerly embraced. When it reappears in Hunt's *Ramona* as the setting for the novel's tragedies, it aided in the elaboration of a mythology whose power Jackson and the Coronels didn't fully realize. Entranced by the Coronels' performance, Jackson made the landscape of Southern California the stage on which sentiments were conjured to give Anglo migrants a sense of place that wasn't their own. Tourists and newcomers slipped into attitudes about the interplay between place and character that Jackson borrowed from the Coronels' performance.

Coronel and his wife—sophisticated negotiators of a borderland—sang and danced, brought out a jumble of relics of "olden times" for Jackson's inspection, and steeped her in the rhythms of the pre-American Los Angeles they chose to represent. And if Californios like the Coronels were now a remnant and their way of life only a memory, then the landscape that had made them remained to remember them. By merging place and identity in *Ramona*, Jackson helped fabricate a fantasy locale that her readers wanted to believe they could visit and even possess. What had begun as the setting for Jackson's novel of protest became its substitute narrative.

Affective Landscapes

Antonio Coronel's evocation of past times, he hoped, might slow the disappearance of the Californio identity that Jackson embedded in the landscape. Like many other Californios, Coronel and his wife wanted to protect their social status and the distinctiveness of their Californio identity at a time when newly arrived Anglos, many from the South and Midwest, saw the Coronels and other Californios merely as Mexicans and therefore a racial threat.

To further his cultural defense project, Coronel urged Jackson to journey through a wider affective landscape—the Del Valles' Rancho Camulos, the Bandini-Couts's Rancho Guajome—where Jackson would see that Californio identity lingered in the places from which it had originally come. Jackson also turned to Antonio and Mariana Coronel for additional details of Californio society, eventually writing to them in November 1883 that she had begun a novel about Anglo treatment of indigenous Californians "in a way to move people's hearts," with "enough of Mexicans and Americans to give it variety." Would the Coronels please send any "romantic incidents, either Mexican or Indian that might work well into a story of Southern California life. I wish I had had this plan in my mind last year when I was in Los Angeles. I would have taken notes of many interesting things you told me."[12]

The Coronels were happy to oblige. And as Jackson wrote *Ramona*, quickly turning out whole chapters based on their remembered "romantic incidents," the Coronels' fandango of Californio memories began to displace the urgency of Jackson's political agenda. Local color of the sort she had put in her magazine pieces took on coherency and appeal as a substitute. The Californio characters in *Ramona* are unbound by history, simultaneously representative of a heroic age of Spanish conquistadors, the mission era of the padres and the pastoral days of the great ranchos. The conflation of these periods into an arcadian timelessness served Jackson's novelistic ends, as contrast to the crass meanness that characterized American California, but it also answered Jackson's need to validate the integrity of Californio culture as an useful alternative to the psychological fractures of post-Civil-War America. Like many of her contemporaries, Jackson was weary of the conflicts—social and economic—shaping a society that delivered so much prosperity while taking away so much of value. The myth of the Californios was Jackson's antidote to the distempers of the age.

Jackson was generous (in print and in her correspondence) in acknowledging the debt she owed the Coronels, although she gives few details of their contributions. It's as if the sentiments Jackson wished to evoke emanate from everywhere, as much from the qualities of the landscape, atmosphere and architecture as from the memories and personalities of the Coronels and the remnant Californios Jackson interviewed.

Perhaps there was nothing else for tourists to embrace in the alien land-scape of Los Angeles other than identification with the easeful, unhurried, and modest Californio ethos that the Coronels made so welcoming of Anglo admiration and, ultimately, Anglo longing. The Coronels hoped that the regard Jackson showed their values would shield Californios from the *mexicanidad* of immigrants coming from south of the border and the racism of American immigrants coming from beyond the Colorado River. For *Ramona*'s uncritical readers, however, the identification of place and sensibility that Jackson found at the Coronel adobe destabilized the novel's social protest and opened a way out of Jackson's uncomfortable critique of Anglo treatment of Native Californians.

Ramona in later years was mocked for having metastasized a host of themed tourist spots and once-popular post-*Ramona* books with titles like *The Genesis of the Story of Ramona* (1899), *The Real Ramona of Helen Hunt Jackson's Famous Novel* (1900), *Through Ramona's Country* (1908), *Ramona's Homeland* (1914), and *The True Story of 'Ramona' Its Facts and Fictions, Inspiration and Purpose* (1914). Tourist guides to Ramonaland were illustrated with images of a beckoning landscape that substituted for a complex borderland of hybrid identities, conflicted history, and genuine grievance. The outcome of "Ramona memories" was, author Carey McWilliams claimed, a faux-Spanish Revival in art, design, advertising, architecture, landscaping, and even urban planning that Anglos mistakenly adopted as the truest expression of what Southern California meant.

The Coronels' mythmaking was an act of resistance against Anglo attitudes that conflated their Californio cultural distinctiveness with the status of working-class Mexicans. Jackson, however, saw romance and not resistance in the intricate steps of the Coronels' fandango. In the affective landscape that the Coronels had sketched and Jackson's travel in Southern California confirmed, she found that a "certain indefinable, delicious aroma from the old, ignorant, picturesque times lingers still, not only in byways and corners, but in the very centres of its newest activities."[13] In the decades that followed the novel's publication, travelers to Los Angeles would read *Ramona* and long to experience the romance of the Californio ethos that the novel identifies with its setting.

Jackson didn't need the Coronels to write a novel of protest about the treatment of Native Americans. But she needed their help to enter a landscape of sentiments where she absorbed the identification of place and sensibility without examining the Coronels' motives. Jackson's readers longed for that identification too. There were many reasons: the trauma that remained after the Civil War, the increasing harshness of industrializing America, the unsettling diversity of an immigrant nation and the problem of imaginatively integrating the West into the American experience. Jackson herself had reasons for embracing a healing Californio ethos: poor health, exhaustion after years of difficult work and the failure of her campaign for Native American justice.

The Coronels hoped that Jackson and other Anglo narrators would support the preservation of Californio social status. It's as if the Coronels had wanted to recolonize American Los Angeles, a *reconquista* that ultimately failed. There were risks, they found, in lending your history. But as historian Phoebe Kropp has noted, when faced with erasure, Californios told their stories even though they couldn't control the way Anglos would read them.[14]

In acquiring the sense of place that *Ramona* invited Anglos to possess, readers of the novel and travelers in the tourism it inspired didn't require the inconvenient presence of actual Californios. The landscape substituted for everything desirable about the Californio ethos Jackson portrayed. Identity had become landscape, which Anglos populated with Days of the Dons festivals, Ramona pageants, Old California-themed films, and mission-style housing projects. Many of these artifacts of Anglo desire are with us still.

Antonio Coronel died in 1894. His obituary, written by a fellow member of the Historical Society of Southern California, included the hope that "Mr. Coronel . . . as he recedes gradually into the distance of the past [will], like many others of his predecessors of Spanish ancestry in the Californias of whom Anglo-Californians of today have but partial knowledge, become more and more a striking figure in the annals of the times in which he lived."[15] Instead, Coronel is nearly forgotten. The steps of the mythmakers' fandango led away from the ends that Coronel and Jackson sought for their stories and toward a constructed sense of place from which Angelenos still take some meaning. Useless to insist that the myth marooned them as presumed exceptions to the American experience.

Eugene Plummer: The Last Californio

Los Angeles, more than any other city in the West, grabs you by the arm—nearly by the throat—and insists you hear another explanation of itself. To the readers of its popular literature after 1900, Los Angeles must have seemed like a city of compulsive memoirists who want you to know why they came here, what they found when they did, and if they stayed or left. Some of these narratives are hilariously unreliable, like Horace Bell's *Reminiscences of a Ranger: Early Times in Southern California* (1881). A few, like Harris Newmark's *Sixty Years in Southern California 1853–1913* (1916) and Sarah Bixby Smith's *Adobe Days* (1926), begin with the personal and end as something like a diary of the city. But many of these narratives are like Jackson Graves's *My Seventy Years in California 1857–1927* (1927), a recasting of the American myth of the self-made man as a myth of a self-made Angeleno. Among the many books are a few, like Leo Carrillo's *The California I Love* (1961), where Southern California is remembered for a former sweetness of life. Not history, exactly, but something deeper, more intensely felt—call it affective history for its ability to touch.

Señor Plummer: The Life and Laughter of an Old-Californian (1942) blends all these modes: history, memoir, comic anecdote, sad reflection, and a meditation on a sense of place. It's an "as told to" book assembled by John Preston Buschlen (writing under the pseudonym of "Don Juan ") and published by the Times-Mirror Company when Eugene Plummer was ninety. The *Los Angeles Times* was then (and would be for another three decades) a principal custodian of the mythology of Los Angeles. The paper used writers like Buschlen (who had turned out novels for a variety of publishers and movie scenarios for Jesse Lasky) to retell the city's myths to successive waves of newcomers.

Plummer, an original resident in the 1870s of what would become Hollywood, could have told a story of placemaking, but Buschlen used Plummer to serve mythology first. The procession from Mission San Gabriel Arcángel to the founding of Los Angeles in September 1781 gets a solemn remembrance of gray-robed Franciscans and banner carrying soldiers with Felipe de Neve, Spanish governor of California, in the lead, although that story was invented a hundred years later by Anglo real estate promoters in need of a colorful beginning to a sales pitch for dusty lots on the fringes of a marginal city. Plummer didn't claim to be at the founding of Los Angeles, but Buschlen has Plummer tell the story as if he had been.

Plummer did have real memories of the era when outlaws like Tiburcio Vasquez troubled the desolate parts of Los Angeles County. Buschlen thought of Vasquez as a Wild West cliché, but Plummer's recollections of Latinx resistance after the Mexican War of 1846–1848 are a signal that Plummer had become a friend to defrauded Californios and exploited mestizo laborers. Plummer worked as a court translator and probably as an informal adviser to Spanish-speaking Angelenos caught in the law. The law catches nearly everyone in *Señor Plummer*—in writs, injunctions, and adverse judgments. American law in *Señor Plummer* is thoroughly Dickensian, a trap for the unwary and a tool of Anglo domination.

The rise of Anglo Los Angeles through property theft was long ago recast as a story of feckless Californios, childlike in their trust, losing their land to sharp Americans with their skill at hard bargaining. The myth of Californio incompetence lingers in Plummer's memories, but you also see Latinx landowners (both men and women) fighting fraudulent deeds and brazen land grabs. They resisted. They went to court and sometimes won. Some chased off Anglo squatters with pistols and shotguns. They persisted, even though the Anglo interpretation of history consigned them to a mythic past of romance and *dolce far niente*—the sweet idleness of California life.

Plummer identifies himself ethnically Mexican American throughout *Señor Plummer*, although his father was an Anglo sea captain and his mother, with connections to the Pacheco family, was born in Toronto. Mythologizing reinvented Eugene Plummer as Eugenio Plummer, the "last of the dons" with tales to tell of the characters—like blustering filibuster Horace Bell—who populated a more colorful Los Angeles before 1900.

In these jokey accounts of drunks and scallywags, *Señor Plummer* trades in stereotypes and rude humor. It's only at the periphery of his anecdotes that something else leaks into the story. Plummer is shown sitting on a fragment of the land his mother homesteaded in what is now West Hollywood, waiting for even these last acres to be foreclosed, while around him in vivid memory are the ranchos and homesteads of his Anglo and Latinx neighbors—a shadow landscape overlaid by the triumphant modern city.

Nearly everything about the way the author presents Eugene Plummer is meant to instigate nostalgia for a place that few Anglo readers in 1942 could remember. But the romance of Old Los Angeles is undercut by Plummer's memories of the real city. Plummer's Los Angeles was small, dusty, violent, and a dumping ground for adventurers who couldn't make it in San Francisco. Beyond the cluster of storefronts, saloons, and hotels around the old plaza, Plummer's Los Angeles is sparsely built up. A lonely, wood-frame house, hardly more than a shack, sits on a homesteaded lot. The next house might be a quarter-mile away across eroded hillsides and empty fields. Those who live there—marginal Anglos and Latinx alike—are sustained by growing an acre of produce, dairying a few cows, raising hogs, running a small business or all of these. Despite the book's comedy and its cast of eccentrics, *Señor Plummer* presents a city where nearly all its residents are dispossessed—the Native Americans by Spaniards and the Californios by conniving Yankees. The waves of immigrant Anglos of Plummer's boyhood were themselves displaced from homes "back East" by distance and often by misfortune. Plummer's own misfortune was the reason for the publication of *Señor Plummer*. Plummer is presented as the last surviving pioneer of Los Angeles and the last Californio to be driven off his land. His book of recollections was part of a fund-raising campaign to keep him there. Missing from the narrative are the descendants of the city's founding Californio families—the Lugos, the Carillos, the del Valles—who persist even today.

Plummer looks back to the fiestas of a Latinx Los Angeles made of adobe. Someone is always singing a ballad there, before the guitars and fiddles pick up a waltz or a polka. But everything there is about to be erased. Eugene Plummer—*Don Eugenio*—outlived the Californios, to whom he was only lightly connected, to become a guarantor of Anglo-made myths. He allowed himself to become a souvenir of Los Angeles. He died in 1943, aged ninety-one. A remnant of his land became Plummer Park.

Los Angeles Sells Itself

The writer for the *Los Angeles Herald* in 1887 knew his stuff. There was, he said, a uniquely favored place in the San Gabriel Valley, just forty-five minutes by train from Los Angeles, that "comprises . . . the finest land on the globe, with ample water rights . . . ." And that wasn't all, the *Herald* reported. "A grand avenue, 88 feet wide, bordered with shade trees and containing two highways, extends from the Sierra Madre to the south side of the tract. In the center of this highway, ten electric masts are being erected so that the great highway that cuts the land into two royal domains will be lighted from (and after) tonight with the pure light borrowed from the sun by the permission of that luminary."[16] According to the *Herald*, Professor Warren, "the electrician in charge of the manufacture of electric energy in Los Angeles," would provide the promised lighting. William Gladstone, several times the Prime Minister of Great Britain, provided the townsite's name. And Gladstone's promoters in that boom year provided, in florid prose, the sales pitch.

Gladstone, "the most beautiful land that the sun ever shone upon," would be the city of destiny for smart buyers who got in early. "Business lots . . . will double in value within a week after the day of sale," developer H.H. Boyce confidently predicted. "Nearly all the land in Gladstone is covered with blooming vineyards and orchards, the latter mostly in orange groves," Boyce claimed. "The capital stock of the company is $1,000,000, of which a large sum has been expended for lands, roads, water pipes, surveying, and electric lights."

The ballyhoo for Gladstone was typical of that nineteenth-century boomtime: a spate of breathless newspaper advertisements; a glowing report in the *Times* or the *Herald*; a bunting-draped bandwagon parading on opening day to the train station to take "anxious speculators" to the townsite where, after a free lunch, the auctioning of lots would begin. Had you gone to Gladstone on its inaugural day in April 1887, you might have wondered what amount of desire could so completely obscure what little was there. Gladstone was a bit more than five hundred acres of pasture and orange grove next to the crossroads settlement of Centra (between what is now Azusa and Glendora). There were a few houses in the neighborhood and a blacksmith and a laundry. There was a post office. There was Captain H. Fuller's hotel, although it was only his house made over for the purpose. But there were big plans, Boyce said, for a bank, a streetcar line, and a genuinely grand hotel to be built in the style of the boomtime—a florid, multi-story confection in millwork and paint that would have, like so many hotels of that year, either burned to the ground or become a church-affiliated college or been cut up and carted away to another speculative townsite to lure the next wave of real estate romantics. In some accounts written in the aftermath of the boom, Gladstone didn't get its hotel. In other accounts, a hotel is built, left vacant, cut up, and reassembled in Azusa.

Maybe the hotel in Gladstone was there; maybe not, like the dam that would power the electric lights, like the quarry that would make dressed stone cheaper than brick for building the new bank and the train depot. Like the bank and the depot, Gladstone existed, if it existed at all, only in the breathless prose of the *Herald* and on a subdivision map (surveyed by V.J. Rowan). Of the actual Gladstone—"The Richest Settlement in Natural Advantages in California"—C.C. Baker later wrote, "there is of record only . . . one block."[17]

In 1887, when commercial lots in Los Angeles that had previously sold for five hundred dollars an acre were offered at five thousand dollars an acre, Gladstone's promise of a 100 percent return in a week seemed realistic. When nearby Azusa was subdivided, J.M. Guinn told the members of the Historical Society of Southern California in 1889, "Two hundred and eighty thousand dollars worth of lots were sold the first day. . . . Not one in a hundred of the purchasers had seen the townsite, and not one in a thousand expected to occupy the land."[18] In 1887, not just Gladstone but all of Los Angeles was busy selling itself into existence in a frenzy of speculation.

The promoters of Gladstone did their part to convince prospective buyers that the selling would go on and on, propelled by the bounty of Southern California and the gullibility of the next wave of buyers. In the paper towns of Los Angeles County, 79,350 subdivided acres had been listed with the county assessor by the fall of 1888, yielding a minimum of 400,000 standard house lots. Guinn, using data he gathered from the Los Angeles County Recorder, estimated that the notional value of real estate transactions had reached $200 million. He surmised that another $200 million in purchase contracts had traded hands in San Diego, San Bernardino, Ventura, and Santa Barbara counties. "Could we have kept the boom running for another year," he told historical society members, "we would have made enough to pay off the national debt."[19]

The boom had begun in the spring of 1886. By the summer of 1888, it had collapsed. In Gladstone, the electric lights went on and then flickered out. The right-of-way for the streetcar line was graded, but the franchise lapsed. Water mains, waterless, rusted in place. The bank never sought a charter. The train depot remained a rumor. The roads of Gladstone led to dead ends. According to C.C. Baker, "newspaper accounts said $100,000 worth of lots were sold. While there was great excitement, there is indisputable proof that nothing was sold. There are of record only two deeds covering bona fide sales by the company, one dated in November 1887, and the other in June 1888, both sales being to [Gladstone] residents, and the consideration amounting to $2862.50."[20] In September 1888, the Gladstone Improvement Company disposed of the few lots it actually owned along with the water mains and electric lighting equipment. "[E]everything except the grading of the streetcar line," as the *Glendora Signal* newspaper put it, was removed.

Guinn in later years lamented that the spectacle of boomtime towns like Gladstone had faded so quickly, that the grand hotels were gone (or been relocated) and the hyperbolic newspaper advertisements—the "literature of the boom"—had been "buried in waste baskets and cremated in kitchen stoves." No one, he said, would remember the location of these paper towns. Guinn wasn't entirely correct. Twenty years and another boomtime later, several of the paper towns of 1887 reappeared as the names of stops along the Pacific Electric trolley lines that Henry Huntington spread across the Los Angeles basin to service his own, better-financed real estate ambitions. Some boomtime subdivisions, like Burbank and Glendale, lay dormant and then revived in the new century.

Memories of the boomtime left Los Angeles with a fractured sense of place. The essential division is still with us. The "literature of the boom" promised that limitless desires would be satisfied here. The history of the boom warned that nothing here was as it seemed. We Angelenos still want so much and are still so deceived.

Climates of Opinion

Spanish *Alta California* in the 1790s was at the edge of the world. For royal officials and Franciscan missionaries, it was a forlorn place, but it wasn't entirely strange. Spain's Mediterranean shore, parts of Mexico and Southern California from San Diego to Santa Barbara are first cousins by way of climate. Los Angeles may have been a cluster of mud-brick hovels during the last decade of the eighteenth century, without even a proper church, but it had the same short, warm winters and long, bright summers as Valencia with its palaces and basilicas.

Thirty years later, the few Americans who drifted into Mexican Los Angeles found the qualities of its climate alien and troubling. Richard Henry Dana, passing through in 1835, admired the mildness of the seasons, but he saw an existential risk in the always sunny skies. What if the climate of Los Angeles was its racial destiny? "In the hands of an enterprising people, what a country this might be," Dana admitted. "Yet how long would a people remain so, in such a country?" The children of industrious Americans, Dana feared, would succumb one day to the indolent climate and be no better than the Californios Dana despised.[21] Thirty years after Dana diagnosed a racial threat in the climate, the region's boosters set out to rewrite its nature to resolve that dilemma. The qualities of climate that degraded indigenous Californians had to be marketed as revitalizing if Southern California was to become the "sanitarium of the Union"[22] where the traumas of the Civil War might be healed.

For Los Angeles boosters, making a new nature also would resolve a lingering question of ownership. Indigenous claimants belonged to a former nature and they to it, and that had made them incapable of holding the land or making it fruitful. Anglo Americans were assembling a fertile, new nature of astonishing vigor. When California Governor George Perkins addressed the growers at a horticultural fair in 1881, he marveled, "A few short years ago and these valleys now emparadised in fruits, cereals, and flowers raised their upturned faces in sullen uninviting barrenness. Surely the approving smile of heaven is upon us." A new nature, realized with every acre sown with wheat and with every honeysuckle, peony, dahlia, and camellia planted, confirmed that this land was now indisputably an American possession. "This vast region," wrote James DeLong in his 1877 Los Angeles guidebook, "which was considered a few years ago a desert . . . is now made to bloom as the rose."[23]

The abundance of this American-made nature was almost hallucinatory. "The floral offerings even in the dead of California winter overwhelmed the senses," the *California Horticulturist and Floral Magazine* enthused in 1874:

> Roses, Pinks, Stocks, Candy-tuft, Sweet Alyssum, Violets, Stevia, Gladiolus, Pelargoniums, Fuchsias, Pansies, Laurustinus, Diosma, Erica, Mignonette, Gypsophila, and Abutilon" as well as greenhouse flowers, "Camellias, Eucharis, Tuberoses, Epiphyllums, Agapanthus, Azalea, Heliotrope . . . Spanish Jasmine, Cyclamen, Poinsettia, Chinese Primrose, Begonia, Cineraria, [and] Orange-blossoms.[24]

In *Our Italy*, Charles Dudley Warner considered how a desert had been transformed into a garden by 1891 and thought that it defied the natural order:

> It is still a wonder that a land in which there was no indigenous product of value, or to which cultivation could give value, should be so hospitable to every sort of tree, shrub, root, grain, and flower that can be brought here from any zone and temperature, and that many of these foreigners to the soil grow here with a vigor and productiveness surpassing those in their native land.[25]

R.W.C. Farnsworth was even more mystified. "Nature assumes many unusual phases in this strange land," he warned in *Southern California Paradise* in 1883. "Squirrels live in the ground and rats in the trees. The songs of birds are heard all winter. The forces of nature have no common season of rest, some taking a little sleep in summer and others in winter." If Southern California was a paradise, Farnsworth complained, it was likely "to confuse the careless sight-seer."[26]

Boosters and the travel writers were uncertain what nature they should describe when selling the qualities of the Southern California landscape. Should they record what was here or imagine what might be? Was the landscape empty or full, alien or familiar? Confusingly, the guide books said it was both. They lacked a word to reconcile the landscape's contradictions.

"Arid" and "tropical," terms that had been occasionally used to characterize the Southern California climate, were loaded with unwanted associations for the boosters. "Arid" had been the description of treeless plains west of the 100th meridian: the Great American Desert of the 1830s. "Tropical" was reserved for the swamps of Louisiana and Florida. Making a new nature for Southern California required more than peonies; it needed a new language.

Subtropical

Geographers had long ago systematized geometric and astronomical subdivisions of the terrestrial globe. Start at a point, they said, exactly half the distance from the North Pole to the South Pole. Draw an imaginary circle around the globe at that point and call it the equator. Walk away from the equator, degree by degree northward, to the last point where, at noon on the longest day of the year, the sun is still directly overhead. The next step north crosses another imaginary circle, the Tropic of Cancer. Between the equator and the Tropic of Cancer (and in the southern hemisphere, between the equator and the Tropic of Capricorn) lie the tropics and in them, images of intense heat, trackless jungle, and barren waste. In North America, the Tropic of Cancer cuts through central Mexico, at around 23.4 degrees north latitude (about the latitude of Mazatlán). Below the Tropic of Cancer are the tropics; above is the Northern Temperate Zone.

It had become a convention by the nineteenth century to divide the temperate zone further. The area between the Tropic of Cancer and about 35 degrees north latitude is cooler in summer than more southern latitudes and warmer in winter than latitudes more northerly. In between—between jungle and snowfall—is the geographer's subtropical zone. Los Angeles is about 34° north latitude, just within the subtropics.

Real estate developers in the 1880s with rancho land to sell were eager to recast the nature of Southern California in ways that implied warmth and plentitude but not a steamy jungle or burning desert. In the subtropical embrace, a farmer could raise familiar fruits and grains as well as every tropical crop—from bananas to passion fruit—without the health risks of life in the actual tropics. Anglo migrants and their progeny could flourish too, without the racial risk that troubled Dana, because Anglo-American husbandry had proved the vigor of transplanted peonies and hydrangeas. "Subtropical" rewrote the nature of Southern California to segregate it from the region's unfruitful, colonial history and to justify its exuberant strangeness.

"California is our own," wrote Charles Nordhoff in the preface to *California:*

For Health, Pleasure, and Residence, his 1873 tourist and immigrant guide:

> [And the first] tropical land which our race has thoroughly mastered and made itself at home in . . . . There, and there only, on this planet, the traveler and resident may enjoy the delights of the tropics, without their penalties; a mild climate, not enervating, but healthful and health-restoring; a wonderfully and variously productive soil, without tropical malaria . . . [and with] strange customs, but neither lawlessness nor semi-barbarism.[27]

Subtropical was the technical term, but not the adjective generally used to describe the climate of Southern California. For boosters like Warner, Nordhoff, and Farnsworth, the "sub" part probably suggested something diminished or subordinate. Warner, adopting a new word for a new nature, called Southern California "semi-tropical." Clipped to "semi-tropic," blurring its image of nature even more, the term could mean whatever you needed it to mean. It was attached to the climate, the landscape, a way of life, a real estate development in San Bernardino, a Spiritualist camp, a school district, and a co-op cotton gin.

Semi-Tropical

"Semi-tropical" contained the marvel that was Southern California, a place that writers regretted they couldn't otherwise adequately define. DeLong complained that "neither pen, pencil, nor painter can describe those lovely places. They must be seen to be appreciated." That didn't stop boosters from extolling the delightful, reviving, and profitable qualities that its semi-tropical nature gave to Southern California. The word threads through the booster narratives of the post-Civil War period, bracketed between Benjamin Truman's *Semi-tropical California: its Climate, Healthfulness, Productiveness, and Scenery* in 1874 and F. Weber Benton's *Semi-Tropic California: The Garden of the World* in 1914. The semi-tropical climate wasn't arid; it was dry. Its warmth didn't breed lethargy; it freed men to work productively year-round. Semi-tropical was semi-miraculous. "Meat suspended in the air dries up but never rots," Truman claimed. "The air when inhaled gives to the individual a stimulus and vital force which only an atmosphere so pure can ever communicate."[28] "Semi-tropical" confirmed the exceptionalism of Southern California, distinguishing it from rival

San Francisco and freeing it from an unwanted Latinx past.

Truman's scrapbook of statistics and newspaper extracts could have been illustrated with some of the hundreds of stereograph views taken by Henry T. Payne. His *Semi-Tropical California Scenery*, drawn from a collection of nearly one thousand views shown at Philadelphia's Centennial Exhibition in 1876, traded on horticultural exoticism—palms, oranges, olive groves, and cacti—but located these unfamiliar forms in the commonplace of suburban and rural Los Angeles. "Semi-tropical" seemed to mean an *agave* blooming in front of a white, wood-frame farmhouse. What was semi-tropical in the scene was the novel juxtaposition. "Semi-tropical" meant that cacti and roses, palms and wisteria had been brought together in Southern California's domesticating garden, just as the Latin and the Anglo-Saxon had been. "Strange customs" from the first; power to control "lawlessness" and "semi-barbarism" from the second. What Anglo Americans wanted in the last decades of the nineteenth century was the new nature that they had summoned from a wasteland and given a name. "Semi-tropical" wasn't an environmental descriptor; it defined everything that Anglo Americans had planted in foreign soil.

To homesick missionaries and Spanish colonial officials in the eighteenth century, Southern California had been uniquely unhealthy, breeding melancholy and hypochondria. The malign environment also explained the degraded state, as defined by the colonizers, of the region's aboriginal inhabitants. American occupiers of Los Angeles after 1850 agreed with this assessment but included their Latinx neighbors in the class of those enfeebled by the qualities of the Los Angeles climate. Its powers of physical and psychological renewal could only be realized now, under a newly Anglo sun. Healing "is not across the ocean or upon some foreign shore . . . but within our own land, under our own flag, and among our own people."[29] For its new American possessors, Los Angeles had become a city of racial health because the climate of Los Angeles had been made white.

Architecture of Dreams

Once upon a time in Los Angeles, you could get a hot dog *from* a hot dog and a tamale *inside* a tamale. You could get a bowl of chili while sitting in a chili bowl, a cup of coffee beneath a coffee cup and a mug of beer in a beer keg. The buildings where hot dogs and tamales were served looked like those things, but they were made cartoonishly huge, as if for a giant's table.

A building that imitates the things sold inside is mimetic architecture. There were even more mimetic buildings in Los Angeles from 1915 to 1955: a camera store that looked like a camera; a piano store shaped like a piano; and a flower shop in the form of a flower pot. But not all the exuberant commercial architecture was an oversize image of what was sold inside. Igloos and icebergs sold ice cream. Snow-capped mountains housed a bar. Windmills advertised baked goods. Bacon and eggs were logically dished inside a stucco pig, but hamburgers were on the menu inside dogs, toads, and an oil can.

Chinese shrines, Art Deco ziggurats, and domed mosques pumped Gilmore, Signal, and Violet Ray gasoline. The wings of a Fokker F-32 airliner, improbably parked at the corner of Wilshire Boulevard and Cochran Avenue, shaded the gas pumps of Bob's Air-Mail Service Station. The Sphinx Realty Company was a (sort of) sphinx. A steamship was (and still is) the Coca-Cola bottling plant in Los Angeles. The Brown Derby on Wilshire Boulevard was an enormous brown derby. The name of the restaurant was the restaurant.

Material dreams like the imitative Tail o' the Pup and the symbolic Coca-Cola Building are collectively called programmatic architecture, where form willfully ignores function. Predictably, Hollywood played a role in making it part of fantasy Los Angeles.

Spectacle and Sham

In 1915, following the success of *Birth of a Nation,* director D.W. Griffith planned his next movie on an even grander scale. Griffith's *Intolerance* would show "Love's Struggle Throughout the Ages" with all the melodrama he could fit into the film's three and a half hours. For scenes set in ancient Babylon, Griffith ordered two rows of 50-foot pillars topped by gigantic rearing elephants to form a processional way. More huge elephants guarded the gates of Babylon, which were 136 feet tall and patterned with crests and frescoed gods. When production of the movie ended, the plaster and plywood set loomed over the intersection of Sunset and Hollywood boulevards, slowly decaying. In 1919, the Los Angeles Fire Department ordered its demolition.

Jim Heimann, who has documented California's unrestrained programmatic architecture in several books, dates its beginning in Los Angeles to the lingering spectacle of Griffith's *Intolerance* set. But there were earlier precedents. Buildings in the amusement zone at San Diego's Panama-California Exposition in 1915—made of plaster, fiber, and chicken wire—looked like toadstools and pagodas. That same year, San Francisco's Panama-Pacific International Exposition had a 120-foot figure of Buddha, an enormous Uncle Sam, and a two-story horse. Griffith was impressed and brought some of the fair's craftsmen to Hollywood to build his Babylon set.

By the early 1920s, Los Angeles builders had access to set designers with the skills to sculpt plaster, stucco, wood, and wire into eye-catching storefronts and freestanding buildings. Los Angeles had the perpetual good weather and a mobile population eager to see the sights from the era's open automobiles. Business operators saw that quirky architecture could attract customers. Sun, speed, wide vistas, and post-war optimism built fakery into the fabric of Los Angeles and into the city's mythology of itself. When Claes Oldenburg and Coosje van Bruggen designed a titanic pair of binoculars as the portal to the Chiat/Day Building in Venice in 1991, they were having postmodern fun with a tradition of shape-shifting Los Angeles architecture. But Angeleno taste for dreamscapes went deeper than novelty buildings.

Dream Houses

Wallace Neff and other architects in the 1920s designed homes in Pasadena and San Marino in the new Spanish Colonial Revival style, which was, architect Richard Requa argued, "the logical, fitting, and altogether appropriate architecture for California ... a style inspired and suggested" by Spain and colonial Mexico.[30] In its cheerful disregard for authenticity and its materialization of a past that ought to have been, the Spanish Colonial Revival prefigured the architectural programs of Disneyland and Universal Citywalk. Developers in Southern California eventually laid out whole cities—"themed communities"—in the new style. Santa Barbara and Ojai remade themselves in white stucco, red tile, and wrought iron. Rancho Santa Fe in San Diego County was newly built beginning in 1921 as a hybrid of Navajo pueblo and Mexican colonial village.

The Spanish Colonial Revival answered the longing of well-to-do home-owners who wanted to be connected to the essence of Southern California, even if that connection was a sham. In the conflation of landscape and dwelling—Ramonaland on a house lot—architects and their clients sought to define a new domesticity intended to rescue modern life from haste and monotony. The Depression ended that project. The Spanish Colonial Revival had a diminished afterlife in working-class suburbs as a white, stuccoed box with red tile trim, a flat roof, and a cement figure of a sleeping Mexican on the porch.

What made it possible to build that kind of sketchy house was the climate that had suggested the revival style to Requa. Houses in Los Angeles need only enough bracing to shed occasional rain, not bear the load of a long winter's snow and ice. Liberated from stone, brick, and a steeply pitched roof, a house in Los Angeles could be anything from a storybook "Hansel and Gretel" cottage, like the Willat/Spadena house, to a docked UFO, like the Chemosphere.

The boisterous architectural freedom that Angelenos embraced propped up a long-lasting critique of Los Angeles, as in the opening pages of Nathanael West's *The Day of the Locust* (1939):

> [N]ot even the soft wash of dusk could help the houses. Only dynamite would be of any use against the Mexican ranch houses, Samoan huts, Mediterranean villas, Egyptian and Japanese temples, Swiss chalets, Tudor cottages, and every possible combination of these styles that lined the slopes of the canyon. . . . On the corner of La Huerta Road was a miniature Rhine castle with tarpaper turrets pierced for archers. Next to it was a little highly colored shack with domes and minarets out of the Arabian Nights. . . . It is hard to laugh at the need for beauty and romance, no matter how tasteless, even horrible, the results of that need are.[31]

Objections to the inauthenticity of Los Angeles architecture mistook what was fundamental about the city. Traditional architectural styles—a department store decorated like a Venetian palazzo, a bank that looked like a Roman temple, a church that pretended to be Gothic—were as inauthentic in Los Angeles as a tire plant in the form of an Assyrian fortress or an apartment building that looked like the bridge of an ocean liner.

Fantasylands

Clifton's Pacific Seas cafeteria entertained bored retirees in a stage set of waterfalls and jungles. Waiting for a fried chicken dinner at Walter Knott's restaurant in Buena Park, patrons wandered through a "real" frontier ghost town. Shoppers at Hollywood's Crossroads of the World loitered among storefronts designed in Old World architectural styles. In 1955, Walt Disney appropriated all these concepts and wrapped a world's fair amusement zone around them. Disneyland's example of programmed fun inside programmatic architecture generated a new industry that blended theme parks with themed shopping malls, inspirations for retail destinations like The Grove and The Americana at Brand. Cultural critics echoed Nathanael West's judgment that the results were often "tasteless, even horrible," yet something in them satisfied. An invitation to escape into an immersive, alternate reality was key to the allure of twentieth-century Los Angeles.

The benign climate, excellent highways, and the skills of Hollywood designers were material causes of our architecture of fakery. Our fondness for it is harder to explain. Rootlessness might be one reason. It defined Los Angeles when it was largely a city of restless exiles. They wouldn't have come here unless they had a thirst for novelty. Distance from disapproving cultural elites might be another reason. Risk-taking entrepreneurs had the freedom to be outlandish in how they sold donuts, ice cream, and pianos. It worked. People talked about a dance hall in the shape of a pumpkin, a lunch counter that looked like a dirigible, and a supper club that imitated a Zuni pueblo. People laughed at the odd buildings of Los Angeles, but they probably remembered the businesses inside.

Some sarcastic observers claimed that the city's streets were lined with weird architecture, proof, if any was needed, that Los Angeles was uniquely crazy.[32] The architectural historian David Gebhard thought that no more than seventy-five programmatic commercial structures were ever built. Perhaps these eccentric buildings weren't vulgar ballyhoo for a city of yokels. Perhaps they defined something positive about who we are and set us apart from other places and the critics who didn't approve. We once wanted to encounter fantastic buildings that made us feel as curious and as small as a child, although there was something forlorn in that wish. A less naïve Los Angeles grew up after 1950, and it expressed its needs and attitudes in a different roadside architecture—in the soaring angles, swooping lines, and neon towers of Googie

Style, made to be easily read at forty-five miles an hour. The look was different, but the impulse to defy convention and make a statement was the same.

When the Hollywood and Highland shopping and theater complex opened in 2001, part of its design echoed the vanished spectacle of D.W. Griffith's gate of Babylon set.

The Hoard of the Lizard Men

The golden thread of lost treasure runs through the American imagination. Fabulous wealth lies hidden—by time or sorcery—under some hill somewhere, left by the Aztecs or pirates or men from Mu, and waiting for a lucky someone to find the gold, seize it, and become rich. The golden thread even runs through California's state motto—Eureka—Greek for "I have found it." "It" being unearned riches panned from a mountain brook or sluiced from a Sierra hillside.

George Warren Shufelt claimed he'd found "it"—golden and fabulous—under Fort Moore Hill, a low rise overlooking the old plaza that had figured in the American occupation of Los Angeles during the Mexican War of 1846–1848. Shufelt, who said he was a mining engineer and an inventor with a mysterious "radio X-ray machine," claimed to have remotely mapped a maze of tunnels and chambers under the site of what had been Fort Moore. According to his partners Rex McCreery and Ray Martin, who spoke of an ancient map that they had, Shufelt's find wasn't a maze but really vaults of looted Spanish gold. Or perhaps the treasure was hidden by Aztecs. It wasn't clear. In early 1933, Shufelt, McCreery, and Martin convinced the five-member Los Angeles County Board of Supervisors that they should be authorized to dig for the riches that waited beneath the hill. The treasure hunters offered an even split with the county. It seemed like a good deal in the worst year of the Great Depression.

By March, a crew of volunteer diggers (hoping for a cut of the gold) had driven a twenty-eight-foot shaft into the hilltop. They found nothing but rocks and clay. Strangely, the treasure shaft was directly over excavation work for the new Broadway tunnel through Fort Moore Hill. The tunnel workers boring through the hill hadn't found any Spanish or Aztec gold either. In September, the disappointed gold seekers let their county permit lapse. Alfred Scott then took up the search, promising the Board of Supervisors that he could reach the treasure with his own pick and shovel. He may have dug, but if he did, he didn't find anything.

Shufelt and his "radio X-ray machine" returned in January 1934 with an even better story. It combined every trope of 1930s super science fiction: Native American legends, a doomed civilization of Lizard people from five thousand years ago, unknown technological marvels, and vast caverns filled with revelations. It wasn't Spanish or even Aztec gold that lay under "the old Banning property," the *Los Angeles Times* soberly reported, but the hoarded wealth of the Lizard Empire. The paper included a helpful map showing the subterranean stronghold in which the Lizard riches lay. Shufelt told the *Times* he'd gone to Arizona to get the whole story directly from Chief Green Leaf (otherwise referred to as L. Macklin in the *Times* account). The Lizard men weren't really lizards but refugees from a West Coast version of Atlantis. It was meteors that sank the Lizard people's first home, according to Macklin's scrambled version of Native American mythology.

Shufelt, with Macklin's guidance, the backing of new partners and another county permit, began a third excavation on Fort Moore Hill in early 1934, hoping to tap the maze of tunnels and storerooms the Lizard folk had bored into the hill using an unknown chemical solution. Shufelt's exploratory shaft eventually reached a depth of 250 feet when the attention of the *Times* ran out and mud and water began pouring in.

If Shufelt and the other treasure hunters on Fort Moore Hill had been running a confidence scam, their victims were remarkably quiet after being burned. Perhaps the investors were so convinced by the story—or stories—that their losses were accounted as bad luck. Maybe they were just embarrassed.

Shufelt stayed, dying in North Hollywood in 1957. By then, the Lizard men and their fabulous possibilities had disappeared, except as a textbook example of "bizarre Los Angeles."

But the Lizard men hadn't really gone. They fled back underground to help populate a mirror empire of paranoia. On late-night talk radio, the golden thread in the imagination of Los Angeles darkens. It doesn't lead to unearned riches but to sinister aliens, ancient conspiracies, and racial suspicions.

Shelter. Fallout.

In 1961, the federal Office of Civil and Defense Mobilization published "The Family Fallout Shelter," a homeowner's guide to nuclear survival, printed on flimsy newsprint and costing ten cents. The OCDM advised worried readers that a substantial, contractor-built fallout shelter would cost about $1,500. Lacking that kind of capital, dad could build a shelter in the basement himself, following the plans in the OCDM guide. A do-it-yourself shelter would cost less than $500. Only no Los Angeles tract house like mine has a basement. The alternative, the OCDM suggested, was huddling in a corner of a room furthest from the direction from which the blast was expected to come. Except houses like mine were built of stucco over chicken wire; they're mostly a thin skin over absence. The OCDM might hope otherwise, but my parents, my brother, and I wouldn't survive the H-bombing of Los Angeles.

Still, my brother and I needed to be toughened up to take our places in the ranks of Cold War fighters. In 1954, the city council in my hometown unanimously passed an ordinance banning the sale of crime and horror comic books, as well as "Communist-slanted" comics, to persons less than eighteen years old. In 1956, the PTA of the neighborhood elementary school held a meeting on "Strengthening the Country through Sports." The subject of a lecture to the members of the junior high school PTA that year was "The Body as Well as the Mind Toughens for the Space Age."

Braced in mind and body, my brother and I waited for the Space Age to blossom atomically. The sequence was easy to remember during the monthly drills that sent us sliding beneath our skimpy desks on our knees, with hands clasped behind our heads looking as if we were tiny POWs of the Sisters of St. Joseph. First in the atomic sequence: the flash that would blind you if you looked. Next: the burst of thermal radiation that would set your clothes afire. Last: the blast wave that would tear you, Sister Isaac Jogues, the school, and your home apart.

I was trained to be a reservist in a battalion of ideological warriors. I was disciplined by a garrison nation. I grew up in an arsenal making ever more terrible weapons. I was a hostage to the doctrine of Mutually Assured Destruction, my life offered as surety that the worst of those weapons wouldn't be used. I think I may suffer from a kind of Cold War PTSD.

The world ended, over and over, during our years in the fallout shelter the Cold War built. In *Dr. Strangelove*, fools and mindless machines do it. In *On the Beach*, drifting fallout does it. In *When Worlds Collide*, a rogue sun passing through the solar system does it. In *Beneath the Planet of the Apes*, the gorillas and we do it to each other. The stories satisfied a need to nervously pick at the scab of our nightmare.

Nuclearland

It's a Friday night in January 1962, and the chill, blue-gray light spilling from the television set in the side room is an episode of *The Twilight Zone*. In it, a megalomaniac millionaire has built a comfortable fallout shelter beneath his downtown office building. He invites the three people he blames for ruining his life to join him there. He indicts each of them in turn. And then—with fake television announcements and staged film clips—he convinces them that the Armageddon everyone expects is about to begin. He taunts his guests with his safety and their vulnerability should they choose to leave the shelter. Each may stay but only by groveling in apology and begging him for the privilege. They don't, because each of them has their own stoic pride. When they have left, the millionaire is stunned to see the H-bombs actually detonate and the city destroyed. In horror, he rushes from the confinement of his shelter and finds himself the sole survivor in a ruined, post-nuclear landscape. He breaks down in his awful solitude. But he'd gone mad long before. He sees a wasteland where he's desperately alone, but in reality he's cowering in the middle of an ordinary urban sidewalk—with cops and pretty girls and cars honking—where nothing at all has happened.

Rod Serling's "One More Pallbearer" episode of *Twilight Zone* dramatized how the habits of the fourteen-year-old Cold War had acclimated us—schoolchildren, suburban housewives, and working-class husbands—to what essayist E.B. White called "the stubborn fact of annihilation." In our nuclear imaginations, we saw mushroom clouds on the horizon shining brighter than the sun even as we shopped and worked and fell in love. We saw concentric rings superimposed at five-mile intervals on our hometown. The rings were labeled "fireball," "peak overpressure zone," "secondary blast damage," and "radiation effects." My house, twenty-four miles southeast of downtown Los Angeles, fell outside the ring of immediate annihilation from a twenty-megaton airburst above Los Angeles City Hall, as calculated by the *Los Angeles Times* in 1961. My house fell inside the ring of secondary effects: fire and radiation. The target rings made some of my neighbors store drinking water in gallon containers in their garage. They planned to survive. The target rings made one neighbor top off his gas tank so that the dashboard gauge never fell below half-full. He planned to escape.

Ground Zero

When I was a boy, one of my favorite shows was *I Led Three Lives*. Richard Carlson played Herb Philbrick, a loving father and husband, a member of a Communist spy ring, and an undercover agent of the FBI. Herb Philbrick lied all the time, with the conviction that lying is a necessity when war is fought in your bedroom, your dad's office, and your older brother's classroom.

In mid-October 1962, during the week of the Cuban missile crisis, my parents stood at the kitchen sink after dinner, washing up and listening to the news. They turned to my brother and me and told us what we should do if something happened. We knew what it would be. My brother and I—he was 16 and I was 14—should not try to come home from our high school. We should go to the school chapel instead to wait. My parents said they would come for us there. My parents mouthed these lies, and my brother and I repeated them. We knew that we lived nearly at our own "ground zero," surrounded by Douglas Aircraft, Rockwell International, a Nike missile battery, and the ports of Long Beach and Los Angeles. We knew that our parents would not come for us and that our school chapel was a fit place in which to die.

The Cold War taught parents the moral imperative to lie to their children. The government played a jingle for kids, reminding them to "duck and cover." That was a lie too.

Survival Shelter

In 2013, the city council of Menifee in Riverside County, after initial reluctance, approved an ordinance allowing residents to build a survival shelter in their backyard. Builders would be issued permits, and city inspections would ensure that the bunkers of Menifee are up to code. Unlike the shelters of the Cold War, which were commendably spartan, the new era of survival aims at relative comfort. As the *Los Angeles Times* reported, one Menifee resident planned to excavate a shelter with space to house twenty people, enough for his extended family and perhaps a friend or two. A company called Vivos offered more—the equivalent of a bunker condominium with space for ten thousand people. It was supposed to come with all the attractions of a spa. It's unclear what would happen should the shelter managers begin voting tenants in arrears out of the bunker's blast-proof doors. Something more modest is available from Atlas Survival Shelters. ASS assembles steel tubes that are designed to be buried twenty feet underground. According to the company's sales pitch, the shelters are supposed to withstand nuclear, chemical, and biological attack. The smaller versions can accommodate three or four people. There's storage space for a year's worth of provisions.

If a year in a steel tube seems like your idea of hell, you might consider the house at 3970 Spencer St. in Las Vegas. The one above ground won't interest you—too easily overrun by biker gangs/plague-infected zombies/UN troops. It's the house below the house you'll want. It's a fantasy of terror and control. Under twenty-six feet of sand and gravel is a two-bedroom, three-bath house with a fake lawn with fake trees, a putting green, a swimming pool, Jacuzzis, a sauna, a dance floor with a small stage, a bar and a barbecue. Light switches that are marked Day, Dusk, Sunset, and Night. The Night setting turns on the stars in the ceiling, which is painted blue with white clouds. The bunker was built in 1978 by entrepreneur Jerry Henderson and his wife, Mary. Later owners lost the house when the bank foreclosed on their $2-million mortgage. The homey bunker wasn't much shelter from the economic collapse of 2008.

Shelters—even fragile ones—serve a purpose. Fears have to be housed as much as hopes. And there are so many fears now. But the questions asked at the shelter door before it clangs shut are the same ones. We'll have to decide who to let in and who to keep out. Survival means above all your survival and that means, as the literature of the Cold War pointed out, killing anyone who wanted your water, food, weapons, and women. The list of those who were expendable began with the next-door neighbors. The Rev. Billy Graham counseled otherwise, but he said that he understood it would be difficult to pass judgment on what a man did—down there in the shelter—to protect his family.

My parents never considered buying or building a fallout shelter. A shelter dealer in Downey, across the street from the Rockwell plant, sold prefabricated fiberglass pods for burial in backyards. No one I knew bought one.

Laurel Canyon Suite

Laurel Canyon in Los Angeles is a landform, a subdivision, and a myth. Predictably for Los Angeles, it's a myth of perfection reached by acquiring a perfect place—a wonderland—except, even as you stretch out your hand to grasp it, wonderland transforms into something more complicated, darker, and touched by tragedy.

Lyre Strings

The myth involves sex and murder. But there are gods in the story and glory of a kind. In one version, the myth begins with a girl—pretty, well-connected, high-strung. This version ends with a divine musician and a laurel tree. But the myth doesn't end there, or rather, it has neither a beginning nor an end—only renditions, sometimes melancholy and bluesy, occasionally raucous and low-down, sometimes elegant and lingering, making the myth even more dream-like, harder to place. Think of it as a concept album on the theme of longing. This being Los Angeles, it's longing for undying beauty and youth.

The girl in the myth is Daphne, a beautiful nymph (already the same old Hollywood story) but uninterested in men (the cause of her aversion is left unexplained). Prince Leucippus falls madly in love with her. Daphne is stand-offish. Maybe it wasn't love that moved the prince but his urgency to possess. Leucippus cross-dresses in a shift and hair ribbon, the only way to linger with Daphne and her virgin girlfriends—Leucippus being as friendly as he can in drag. (Unbelievable, but the point of the story is erotic fervor not low comedy.) The girls go swimming one day; "she" being a "he" means Leucippus can't strip. Daphne demands to know why. He backs off. The girls get the picture. He's exposed. They kill him.

They bring down Leucippus, pierced "with their javelins and daggers," the first of the tragic ends in this story. Then the gods Apollo and Eros are arguing over reason versus passion and which is more potent. To demonstrate his point that passion reigns, Eros pierces rational Apollo with the golden arrow of desire and Daphne with an arrow of disdainful lead. (But why this divine intervention? She had made her choice of what not to love with Leucippus's murder.) Divinely besotted, Apollo pursues Daphne. He must; not even a god can solve the problem of desire. Daphne flees Apollo's doubly unwanted advances. She prays to Mother Earth for escape, for rescue from the bitter ordinariness of being a footnote in the many conquests of a divine hero. And in her headlong flight from the god, when swift Apollo's outstretched arm encircles Daphne's waist and Apollo's hand—a musician's hand with a lyre player's slim fingers—lifts to cup her breast, Mother Earth answers Daphne's plea. Daphne metamorphoses into a laurel tree. Feet, waist, arms, and hair are roots, trunk, limbs, and leaves.

Agreeable, although he's been stiffed (this is even more unbelievable), Apollo plucks one of Daphne's evergreen boughs and plaits for himself a victor's wreath—the laurel crown that Olympic winners will wear, that modern poets laureate symbolically hang from their even more symbolic lyres. These are the laurels that champions in their triumphs will be given as they stand above the cheering crowd gathered at the foot of the rostrum. If the gods/heroes/celebrities remember the source of the laurel wreaths they wear, they'll know that the prize they most wanted eluded them—that it will always elude them.

Risks

Laurus nobilis—the noble laurel—is the tree Daphne changed into in Ovid's version of the myth. The similar tree indigenous to Los Angeles is *Umbellularia californica*, also called the California bay laurel. Like many things in myths and in Los Angeles, our laurel is a substitute standing in for virtuous Daphne, for the savory leaf flavoring a bouillabaisse, for the plaited crown of a hero. With larger leaves and a bitter taste, the California bay laurel doesn't make it onto the brows of victors or into bowls of fish stew. There's even some question if our tree is poisonous. The United States Department of Agriculture posts a toxicity warning in its profile of *U. californica*. Other sources, mostly from the nineteenth century, make claims for our laurel's beneficial properties. Tea from laurel berries will treat dysentery. A poultice of boiled laurel leaves and olive oil will heal wounds. Crushed, the leaves cure headaches. Or maybe they cause them. It's not clear. And our tree has another power, as lethal as wildfire. The California bay laurel nurtures the pathogen that causes Sudden Oak Death.

Our laurel—heady with too much perfume and risk—isn't what you'd wish it to be, although it looks as if it might be, but only if your glance is distracted, only if you see it in the glare of klieg lights, only if you're speeding along a canyon road hoping that the city below will reveal itself, that Los Angeles will stop escaping your grasp, stop turning into something else, something that may be lethal or not, healing or not. It's never very clear.

Clefts in a World

The Santa Monica Mountains rise in a jumble of geologic blocks thrust up like titanic pistons, first as islands edged by submarine trenches and then on shore as a granite wedge that arrows easterly. The body of the wedge is pleated into a row of neat north-south arroyos. The ridges between are dissected by lesser clefts like veins in a leaf, like the gathers of a skirt falling from around a woman's waist. These mountains are moving north and west as the Pacific plate rubs past the North American continental plate, which is moving south and east. These mountains are still rising. Erosion plays counterpoint to their continued uplift.

Ages of winter rains blowing from the south and west made streams that cut long-legged canyons in the hillsides. The water that flowed in them pooled in basins or turned subterranean and reappeared as perennial springs or canyon streams. The canyons from Topanga to Cahuenga were a whole world once. And when the heat of early autumn burned the grasses of the coastal plain gold and brown, the canyons lay cool and wet beneath their laurels.

Near the tip of the mountain wedge, before it narrows to a point and hooks slightly, the contours of the ridges soften; the canyons splay more. "Subdued" is the word used in Bulletin 158 of the Department of Natural Resources of the California State Division of Mines to describe Laurel Canyon. Subdued but only partly. Just as Prince Leucippus discovered there are risks cavorting in nature, Laurel Canyon isn't exactly what you might most desire. Laurel Canyon has burned throughout its history and will again. It has trembled in earthquakes and will again. In flood years, mudslides from the hillsides have gagged the canyon's mouth. They may again.

Other Gods

Dancing and singing, said the First People of Laurel Canyon,[33] the gods created the mountains and the canyons, the deer and the geese, the oaks and the laurels, the willows and the marsh reeds (bent into domed shelters, plaited into baskets). To improve their world of foothill and canyon, the First People were taught mastery of fire. Deliberate burning killed the seedlings that competed with the oaks that gave acorns for food. Fire opened the ground for hunting near the stream that flowed from Laurel Canyon onto the plain. Fire completed the work of the gods, who had made the hot, dry winds of autumn to stoke the flames in the flue-like canyons. They had made the seed heads of native flowers burst only after flames had touched them, sowing another spring.

From time to time, the First People set fire to their willow and reed shelters and plaited new shelters at the mouth of Laurel Canyon. In their season, boys became men hallucinating on a decoction of the jimsonweed that grew there. Girls became women, dancing and singing in their circle. In wet years, hunters pushed off in reed canoes to cross the marshy *ciénegas* to hunt and trap. In drought years, the famished dead were burned with what little they had. Afterward, the dead were said to become stars. There must have been more knowledge than this, accounts as full as the myths told of Apollo, Daphne, and Leucippus, but all we have now are a few transcriptions of native stories. There are even a few wax cylinder recordings of voices. We have an incomplete dictionary and some grammar, an echo. It's as if we had only a single torn page from a literature that flourished for a thousand years.

The world of the canyon's First People was gone so quickly after Europeans trespassed it that shamans had no time to add European honeybees to the inventory of their jimsonweed dreams or discover which preparation of laurel leaves would ease the symptoms of the smallpox and measles that accompanied the Spanish. The shamans had no time before they and their visions were swallowed up by Fray Junípero Serra's mission system in the 1770s; no time before disease and liquor burned through Native villages after the missions were secularized in the 1830s. When Americans in the 1850s crossed the plain below the mouth of Laurel Canyon, they saw only cattle and horses on a thousand hillsides. They saw the thick stalks of mustard plants, successful invaders, too, vivid with yellow flowers in spring and rising chest high to a man riding on horseback. The fields of wild mustard stretched to the horizon, and riders saw no one living there.

Subdivided Mythology

One version of the myth of Los Angeles begins with that man on horseback riding through a landscape assembled by forces he doesn't understand and shaped by the actions of indigenous men and women he mistakenly believes had done nothing with their land. The man on horseback believes he sees Laurel Canyon as it has always been, as golden as mustard flowers. He believes that no one before him has thought to improve it. He believes that the land will yield to him whenever he puts his hand to it. He's untroubled by the ironies of improvement. Not a single story clings to him, he believes, that he can't revise again and again. He thinks that he has been made new out of his willful ignorance.

The man on horseback, cutting through the tall mustard stalks, is replaced in a few years by another man in a buckboard on a rutted country road (it will become Sunset Boulevard) to be replaced by men stringing electrical wires to power a "trackless trolley" up a newly laid gravel road that branches off Sunset before it dead-ends in a rustic subdivision in the upper part of Laurel Canyon. The subdivision is called Bungalow Land.

"The Laurel Canyon Land Company," reported the *Los Angeles Herald* in 1909, "has erected a bungalow inn and a number of small bungalows for rental purposes, affording the visitors an opportunity to enjoy the mountain environments for an indefinite time, as they may desire. Numerous side roads and trails have been constructed, affording magnificent viewpoints for those who take the mountain climb."[34] The *Los Angeles Examiner* enthused that "the many pretty curves along the way ... will make it one of the most famous drives of Southern California." County Supervisor S. Tuston Eldridge thought so, too. He built a summer home along the canyon road, the *Examiner* reported. The house was said to be "elegant in the extreme."[35]

The electrified "trackless trolley" ascending Laurel Canyon was on "a road to nowhere," the editors of the *Herald* later complained. The nowhere was a collection of intersecting ridges and folds that Laurel Canyon Land Company subdivided into house lots to sell to enchanted tourists who would ride the trolley up the canyon to marvel at the views of Los Angeles and the Pacific Ocean from Lookout Mountain. The tourists got a sales pitch before they got to the view:

Nearly every type of real estate development and its consequent increase in value has been offered to you at one time or another—except mountain or canyon property.... [I]t is another one of Los Angeles' opportunity offerings. Are you going to avail yourself of the chance this time—or wait again to tell the later-comer how much you "might have made" and didn't? And don't forget that as he listens, Mr. Later-Comer has an opinion of you that he mentally reserves but would do you good if he gave it voice.[36]

The road that potential buyers took to Bungalow Land, the *Herald* complained, was paid for by diverting $30,000 in county highway repair funds.[37] The *Herald* accused County Supervisor "Tuss" Eldridge of engineering the swindle. Eldridge and Charles Spencer Mann, it turned out, were co-owners of Laurel Canyon Land Company. They had thought it a good idea to get Eldridge elected to the Board of Supervisors in 1906 on a platform of road improvement. Eldridge and Mann had only one improvement in mind. The county's new road in 1908 went nowhere except to the lots that Eldridge and Mann had for sale in what the developers pitched as a better paradise, better than the one that Los Angeles was already supposed to be. It wasn't, for reasons of fire and mudslide. Bungalow Land Company intended to convert dirt into desire but, true to the story, some disappointment followed, just as Apollo found when unyielding Daphne turned into a laurel tree.

Scenes in Wonderland

Mann, aided by the unapologetic graft of Supervisor Eldridge, subdivided Laurel Canyon as it steps up to the ridges that divide Hollywood from the San Fernando Valley. He made the same prodigiously hopeful sales pitch that other developers did for Los Angeles in its early twentieth-century springtime. Hillsides in Los Angeles have always been imagined as a place apart, not just for their beauty but literally, because they're above, reaching for what Los Angeles promises but never fully delivers no matter how high you go. The climate of the canyon was even more perfect than the famous climate of Los Angeles. The air was purer and well above summer fog. Redemptive Nature was near at hand. "Out of sight and sound of the city, yet near to it," the advertisements promised, "always healthful, always delightful, always natural," which were the original promises in the myth of Los Angeles, that development improved its perfect nature. Mann named part of his subdivision Wonderland Park.

Mann made a fetish of who the buyers should be. "Extreme care is taken in choosing purchasers; only the desirable welcomed," claimed one advertisement. Only "people of a high plane of living, of thought, and of conduct" were permitted to buy, according to another. "A person disorderly or vicious is seldom found among Bungalow Land crowds of visitors," remarked an ad (without resolving what "seldom" implied). In Bungalow Land, an ad in the *Los Angeles Times* in 1909 promised, "liquor and race restrictions [insure] good conduct and desirable people for all time to come."[38] Improvement of Laurel Canyon required policing "for all time to come." Desire needed management.

Mann eventually left Laurel Canyon and went higher, developing Crestline in the San Bernardino Mountains. Supervisor Eldridge, tied to other scandals, was defeated for re-election in 1910. There was some poetic justice in his loss to Sidney A. Butler, who was chairman of the county's Good Roads Advisory Committee. The "trackless trolley" to Bungalow Land stopped running in 1915, worn out by the grade. But the real estate ads continued to promise that owning a piece of Laurel Canyon was entry into a world apart, above the flats of Hollywood soon to be covered by gas stations, apartment blocks, and the rest of ordinary Los Angeles under its extraordinary sun.

Laurel Canyon by then had a few estate-size lots along the canyon road, setting up their excavated hillsides to fail in future winters, their ornamental trees to burn in future autumns. The well-to-do and people in the movies bought the big lots and the eloquent views. In the narrower folds away from the highway, the promises of Laurel Canyon were subdivided more cheaply. Workmen graded hillsides into fractions of an acre and fronted them with a network of roadways barely a Ford Model-T wide.

With its fire-knowledgeable Native cultivators dispossessed, Laurel Canyon returned to a primordial rhythm of uncontrolled burning. The canyon burned in 1904 (destroying several homes), in 1918 (consuming the Lookout Mountain Inn and adjacent bungalows), and in 1921 (destroying more homes). Lesser fires burned in 1935, 1941, 1949, and 1956. A disastrous fire in 1959 destroyed more than thirty homes. Another fire in 1979 took twenty-three homes, most of them before the Los Angeles Fire Department could lay its first hose line. As the department's report explained, "The topography of the fire area is comprised of steep hills, heavy brush, very winding narrow streets with single ingress and egress, and a heavy concentration of older structures built in close proximity to each other on top of ridges."[39] In Los Angeles, the image of beauty and perfection is always paired with loss.

Burned Out

Up in the canyon, the houses on the wayward, dead-end streets were often owner-built, originally only for weekend use. A few were an idiosyncratic jumble of compromises with the slant of the lot, the builder's finances and the drift of time, perfect for renting or selling to people whose "plane of living, of thought, and of conduct" often started with the unconventional and sometimes ended in violence. By the 1960s, the free-spirited people in those makeshift houses were having chemically induced visions as they sang and danced. The canyon itself was the subject of some of their songs: John Mayall's "Laurel Canyon Home," Jackie DeShannon's "Laurel Canyon," Van Dyke Parks's "Laurel Canyon Boulevard," and Joni Mitchell's "Ladies of the Canyon." The music of new gods flowed out of Laurel Canyon like winter floods, like autumn wildfire. "From the mid-1960s to the early 1970s, some of the most melodic, atmospheric, and subtly political American popular music was written by residents of, or those associated with, Laurel Canyon," wrote Lisa Robinson in *Vanity Fair* in 2015:

> . . . including Joni Mitchell, Neil Young, David Crosby, Stephen Stills, Graham Nash, Chris Hillman, Roger McGuinn, J.D. Souther, Judee Sill, the Mamas and the Papas, Carole King, the Eagles, Richie Furay (in Buffalo Springfield and Poco), and many more. They made music together, played songs for one another with acoustic guitars in all-night jam sessions in each other's houses. . . . They took drugs together, formed bands together, broke up those bands and formed other bands. Many of them slept with each other. The music was mislabeled "soft rock" or "folk rock," especially in the Northeast, where critics panned it as granola-infused hippie music—too "mellow" and too white. But in truth, it was an amalgam of influences that included blues, rock and roll, jazz, Latin, country and western, psychedelia, bluegrass, and folk.[40]

When Laurel Canyon was a scene, Jimi Hendrix, James Taylor, Cass Elliot, Marianne Faithfull, Jeff Beck, David Crosby, Graham Nash, Jim Morrison, Frank Zappa, Dusty Springfield, Neil Young, and Michelle Phillips hallucinated under California laurels that may or may not be toxic. And then, like the shamans' jimsonweed dreams, like the man on horseback, like the schemes of subdividers, the scene was gone. "Scenes aren't meant to last," music producer David Geffen told *Vanity Fair*. "They sparkle with activity, flourish, then burn out. The California music scene of the late 1960s and early 1970s fell apart because of drugs, money, success, Altamont, money, drugs, burnout, and new musical trends."[41] Like Laurel Canyon itself, it was never clear what would satisfy—if only briefly—desire for fame, for endless youth, for the unobtainable.

PART 2

Becoming Los Angeles

BECOMING MIGHT BE the definition of Los Angeles, but what we're becoming has always been uncertain (*Who Do You Say I Am?*) and subject to revision (*Coming Here* and *Some Assembly Required*) or casually discarded (*The Death of Riley*). Becoming was pitiless for some Angelenos (*Don't Be Lonesome* and *Becoming Homeless*). In my suburban childhood, becoming was toxic (*I'm Dreaming of a Smoggy Christmas*), mediated by black-and-white television (*Over Los Angeles* and *Tom Hatten: Rascals and Stooges*), and lived as a regime of speed (*Los Angeles Loves Wheels*).

Ways of becoming constrained some Angelenos (*Signs and Wonders, What We Talk About,* and *Stupid, Unproductive, Gullible*) and gave meaning to others, as profiles in the following pages suggest. And when Angelenos felt most bereft, there was *La Virgen,* comforter of the wayward.

Who Do You Say I Am?

According to the *Inmortales* of the Real Academia Española, we're angelinos. The emblem of Spain's royal academy is a refining crucible, wreathed in fire, with the motto *Limpia, fija y da esplendor*. The RAE has been purging, pinning down, and burnishing Spanish since 1713. Its language fixes were royal decrees in 1844. Today, the academy continues more democratically to wrangle into order the grammar, spelling, and vocabulary of Spain and its former colonies.

We became angelinos because of basketball. When the Los Angeles Lakers signed the Catalán forward Pau Gasol in 2008, Spain's sports writers needed a ruling on what to call Los Angeles basketball fans. It was unclear if they should be *angelinos, angeleños, angelopolitanos*, or another *gentilicio* (which in Spanish denotes a people). The rapid response unit of the royal academy—the Fundación del Español Urgente (Foundation for Emerging Spanish)—picked *angelino*, a *gentilicio* already in Spanish dictionaries and used by some Spanish-speaking residents of Los Angeles to name themselves.[1]

America doesn't have an academy for fixing its language, but it did have H.L. Mencken—journalist, bigot, and scholar of how Americans speak. Mencken was committed to American English in all its ways and varieties (called descriptivism by linguists, in contrast to the prescriptivism of the royal academy). In 1936, he mused in *The New Yorker* on the words commonly used to name a city's residents:

> The citizen of New York calls himself a New Yorker, the citizen of Chicago calls himself a Chicagoan, the citizen of Buffalo calls himself a Buffalonian, the citizen of Seattle calls himself a Seattleite, and the citizen of Los Angeles calls himself an Angeleño. . . . In Los Angeles, of course, Angeleño is seldom used by the great masses of Bible students and hopeful Utopians, most of whom think and speak of themselves not as citizens of the place at all but as Iowans, Nebraskans, North and South Dakotans, and so on. But the local newspapers like to show off Angeleño, though they always forget the tilde.[2]

Mencken hated Los Angeles for its provincialism, which may explain in part why he favored "Angeleño," the least common, least Iowan, and most musical word to bind a heedless people to their place. Mencken presumed that the tilde in Angeleño was an accent mark that careless typesetters forgot. It isn't. The unfamiliar ñ—eñe (pronounced "enyá")—has been a separate letter in the Spanish alphabet since the eighteenth century. (Think of the "nyon" sound in *cañon*, although that's not exactly it either.) Angeleño to Mencken may have sounded something like "ăn'-hə-lənyō" or perhaps "ăn'-hə-lānyo," with stress on the first syllable which sounded more like "awn" and less like "ann."

Angeleño wasn't a word residents of Los Angeles would have seen in the *Los Angeles Times* in 1936. Mencken was right that the most-used Los Angeles demonym (the technical term for a place-based name) was Angeleno, without the eñe. The *Times* spelled it that way in more than seven hundred articles in 1936 alone (and at least ten thousand times between 1930 and 1950). Angeleno—usually pronounced "ăn'-jə-lē'-nō"—stresses the first and third syllables and sounds like nothing in Spanish.

In picking Angeleño, Mencken, perhaps unthinking, had fallen into the prescriptivist trap. When an expert makes a definitive choice—and Mencken was an expert[3]—it's understood to be the "right way" to say something. But the people of Los Angeles didn't have the perfect word for themselves even before the diaspora of flat-voweled Midwesterners arrived in the 1920s. We still don't have one word that holds us all.

Disappearing Ñ

A 2015 report to the Los Angeles Cultural Heritage Commission, in a filing to give historical status to an Edwardian-era house, named its location as Angelino Heights, Angeleno Heights, and Angeleño Heights almost interchangeably. Naming the heights—the city's first suburb in 1886—lays a sequence of mutating demonyms on the landscape of Los Angeles and threads them through the city's history. The maps that parceled out lots on a ridge overlooking downtown were headed with the title Angeleño Heights. The tract's name became Angeleno Heights in the advertising copy of the *Los Angeles Times* and the *Los Angeles Herald*, probably because the decorative typefaces used by compositors for real estate ads lacked the eñe character. The *Herald* did use Angeleño Heights in other contexts after 1886 but not exclusively. The *Times* used Angeleno Heights in classified ads and news stories, but a few listings and location references used Angeleño Heights instead. The Birdseye View Publishing Co. rendered virtually every building in Los Angeles on a 1909 map. A block of houses on a ridge along Kensington Road, still isolated among empty fields, is labeled Angeleño Heights. By 1918, Angeleño Heights had disappeared. Angelino Heights rarely appeared, except in a few house-for-sale ads, probably typeset that way when the seller telephoned the ad. It's an easy error to make when spelling by ear. For English-only speakers, both Angelino and Angeleno will sound the same.

Anecdotal accounts suggest that spelling by ear led city planners in the 1950s to permanently anglicize the neighborhood's name as Angelino Heights. Highway directional signs continued to point to Angelino Heights until 2008, when Los Angeles City Councilman Ed Reyes had them replaced, correcting the signs but only to the first, eñe-less error. Eventually, a truce was called. At Bellevue Avenue and East Edgeware Road are two signs that spell out the neighborhood differently: Angeleno Heights is on the highway directional sign; the city's historic marker uses Angelino Heights.

Angeleño, Angeleno, Angelino

The 130-year drift from Angeleño to Angeleno to Angelino back to Angeleno parallels the uncertainties that linger in our name for ourselves. In 1850, when the Mexican Ciudad de los Ángeles abruptly became the American city of Los Angeles, its tiny anglophone population was necessarily bilingual in borderlands Spanish. Court proceedings, ordinances, and city council meetings were in English and Spanish (and sometimes only in Spanish). What the city's new Americans called themselves isn't clear. It may even have been Angeleño. The eñe was still in the type fonts of printers. *The Star/La Estrella*—the city's bilingual newspaper—accurately characterized travelers from Sonora as Sonoreños in 1853. But the paper apparently had no collective name for Los Angeles residents, identifying them as Americans, Californians, and Mexicans in the English language columns and as *americanos*, *californios*, and *mejicanos/mexicanos* on its Spanish pages. El Clamor Publico—the city's Spanish language newspaper in the 1850s—did the same. It wasn't until January 1878 that the *Los Angeles Herald* listed the names of residents as Los Angeleños. By 1880, the *Herald* had clipped this to Angeleños, a spelling the paper continued to use intermittently with Angelenos through early 1895. The *Herald* then carried on without an eñe until the paper merged with the *Los Angeles Evening Express* in 1921. The *Los Angeles Times* was equally inconsistent. In 1882, less than a year after its first edition, the paper was regularly referring to Angeleños collectively. Angeleños (sometimes with "Los") appeared in news and society columns through mid-1910, a linguistic puzzle for the growing number of residents who had never heard their demonym spoken. But some writers in Los Angeles had heard its echo.

In 1888, Walter Lindley and J.P. Widney referenced Angeleños in their popular guidebook, as did Charles Lummis in *Out West* magazine in the late 1890s. T. Corry Conner's city guide in 1902 and J.M. Guinn's history of California in 1907 both used Angeleño to name Los Angeles residents. Harris Newmark—who had arrived in 1853 from Germany and who spoke Spanish as often as he did English in those days—used Angeleño throughout his 1916 memoir. Even as the twentieth century began, the eñe in Angeleño lingered at the margins of the city's self-image, a fading music.

But had that music ever actually played?

Orthographic Salsa

In 1948, the *Los Angeles Times* style guide directed the paper's copyeditors to reference Angeleno/Angelenos exclusively. Angelino/Angelinos made it into other papers, spelled in imitation of the sound that transplants gave to the last syllable of "loss an´-je-leeze" (when they didn't pronounce Los Angeles as "loss-sang'-liss"). Angeleno/Angelenos made it into dictionaries: in the second edition of the *Oxford English Dictionary* (which gave Angeleño as an alternative); in the third unabridged *Merriam-Webster Dictionary* (which offered Angelino as an alternative); and in the current *American Heritage Dictionary* (with no alternate spelling).

Dictionaries that provide word origins point to *angeleño* and the Spanish eño morpheme as the source from which American English Angeleno was derived. It makes a neat evolutionary tree. Angeleño (hard for English-only speakers) begets Angeleno (easier but unclear about the value of the second e), which becomes Angelino (finally pinning down that value). Except the Angeleño root may be conjectural. The *OED* dates Angeleño's first appearance to 1888 in the Lindley and Widney guidebook. The appearance of Angeleño in the *Los Angeles Herald* in 1878 pushes back the word's first use in print, but 1878 is a decade after the city ceased to be casually bilingual.

For Robert D. Angus, writing in *California Linguistic Notes*, the Angeleño origin story is unlikely, and the word is probably an Anglo invention. Angeleño "appears to be a self-conscious and intentional (but erroneous) emulation of a Spanish looking and sounding form, a kind of fashionable hypercorrection, garnishing an article in a trendy publication like a dab of orthographic salsa."[4] Despite the appearance of Angeleño/Angeleños in contemporary publications in Latin America (and even in the English language newspaper published in the Filipino city of Angeles), each fresh occurrence of the eñe might be another instance of spreading Anglo orthographic salsa. The pull of American English, Angus thought, would naturally end the confusion, and we would properly be Los Angeleans one day.

Who Do You Say We Are?

Comb through books in English published since 1950 for the names that the people of Los Angeles have been given, and Angelenos tops the other alternatives: angelinos, angeleños, and Angeleans. That doesn't make Angeleno the right (prescriptivist) way to identify us but only the typical (descriptivist) way. No more right is angelino (with an aspirated g that breathes into the following e: "ăn'-həl-ēnō"), despite the royal academy's decision to fix our *gentilicio*. Nor is Angeleño more correct, despite my own attempts (and of some in the Latinx community) to foster that name back into use. Angeleño might be a linguistic myth and a reminder of Anglo nostalgia for the fantasy romance of Spanish Los Angeles, but that the name may be a myth is inconsequential. Angeleño is in the reality of Los Angeles.

Although we're no longer Mencken's tribes of "Iowans, Nebraskans, North and South Dakotans, and so on," a worse alternative for the future would be two permanently divergent language streams, their Spanish and English histories separated although they share the same place. A Latinx resident of Boyle Heights could choose to be an *angelino/ăn'-həl-ēnō*, the Anglo Westsider would always be an Angeleno/ăn'-jə-lē'-nō, and neither *angelinos* nor Angelenos would know the full music of the other, depriving both speakers of some of the hybridizing *mestizaje* of Los Angeles. They would never experience the strangeness that Jesuit philosopher Michel de Certeau thought was necessary to make the everyday more difficult in order to make it more truly felt. They wouldn't know the many stories of their place and end by not knowing their place at all. "Through stories about places," de Certeau wrote, "they become habitable. . . . One must awaken the stories that sleep in the streets and that sometimes lie within a simple name."[5]

Los Angeles existed first in the mouth. It was spoken before it was. It was inhabited with words before it was lived in by us. In the process, Los Angeles has gathered many names. All of them have entered into language and the imagination and thus into history. Angelino, Angeleno, and Angeleño (even Angelean) are part of who we are, part of our sense of self and of place. We're all those names.

Coming Here

Publisher Harrison Gray Otis was looking for an editor in 1884 to write for the *Los Angeles Daily Times*. The four-page paper bragged to its readers that it was "the county's official paper." The county had just thirty-four thousand residents. The Southern Pacific had linked Los Angeles to the transcontinental rail network less than a decade before. (It wouldn't be until 1888 that trains arrived directly from the Midwest.) The city's first paved road—Main Street—had been laid down less than four years before.

Los Angeles itself had thirteen thousand residents, but more would come, Otis was sure. Already an "orange empire" in the inland valleys had begun to boom, proving the agricultural abundance of Southern California. Civil War veterans with shattered nerves and "lungers" suffering the urban scourge of tuberculosis were redeeming another promise—renewed health and vitality in the sunshine and clear air of Los Angeles.

Otis was confident that Los Angeles, so favored, wasn't destined to remain in the shadow of San Francisco, then the center of industry, finance, and population in California. What Los Angeles needed, Otis thought, was a journalist and storyteller, a weaver of tales, and a poet to further Otis's demand that the city deliver on another promise. Otis intended to turn the vacant, dusty acres of Los Angeles County into farms, orchards, and house lots for the thousands of migrants who could be enchanted to come and make Otis rich.

He found his editor and storyteller in twenty-four-year-old Charles Fletcher Lummis, who pitched himself perfectly to the *Daily Times* publisher. Los Angeles was a promise of adventure and romance for Lummis. He planned to get both by convincing Otis of his Republican Party loyalty, his journalistic bravado, and his capacity for the strenuous life. Otis was impressed by Lummis's skill in selling himself but even more by Lummis's proposal to walk a meandering 3,500 miles from his home in Chillicothe, Ohio, to Los Angeles, sending newspaper dispatches along the way to be published in the *Daily Times*. Half a year later, Otis greeted Lummis in San Gabriel. Lummis had nearly died in the snows of Colorado and later New Mexico. He had broken his arm while crossing the Arizona desert after which he set the bone himself. Otis offered him the job as editor and walked the last ten miles to Los Angeles with him.

For all its real dangers, walking to Los Angeles in 1884 was essentially a stunt, a way for Lummis to replay for *Daily Times* subscribers the heroic narrative that heading west had already become in the Californian imagination. Getting here had become part of what being here meant. The more arduous, the more demanding the passage, the more legitimate was the migrant's claim to the promises of California. Lummis's suffering, even as part of a stunt, seemed to prove that he'd earned the golden destiny that Otis imagined for Los Angeles.

El Dorado and Donner Pass

Joan Didion, a Sacramento native, has framed her family's pioneer journey west in terms that Lummis would have understood. Didion's family had crossed mountains and deserts in a train of covered wagons to come west in the 1840s. Along the way, they had pitched over the wagon's side nearly all the finer things they had accumulated until they, like other migrants, had only the things that were needed to survive. A reed organ was left by the trail. Babies dead along the way were buried there. So were husbands and wives. So were certain assumptions about coming to California.

What the survivors of the passage gained in exchange, Didion argued, was a stripped-down "wagon train morality" that she thought could still be found in the descendants of pioneer migrants. "One of the promises we make to one another," she writes in "On Morality," "is that we will try to retrieve our casualties, try not to abandon our dead to the coyotes. If we have been taught to keep our promises—if, in the simplest terms, our upbringing is good enough—we stay with the body, or have bad dreams."[6]

But Didion suspects that the journey had other lessons. Crossing Death Valley and the Sierra Nevada "might not, after all, be a noble odyssey, might instead be a mean scrambling for survival."[7] What if what you earned in coming to California wasn't a golden El Dorado but snowbound Donner Pass in the winter of 1846, not a gift of fortune but a dehumanizing fall into despair, brutality, and cannibalism? The living who survived Donner Pass were coyotes to their dead. They had "somewhere abdicated their responsibilities, somehow breached their primary loyalties, or they would not have found themselves helpless in the mountain winter ... would not have given way to acrimony, would not have deserted one another, would not have failed." Didion's ancestors hadn't failed. Josephus and Nancy Cornwall (Didion's great-great-grandparents), heading for Oregon, split off from the Donner wagon train before the fatal error of taking a shortcut to California. Shortcuts expose character flaws. Flying to Los Angeles from New York, Didion felt strangely guilty. "The more comfortable the flight, the more obscurely miserable I would be, for it weighs heavily upon my kind that we could perhaps not make it by wagon."[8]

And what if getting to California wasn't the Cornwalls' righteous odyssey but something the strong snatched from the weak? Broken wagons were abandoned along the pioneer trail, as were broken men and women, so as not to delay passage, not to risk being lost yourself. If surviving said that you were worthy to inherit the promises of California, then the only imperative was survival. "The redemptive power of the crossing was . . . the fixed idea of the California settlement . . . ." Didion observed. But your survival raised a further question. "[F]or what exactly, and at what cost, had one been redeemed? When you jettison others so as not to be 'caught by winter in the Sierra Nevada mountains,' do you deserve not to be caught?" If coming here was both test and moral instruction, what kind of Californian had you become in taking lessons from its pitiless landscape? "When you survive at the cost of [fellow migrants], do you survive at all?"[9]

Complicating the redeeming test of coming here were newer migrants, including the parents of the teenagers with whom Didion went to high school in Sacramento in the 1950s. Many of them had put the tragedies of the Dust Bowl and the Depression behind them by coming here. By the end of 1945, an estimated six hundred thousand internal migrants had arrived to work in the orchards and oil camps of the Central Valley and then the shipyards of San Francisco and Long Beach and the defense plants of Santa Monica and San Diego. Didion has noted the parallels between the Cornwalls in their covered wagon in 1846 and the migrants in battered Fords and Chevrolets in 1936 who rode the same trails—now national highways—to California. The Depression immigrants ended their journey years later in a tract house suburb like mine. Didion wondered if Nancy and Josephus Cornwall would have recognized them as inheritors of California, would have seen them as "their kind." Didion regretted that those who came in Chevrolets weren't as truly Californian as those who came in Conestoga wagons.

When I was young, I lived among suburban Okies and Arkies and other Dusters from the margins of the South and Midwest. They had jobs, paid the mortgage on a small house, followed milder forms of faith than the strenuous religion of their grandparents, and listened to the country western music coming out of Bakersfield for consolation. Within the compass of their lives, California seemed to have delivered on as many of its golden promises as they were likely to get. They didn't expect more, only enough. Didion thought of my not-quite-middle-class neighbors as an "artificial ownership class"[10] of insubstantial believers in false promises who hadn't earned what they had, unlike the lucky or heartless realists whose survival meant they deserved El Dorado.

Even if coming here was morally suspect and the promises turned out to be a scheme to sell real estate, the sons and daughters of wagon train migrants still wanted to say who could become Californian. Mexicans were excluded by long habit. Chinese were excluded by law in 1882, as were Japanese in 1924. State police turned Dusters away at the Arizona border in the first years of the Depression. African Americans were segregated; Japanese Americans interned. The terms of the journey here still filter Californians from those who can't ever be.

When these unwanted dreamers of the golden dream arrive, legally or illegally, their journey has taught them something, perhaps less about "wagon train morality" and more about the fierceness of desire. Ask Gustavo Arellano, a writer for the *Los Angeles Times* and a memoirist of his family's migration north, which he understands to be as storied as the Cornwalls. "My father?" he wrote in 2008, "He fondly remembers the comfortable space in the trunk of a Chevy Bel Air that was his ticket to the American dream. In 1968, Dad left his dying village of Jomulquillo, in the Mexican state of Zacatecas, to join his three older brothers in East Los Angeles."[11] Lorenzo Arellano was eighteen, another young man full of bravado with a fourth-grade education. Lingering in the Californian imagination is a paradox—avoiding the tragedy of Donner Pass legitimized your claim to be Californian in 1846 but avoiding the agents of *La Migra* in 1964 didn't.

Lorenzo Arellano had to make the journey north over and over, twice cutting through the fence that secured the border and once crawling through a sewage-choked drain that entered California near a McDonald's in San Ysidro. Arellano, now a naturalized citizen, "never tires of telling these stories to anyone who'll listen—his eyes light up, he gestures wildly, and a smile always cracks wide." His journey here had become another instructional narrative, a mixture of humiliation and triumph. Gustavo Arellano doesn't say what promise of California his father dreamed of. Perhaps there was none except the bare possibility of something better than Jomulquillo. The younger Arellano doesn't wonder if the California his father crawled through sewage to reach was a mirage. He doesn't doubt that his father earned his California.

Perversely Resilient

Coming to California—and specifically to Los Angeles—became satire in the literary tradition that runs from H.L. Mencken through Nathanael West, F. Scott Fitzgerald, William Faulkner, and Evelyn Waugh to Peter Plagens, Bruce Wagner, and Geoff Dyer. Los Angeles is an absurd place at a journey's end, a place whose people, climate, and architecture are contemptibly insubstantial yet perversely resilient. Wave after wave of migrants came only because they had substituted for the deficiencies of the city its false promises: Hollywood stardom, a house in the suburbs, a reinvented identity, a second chance, an escape. Seduction by the malign power of Los Angeles was equally toxic for seekers after the "station wagon way of life" in the 1960s, for African Americans getting out of the segregated South in the 1950s, and for chamber of commerce beauty queens getting out of small towns in the 1940s. For the skeptics, there are no legitimate reasons to come to Los Angeles. The painter David Hockney thought there was at least one good reason, as he explained to Lawrence Weschler:

> As a child, growing up in Bradford in the north of England, across the gothic gloom of those endless winters, I remember how my father used to take me along with him to see the Laurel and Hardy movies; and one of the things I noticed right away, long before I could even articulate it exactly, was how Stanley and Oliver, bundled in their winter overcoats, were casting these wonderfully strong, crisp shadows. We never got shadows of any sort in winter. And already I knew that someday I wanted to settle in a place with winter shadows like that. In fact years later, when I staged *The Magic Flute*, it's that aspect of the story that I keyed onto—this journey from darkness toward the light, how the light pulls and pulls you. It certainly did me, anyway: the light and those strong, crisp shadows.[12]

It was preserved light—the bright light insensitive film stock required—that transported Hockney. His reason to come to Los Angeles, after watching a train of moving shadows in a Yorkshire theater, was grounded on everything that shadows in winter light implied. As so many of us did, Hockney became an Angeleno at the movies long before he came to Los Angeles.

William Faulkner, bitter about being in Hollywood (which he mistook for Los Angeles), found the light of Hockney's dreams ironic and perverse. In "Golden Land," a short story from 1935, the awful light breeds lush inauthenticity:

> The sun, strained by the vague high soft almost nebulous California haze, fell upon the terrace with a kind of treacherous unbrightness. The terrace, the sun-drenched terracotta tiles, butted into a rough and savage shear of canyon-wall bare yet without dust, on or against which a solid mat of flowers bloomed in fierce lush myriad-colored paradox as though in place of being rooted into and drawing from the soil they lived upon air alone and had been merely leaned intact against the sustenanceless lava-wall by someone who would later return and take them away.[13]

Faulkner's light is already Los Angeles noir. It's the dull light of Pasadena congealing into malice in *Mildred Pierce* (1941). It's the harsh light in Glendale turning to murderous night in *Double Indemnity* (1943). It's the light that conceals Los Angeles for the clueless Jake Gittes in *Chinatown* (1974).

Did the members of the Donner wagon train, rising into the foothills of the Sierra Nevada, travel in that treacherous light and were they deceived by it? Did Josephus Cornwall, a Presbyterian minister, receive by the light of faith the grace to turn away from Donner's tragic shortcut, or was it only a lucky accident? Do our stories of coming to Los Angeles record what has been hard won, or do they merely dress up the illusions from which Los Angeles is made? Has there been no one who earned becoming Californian?

Some Assembly Required

The founders of Los Angeles ended their ten-mile walk southwest from Mission San Gabriel Arcángel in September 1781. They came down a low ridge whose slopes were dotted with clumps of white sage and saw smoke rising from the cooking fires of the Tongva village of Yangna. The colonists were assigned farm plots along the western bank of a little river and marked the corners of a plaza before they began building shelters for their first night in the new pueblo of Los Angeles.

The pueblo and the Native village perched on the same riverbank, but the pueblo was structurally distinct from the village. Pueblo de Nuestra Señora de los Ángeles was a creation of eighteenth-century rationalism, most of all in its grid of fields and town lots drawn on a sheet of notepaper before the first house was built. Yangna, its organization drawn from tradition and deep knowledge of the terrain, remained a separate center of daily life.

The Franciscan friars at the San Gabriel mission were skeptical of the secular pueblo and the habits it would plant among Yangna's gentiles (as the priests called the unchristianized Tongva), possibly infecting the neophytes laboring at the mission and awaiting baptism. The friars viewed the lax morals and doubtful parentage of the pueblo's founders with such suspicion that they would meet their religious needs only intermittently for the next forty years. Not until the 1820s did Los Angeles have a proper church and full-time pastor. The mission stayed institutionally aloof until the mission system ended.

When United States troops occupied Los Angeles during the 1846–1848 Mexican War, decades of provincial grants had additionally fractured the region into a patchwork of more than thirty ranchos. Few of them were smaller than two thousand acres; some were more than a hundred thousand. Each was nearly self-sufficient, trading hides and tallow for luxury goods and manufactured items but growing or crafting everything else. Los Angeles, now a ciudad (a city, at least provisionally) was the center of civil and social life for the rancheros, but their homes were on the coastal plain and in the valleys to the north and east.

Pueblo, Native village, mission, ranchos—Los Angeles had begun as a collection of centers and edges. It continued to be after 1850.

Speed and Seduction

When drought and the end of the Gold Rush collapsed the rancheros' cattle economy, population leaked out of Los Angeles, depressing land values and leaving the great ranchos in debt but largely intact. In a region lightly tethered to its urban core—the city of Los Angeles grew to only 5,728 residents between 1850 and 1870—the essential socio-economic problem was empty space. To propel Los Angeles from vacant land to boomtown, the missing element was speed.

In the magical years between 1886 and 1888, the steam-driven speed of rival railroads remade Los Angeles. One-way fares from the Midwest dropped below $5 and twenty-five new towns were platted by speculators on former rancho land. The boom of the 1880s ended with the suddenness of a train wreck in 1888, stranding new towns that existed mainly on paper. Another season of intense growth in the following decade accelerated the dispersal of the region's population and established a grid of irrigation systems that eventually became suburban water companies servicing the small farms, orchards, and homes that clustered along the mainline railroad tracks.

The buyers of those homes and farms were immigrants from the East and Midwest lured by glowing advertisements paid for by the Los Angeles Chamber of Commerce. The buyers settled in towns that had begun in the 1870s as semi-rural enclaves for like-minded Republicans and churchgoers who came as a group from the same hometown in Indiana, Ohio, or Iowa. The right-thinking residents of Pasadena (incorporated in 1875), Monrovia (1875), Long Beach (1880), Whittier (1887), and Claremont (1887) shared a peculiarly American sensibility that mixed social uplift, fear of ethnic contagion, and entrepreneurial ambition. As one booster pitched it, Claremont was "the mountain home, the place of rest, the sanitarium," and in his haste to sell another lot to another newcomer, his sales pitch elided metaphors of a tamed wilderness, redemptive healing, and flight from disorder. In effect, you came to Claremont or Glendale or Long Beach to live among white, middle-class property owners who were farmers or shopkeepers as well as part-time real estate speculators. In buying Los Angeles acreage, you hoped to acquire for yourself a utopian amalgam of domesticity, modernity, and profitable leisure, just as the boosters promised. If you could, you purchased this dream whole in the form of an orange grove whose ordered grid defined the image of Los Angeles as a house set apart in a garden. If you couldn't afford an orange grove, you could buy a house lot planted with a single orange tree. The purchase, in either case, implied that, in acquiring any part of Los Angeles, you acquired all of nature and all of civilization.

What you wanted from Los Angeles wasn't centered in a particular place; it was everywhere. What you feared was centered in the Los Angeles Chinatown and the Sonoratown barrio at the edge of the plaza that had been marked out a hundred years before, in September 1781.

Potential Subdivisions

The twentieth century quickened the pace of geographic and social decentralization to the speed of electricity. Already by 1898, Los Angeles had a rudimentary transit system that included a line between downtown and Pasadena. A group of shrewd investors—including Collis Huntington, president of the Southern Pacific Railroad, and his nephew Henry Huntington—saw the possibilities in electrified transit to transform square miles of former rancho land into suburbs, in the same way steam railways in the 1880s had turned the valleys and foothills around Los Angeles into orchards, vineyards, and farm towns.

Henry Huntington began buying cheap land and, in 1901, established the Pacific Electric Railway to tie his scattered properties together. The Old Mission Route went to San Gabriel and Pasadena before returning to Los Angeles. The Balloon Route ran west from downtown through Hollywood, Santa Monica and Venice, and returned through Culver City. The Triangle Trolley went to San Pedro, Long Beach, south to Balboa, east to Santa Ana, and back to Los Angeles. By 1914, Huntington's trolleys took potential homebuyers to destinations as distant as San Bernardino, Redlands, Santa Ana, and Yorba Linda. Every trolley stop had the potential to become another subdivision, many of them developed by Huntington.

Between 1900 and 1920, Los Angeles County's population grew from 170,298 to 936,455, and twenty-four new cities incorporated. By 1930, the population had swelled to 2,208,492, and Los Angeles County had forty-four cities. Speed had taken the embryonic distinctions in the structure of pueblo, mission, and rancho and made these distinctions the texture of Los Angeles.

Suburban Segregation

Population dispersal, hastened by the Pacific Electric system and made permanent by the freeway system after 1940, encouraged segmentation of the Los

Angeles basin by class. The quietly rich could buy an acre or two near Henry Huntington's estate in San Marino, a city so sedate that it restricted hospitals and mortuaries from its business district. (The Bel-Air development was so exclusive that it eliminated businesses entirely, except for the Bel Air Hotel.) The merely rich could live in Beverly Hills, with the added advantage that motion picture money and Jewish movie moguls were welcome there. Well-to-do Progressives could choose to live in Palos Verdes, a garden suburb designed by the Olmsted brothers in which nearly half the area was set aside as park-like open space. Developers of middle-class subdivisions—Glendale, Arcadia, Monrovia, and the Leimert Park district of Los Angeles, among others—adopted the aesthetics of a planned community while emphasizing rail and highway mobility. Some developments blended the suburb and the farm. In the San Fernando Valley, it was common until the end of the 1940s for owners of a house lot to plant an orchard, keep a kitchen garden, and raise chickens and rabbits for sale. Bellflower was on the Pacific Electric line from Orange County to downtown, making it possible to be an office worker during the week and a farmer on weekends.

The builders of grittier, working-class suburbs promised access to jobs, but residents had to accept industrial noise and pollution. Compton, Bell Gardens, El Segundo, Hawthorne, Torrance, and other blue-collar communities clustered small houses on small lots next to the factories of the region's expanding manufacturing base. The contingencies of oil discovery, the placement of power plants and sewage treatment facilities, and the likelihood of seasonal flooding determined where the modest homes of working-class Angelenos would be built.

Center and Edge

None of the previous subdivisions of Los Angeles—orange grove estate, garden suburb, industrial housing tract, urban core, or suburban farm—could put up homes fast enough to satisfy the waves of new immigrants who came during World War II and who continued to come with the build-up of defense industries at the start of the Cold War. The urgent desires of the region's newest residents required instant suburbs, built on an enormous scale for wage earners whose aspirations were a home, a yard, and a neighborhood for their kids. In West Los Angeles between the harbor and Santa Monica, in the southeast along the border of Los Angeles and Orange counties and in the San Fernando Valley, a new kind of builder engineered the mass-produced, tract-house suburb that would satisfy mid-century longings. Beginning in 1946, these builders used an assembly line model derived from wartime ship and aircraft construction to put up tens of thousands of new housing units.

Among these builders were Fritz Burns and Henry Kaiser, whose Kaiser Community Homes developed Westchester near the Los Angeles airport and Panorama City in the San Fernando Valley. Panorama City's sales pitch emphasized the planned community aspects of a street grid that integrated homes, schools, playgrounds, shopping centers, and highway access. The houses—priced at $9,150 to $10,500—shared a common interior layout relieved by the application of a few design elements to produce seventy exterior elevations. The New Englander had columns in front. The Panorama model included a picture window. The Catalina design put the garage at the end of a slightly longer driveway.

Tract houses in post-war Los Angeles were bought with low-interest loans guaranteed by the Federal Housing Authority or through the Veterans Administration under the Servicemen's Readjustment Act of 1944 (better known as the GI Bill). Despite the easy terms, these houses weren't for everyone. Among the Conditions, Covenants, Restrictions in the deeds in Panorama City was a declaration that no lot could be "used or occupied by any person whose blood is not entirely that of the white or Caucasian race."[14] Racial restrictions were almost universal in Los Angeles, based on the redlining standards in the 1938 Underwriting Manual issued by the Federal Housing Administration: "If a neighborhood is to retain stability, it is necessary that properties shall continue to be occupied by the same social and racial classes. A change in social or racial occupancy generally leads to instability and a reduction in value." The manual recommended "suitable restrictions" to achieve "stability."

A landmark 1948 Supreme Court decision ended judicial enforcement of racial covenants, but the covenants themselves weren't declared invalid. Nearly all builders continued to issue deeds that included them, if only by reference, and the *Los Angeles Times* and other newspapers continued to accept advertising for developments that declared they were racially restricted. With covenants and the practice of steering, real estate salesmen made sure that non-white buyers found housing only in the "right," racially defined neighborhoods.

For white aspirants, however, the two-or-three-bedroom, one-bath, "minimum traditional house" (standardized from federal housing regulations) provided an affordable simulation of the golden promise of Los Angeles. "Visit this dramatic new city being built," said one Panorama City advertisement. "See how well Kaiser engineers and architects have interpreted the desires of 'Mr. and Mrs. Modern.'" In Lakewood, built between 1950 and 1953, being modern meant aluminum window screens, stainless steel countertops, and a garbage disposal unit in every kitchen sink, making Lakewood, the sales brochure said, "America's first garbage-free city." Subdividing working-class desires was a formula: a 900-square-foot house on a 50-by-100-foot lot in a neighborhood of more of the same extending as far as the street grid of Panorama City or Lakewood allowed.

There were alternatives. Well-designed public housing in Los Angeles had been built during the war years, including Richard Neutra's Channel Heights and the two-thousand-unit Banning Homes in the harbor district of Los Angeles. The Park La Brea development near Wilshire Boulevard showed how low- and mid-rise apartment blocks might be integrated into an existing grid of single-family homes. The Case Study Houses, built between 1945 and 1966, demonstrated how European modernism could be translated into homes for sophisticated, middle-class Angelenos. Beginning in 1948, Joseph Eichler built neighborhoods that brought the look of the Case Study houses to tract developments. Eichler's neighborhoods still required an automobile for most activities because public transit hardly accommodated the scattered destinations that daily life required: to downtown in Long Beach, Burbank, or Glendale for work, across the Los Angeles basin for the beach or the mountains, to the edge of the subdivision for shopping and on to newer and more distant suburbs with their lure of possibilities.

The grid of suburban streets, which had opened outward in the 1950s, closed in the 1960s and 1970s into confusing loops and cul-de-sacs. The suburbs of the 1980s and 1990s acquired walls, an entrance gate, and perhaps an armed guard. Inside the gated subdivision, variations of the typical wood frame and stucco house strived for unearned nostalgia. Outside, the aging, mid-century suburbs of the San Fernando Valley, the San Gabriel Valley, and the Los Angeles plain evolved into a racially diverse and organizationally complex metropolitan region not conventionally suburban or urban and where the lack of a well-defined center seemed to matter very little. More than two centuries of multiple centers and edges had made Los Angeles what it is today: suburban appearing but with an urban level of density.

Much of Los Angeles County—even in the parts some white Angelenos avoid—is a middling landscape where millions of people of all races express their idea of home. Flawed in 1950, certainly, because suburban Los Angeles had little room for people of color, and flawed today because Los Angeles isn't adequate to every demand we make of it. But hopeful now as then because dignified lives can be lived there.

The categories of urban and suburban hardly make sense when describing a place whose development has had a trajectory unlike the typical American metropolis. From its beginning, Los Angeles has been a multitude of oppositional places—religious and secular, indigenous and colonial, Anglo and mestizo, familiar and alien, real and imagined—and some assembly of its dissonant parts will always be required.

Stupid, Unproductive, Gullible

> [Y]oung men in trunks, and young girls in little more, with bronzed, unselfconscious bodies . . . they seemed to walk along the rim of the world as though they and their kind alone inhabited it . . . and they turn into precursors of a new race not yet seen on the earth: of men and women without age, beautiful as gods and goddesses, with the minds of infants.
>
> — William Faulkner, "Golden Land" (1935)

The summer weather has shifted in my southeastern corner of Los Angeles County. Gloomy mornings open up to gloriously breezy afternoons. The temperature rises to a gentle 75 degrees and stops rising. By a quirk of the onshore flow, which rarely extends this far inland, we're getting the moderating, midday overcast of Malibu.

The weather has been delightful, and that's a terrible problem. According to a report in *The New Yorker*, research on the psychological effect of weather supports the conclusion that a nice day is poison to eyes-on-the-prize mental focus. A day with nothing but blue skies, it seems, is like a day spent smoking Maui Wowie.[15] A 2008 study, using data from the American Time Use Survey, found that, on rainy days, men spent on average thirty more minutes at work than they did on comparatively sunny days. In 2012, a group of researchers from Harvard University and the University of North Carolina at Chapel Hill conducted a field study of Japanese bank workers and found a similar pattern: bad weather made workers more productive, as measured by the time it took them to complete rote tasks in processing a loan application. Even thinking about a nice day is nearly as corrosive to salaryman doggedness. "[R]esearchers found that participants were less productive when they'd viewed pleasant outdoor photographs. Instead of focusing on their work, they focused on what they'd rather be doing—whether or not it was actually sunny or rainy outside . . . . The mere thought of pleasant alternatives made people concentrate less."

> When it's 105 in New York City, it's 78 in L.A. When it's 20 below in New York City, it's 78 in L.A. Of course, there are 11 million interesting people in New York City and only 78 in L.A. Los Angeles—It's like paradise with a lobotomy.
>
> — Neil Simon, *California Suite* (1976)

Angelenos should have known the perverse connection between climate and intellectual and moral stamina. The region's moderate temperatures and cloudless skies have been criticized since the early nineteenth century. Bostonian Richard Henry Dana wrinkled his patrician nose at the indolence of Angelenos as early as 1836 and blamed the ease of life here. Robert Benchley, Thomas Mann, Evelyn Waugh, Dorothy Parker, F. Scott Fitzgerald, H.L. Mencken, and pretty much any writer who spent a balmy week in Los Angeles between 1920 and 2000 had dark opinions about the sunshine. In Los Angeles, where nice days repeat interminably, it's conventional wisdom that the locals lack the rigor of those who face the challenges of real weather. As a result, Angelenos are unable to distinguish fact from flimflam:

> In 1994, (researcher) Gerald Clore . . . found that pleasant weather can often lead to a disconcerting lapse in thoughtfulness. Clore's team approached a hundred and twenty-two undergraduates on days with either good or bad weather and asked them to participate in a survey on higher education. The better the weather, the easier it was to get the students to buy into a less-than-solid argument . . . . When the weather was rainy, cloudy, and cold, their critical faculties improved . . . . Clore and his colleagues concluded that pleasant weather led people to embrace more heuristic-based thinking—that is, they relied heavily on mental shortcuts at the expense of actual analysis.[16]

I thought the worst that could be said about Angelenos is that they're cheerful hedonists. We're actually "whatever works" heuristicians running on sunshine and instinct. And according to other studies, when summer heat lingers above 81 degrees—September weather—reason fails entirely. The hotter it gets, the less likely we're able to question what we're told. "In one recent project, the psychologist Uri Simonsohn found that students were more likely to enroll in a university that was famous for its academic rigor if they visited on cloudy days. When the weather turned sour, he concluded, the value they placed on academics increased."

> I never felt sadder in my life. LA is the loneliest and most brutal of American cities; New York gets godawful cold in the winter but there's a feeling of wacky comradeship somewhere in some streets. LA is a jungle.
>
> — Jack Kerouac, *On the Road* (1957)

Sadly, fair weather doesn't make us happier than the American average, although we may be too blissed out to realize how miserable we are. Multiple studies show that Angelenos are no happier than the clear-thinking people who live in Dubuque or Schenectady, who know they're happy because the snowdrifts have begun to melt. Angelenos, however, cherish the delusion that what they feel under the sun is joy.

I've lived in Southern California my entire life. I shiver when the temperature falls below 60 degrees. Thanks to the climate, my powers of judgment are comparable to a garden gnome's. Gullible me, I've fallen hard for the booster sales pitch that this a land of sunshine. I've written and sold a screenplay, a sure marker of climate-induced intellectual vacuity. And I couldn't care less that the script is unlikely ever to be produced. Blame the awfully good weather.

What We Talk About

Jeff Turrentine, a columnist and a Brooklyn transplant, often writes about urban sustainability and what makes a livable city. He became a Los Angeles resident in 1998. His experience of the city and what he knows of its history led him to imagine, with considerable optimism, what Los Angeles might become. His optimism cheers me, but what interested me was Turrentine's choice of what to talk about when he talked about Los Angeles.

Edenic Los Angeles

The backyard of the house Turrentine rented was a "bounteous garden" that's almost too generous.

> I happily made my way from the brilliant birds of paradise to the pink-petaled bougainvillea to the explosive blue hydrangeas to the dripping honeysuckle vines, giving all a proper soaking before completing the circuit at the base of the lemon tree—our own lemon tree!— right outside our door.[17]

Getting Midwesterners and East Coasters to swoon over Edenic Los Angeles was the response cultivated by the spinners of the city's sales pitch beginning in the 1870s. Turrentine's lone lemon tree was meant to evoke the domesticated world of the citrus orchard, and Turrentine's lush yard was intended to substitute for all of nature. But with "all of nature" in the backyard, Angelenos often had little imaginative space left for the nature outside their backyard fences. As a result, Los Angeles is park poor.

"We had been lured to Los Angeles by a mythic sales pitch," Turrentine ruefully admits,

> depicting sunny skies, palm trees, ocean breezes, new creative opportunities, and the freedom to stretch one's legs and move about. But quickly we would come to appreciate an inescapable irony: the pitch had proved too effective. So many had heard it and heeded it over the years that Los Angeles had become a standing-room-only Shangri-La.

Los Angeles, it seems, is best understood as a fable of irony: Los Angeles was a perfect place—perfect once upon a time—and that time was shortly before an even newer wave of transplants followed you here. Just as all of nature could be distilled into Turrentine's backyard, all of what Los Angeles fails to be is typically reduced to the frustrations of driving the gridlocked 405.

Menacing Los Angeles

After watering his private Eden, Turrentine considered where it's located.

> I looked out the window: there was my green grass, my well-watered garden, my lemon tree. I looked at the television: there was a never-ending freeway jammed with cars, lined with nondescript strip malls, marked by menace.

An Eden embedded in menace has been the image of Los Angeles ever since the *ciudad de los Angeles* was first occupied by the US military in 1847. Because of its Catholic past, its capture in war, and fear of Mexican irredentism and the racism of its Anglo ascendancy, Los Angeles, from its re-founding in as an American city in 1850, was a threatened city. Everything that makes it a place to live—Owens Valley water, tract house suburbs, auto-centered transit—is perversely what makes the city unlivable. Turrentine looks over his backyard fence and hears "the staccato song of the city's official bird, as a pair of police choppers hovered overhead," and finds that his "fantastical garden oasis was surrounded on all sides by drab, squat, utilitarian apartment complexes." The form of the city and its supporting infrastructure, which made Turrentine's stucco bungalow and semi-tropical backyard possible, are part of a "Faustian bargain."

Turrentine's tour around his backyard sketches a history of Los Angeles in which Edenic wholeness declines into suburban sprawl. Despite the city's decline, Turrentine plans to stay here and see what happens next. Even as he conjures up the threatening places that substitute for everyday Los Angeles, he applies the city's core myth—limitless re-invention—to the city's crises of livability.

> [B]old plans for decreasing L.A.'s need for distantly sourced water, reducing its reliance on the single-passenger automobile and reshaping its communities to mitigate the ill effects of sprawl represent a change

in the way the region will look and function over the century to come, but also an equally dramatic shift in how its millions of residents are coming to perceive themselves . . . . The capital of starting over is starting over . . . .

The brave hope in that claim lifts my spirits, but my faith is harder to kindle. The endless futurity of Los Angeles is one of our weaknesses. Los Angeles is always one more improvement away from someone's idea of perfection. If only "bold plans" would unmake the unsatisfactory Los Angeles we have, we could remake it in the better image of our desire. The bold plans never seem to realize what we dream, and so more plans are needed, more perfecting is required.

We talk about dreams a lot in Los Angeles—hopeful dreams and blighted ones and modest dreams not accounted for in bold plans. Perhaps it would be better if we talked about something else, something other than Manhattan and airliner views and a "Prius-driving, yoga-practicing, organic-kale-munching town" that's a "gaudy mirage" and "uniquely cursed."

Turrentine has perceptive things to say about transit, water conservation and reuse, and the momentum for change in Los Angeles. About these, I know Turrentine is right, even though this isn't enough to resolve the contradiction at the heart of what we talk about when we talk about Los Angeles. Failure to reconcile this contradiction leaves our conversation as stuck in clichés in the way the fiberglass replicas of mammoths are stuck in the La Brea tar pits. When we talk about Los Angeles, dystopian and utopian images crowd into the conversation.

Shouldn't we be talking about something else?

Red Flags over Los Angeles

Prologue

Few today remember the tragedy that shaped twentieth-century Los Angeles. The glum slab of the former Los Angeles Times Building on Spring Street remembers for us. The Times Building is a cenotaph for the pressmen and linotype operators who were flung into fire and collapsing masonry in October 1910. But the bombing of the *Times* wrecked more than the building. The reputations of national union leaders were ruined. A coalition of Socialist Party activists, union members, and progressives was shattered. Government reform in Los Angeles was suspended for almost a hundred years. And the reactionary *Los Angeles Times* became the dominant political power in Southern California, the paper's anti-union motto "True Industrial Freedom" printed in every edition and etched deeply into the façade of the new Times Building.

Socialism and Reaction

The *Los Angeles Times* was uninterested in political reform. Harrison Gray Otis, the *Times*'s belligerent owner, and Harry Chandler, his son-in-law and the paper's general manager, focused on keeping out organized labor, enforced by a corrupt city administration, a compliant police force, and the financial support of the Merchants & Manufacturers Association. In response, national unions made Los Angeles the focus of aggressive organizing. From 1901 to 1910, union members in Los Angeles rallied, struck, and picketed for shorter hours, better pay, job security, and a union shop.

Los Angeles socialists had other goals. The local branch of the Socialist Party campaigned for municipal ownership of utilities, reservation of Owens Valley water for city residents, public ownership of the industrial property around the new harbor, a graduated property tax, and better services for the working poor. The party opposed unions on ideological grounds and distrusted "good government" reformers because of their willingness to compromise with the city's political bosses. Socialist Los Angeles was middle-class, bookish, and anti-immigrant. Marxist theory meant more than coalition building.

Inevitably, corporate resistance to union organizing—backed by the *Times*'s fiery anti-union editorials—degenerated into repression: strike breaking, police raids on union offices, and city ordinances that threatened union organizing. Repression further radicalized union members and eventually energized support from the Los Angeles branch of the Socialist Party. Over the objections of hesitant union officials, the Los Angeles Council of Labor adopted the political goals of the Socialist Party, and party members became pro-union.

A fusion Union-Labor Party organized for the 1902 municipal election and put up a slate of mostly Socialist Party members. On Election Day, Socialist supporters were out in force, but the results were disappointing. The Democratic candidate for mayor drew nine thousand votes; the Republican trailed with about six thousand. The Union-Labor candidate was a distant third with just over three thousand votes.

The failure of the 1902 coalition opened a split in the California Socialist Party that nearly destroyed the statewide apparatus. Purists in the Los Angeles branch rejected the wage and working condition aims of union organizers and saw the proliferation of competing unions as undermining working-class solidarity.

Accommodationists (based in the powerful San Francisco branch of the party) argued that support for union interests had won municipal elections for Socialist candidates elsewhere and could win in Los Angeles. By 1905, the north/south rift had hardened into inflexibility. The leaders of the tightly disciplined Los Angeles branch of the party stepped back from the union cause. In 1908, the cause came to them. A city ordinance already outlawed unpermitted street meetings and gave the police commission authority to issue permits to whomever the commissioners chose. During the panic winter of 1907–1908, when values on the New York Stock Exchange fell 50 percent and Los Angeles banks failed, worried commissioners silenced anyone who argued on street corners for better wages and workers' rights. There were no permits for labor rallies.

On July 1, 1908, two thousand Socialist Party supporters gathered at the intersection of 7th Street and Grand Avenue to demonstrate their opposition to the commission's no-permit policy. Jack Wood, a local party leader, was arrested. On July 17, six thousand free speech advocates marched, and more party members were arrested, some of them women. On July 18, two thousand Socialist Party and Democratic Party members joined in a march down Broadway to city hall. They arrived to hear Job Harriman, a leader in the statewide Socialist Party, declare that party members who defied the police commission were martyrs for constitutional rights. Trials of jailed Socialists followed, as did daily pro-union demonstrations in front of city hall. In August, the city council conceded and withdrew the permit requirement.

Victory had several outcomes. Progressive civic reformers now saw moderate Socialists like Harriman as protectors of civil rights. Union leaders accepted middle-class Socialists as allies. And Job Harriman had been made an attractive candidate for mayor in the next election. He was photogenic, still youthful, and a passionate orator in an era when public speaking was an essential political skill. He had been the gubernatorial candidate of the Socialist Labor Party in 1898, campaigning from the deck of a horse-drawn caravan rigged to project glass slides that illustrated economic inequality in California. In 1900, as a representative of the Socialist Party, Harriman had been the vice-presidential candidate on a coalition ticket with Eugene V. Debs, who ran as the presidential candidate of the Social Democratic Party. Part of Harriman's appeal to union leaders and civic reformers was his support for the moderate majority of Socialists led by Debs and not the faction led by Daniel De Leon, one of the founders of the radical Industrial Workers of the World. Harriman made himself the spokesman for a fusion politics that blended working-class economic aspirations with socialist ideology. It was "the organized wage-workers," Harriman wrote in the *Los Angeles Socialist* in 1902, "which should, and ultimately will, lead the Socialist movement."[18] Under Harriman, Los Angeles was to be reformed by union solidarity, Socialist Party leadership, and votes for women, not by bombs and bullets.

The events of 1910–1911 tested each of these propositions.

No Union Man

It was a season of labor militancy. Garment workers were on strike in Chicago and New York. Transit workers led a general strike in Boston and Philadelphia. Miners picketed in Colorado and Texas and steelworkers in Pennsylvania. In Los Angeles, members of the pressmen's union were on strike against the *Times*. With the support of the city's Central Labor Council, butchers, trolley drivers, brewers, and other trade workers would join the *Times* strikers by the end of 1910.

It also was a season of anti-labor violence. Police used billy clubs to break up picket lines in New York, Chicago, Philadelphia, and San Francisco.

Strikebreakers and goon squads used their fists. Union members fought back, sometimes with greater violence. Since 1906, the ironworkers union had conducted a campaign of dynamiting non-union plants. More than a hundred bombs set at ironworks around the nation had caused several thousand dollars' worth of damage but as yet no injuries or deaths.

In June 1910, workers in the metal trades in Los Angeles, including members of the ironworkers union, went on strike for a minimum wage and an eight-hour day. Goaded by the *Times*, the Merchant & Manufacturers Association raised $350,000 to break the strike with scab replacements. According to the *San Francisco Bulletin*, the members of the association had only one principle: "We will employ no union man."[19] In July, the Los Angeles City Council unanimously passed an anti-picketing ordinance that criminalized "speaking in public streets in a loud or unusual tone." Union picketers refused to be silenced, and nearly five hundred were arrested, crowding the city jail and the municipal courts. Union organizers made use of public sympathy for the jailed strikers, forming thirteen new locals by September and more than doubling union membership.

As union organizing gained momentum and the Los Angeles branch of the Socialist Party prepared for municipal elections in 1911, the Iron Workers' bombing campaign came to Los Angeles. Shortly after midnight on Saturday, October 1, while non-union typesetters and pressmen put out the morning edition, a clockwork bomb—a bundle of sixteen dynamite sticks of 80 percent nitroglycerine—tore a hole in the side of the *Times*'s building and ignited barrels of flammable ink in the basement. The fire quickly reached a damaged gas main. The explosion and gas-fed fire consumed the interior of the building and collapsed its masonry walls. At least twenty employees died; a hundred more were injured. Later that morning, unexploded dynamite bombs were found at Otis's home and the home of the executive director of the Merchant & Manufacturers Association.

Otis and Chandler had anticipated an attack on the *Times*. They even may have known the outline of the dynamite plot through a paid informant who was a member of the Iron Workers executive council. As the remains of the Times Building smoldered, Otis and Chandler activated a secret, second newsroom and printed a one-page edition whose headline screamed "Unionist Bombs Wreck the Times." A manhunt to find the bombers fanned out across the nation.

The "crime of the century" became the "trial of the century" in May 1911 when two union organizers—brothers James and John McNamara—were indicted for murder and twenty other criminal charges connected to dynamiting the Times Building. Samuel Gompers, president of the American Federation of Labor, immediately claimed that Otis and the Merchants & Manufacturers Association had railroaded the McNamaras. Debs hinted that Otis and Chandler may have planted the bomb themselves to discredit union organizers and smear Job Harriman before the 1911 election. Gompers, fearing that unions would abandon organizing if the union men were found guilty, pledged $200,000 toward the McNamaras' defense and another $50,000 to retain a reluctant Clarence Darrow as their attorney. Gompers directed union locals to donate twenty-five cents for each member and to set up McNamara defense committees to sustain popular support. Pins and other memorabilia were sold to raise even more money. *A Martyr to His Cause*, a defense of the McNamaras and the first film produced by organized labor, premiered in Cincinnati, where an estimated fifty thousand tickets were sold. Thousands more saw the film in other cities. In Los Angeles, Eugene Debs made support for the McNamaras a test of Socialist Party strength under the slogan "Fight Otis, organize the city, and elect a Socialist mayor—Job Harriman." Harriman's defense of the McNamara brothers colored his campaign even more. Supporters wore buttons that read "McNamaras Innocent—Vote for Harriman."[20]

Votes for Women

Job Harriman—defender of free speech, crusading Socialist, champion of votes for women—was the obvious fusion candidate of Socialists, union members, and good government activists in 1911. He and a slate of city council candidates (one of which was African American) campaigned on a platform of progressive causes that were popular among middle-class Angelenos. Harriman's faced incumbent Mayor George Alexander, a respected good government reformer who had won a recall election in 1909 that swept out the flamboyantly corrupt Arthur C. Harper, one of the many political hacks the *Times* supported. In the primary election, Harriman beat Alexander by nearly four thousand votes in a three-way race, but he failed to reach an outright majority. A runoff election was scheduled for December 5. Fearing that the election might already be lost, the *Times* reacted with its usual vehemence. "The election of Harriman," the *Times*'s editorial page fulminated, "would result in an orgy of evil, in a season of stagnation in businesses, in the curtailment of building, in the withdrawal of capital, in hunger in the homes and rioting in the highways."[21]

New voters would determine if Harriman and the Socialists or Alexander and the Good Government League would run city government. A state constitutional amendment had given women the vote in October, making California the fifth state to grant women suffrage. As an article in *Collier's* magazine pointed out, women would decide who will be the next mayor of Los Angeles. Both the Socialists and Alexander's backers hurried to register the estimated sixty thousand women who were now eligible to vote in Los Angeles. Harriman confidently predicted that working-class women would vote their economic interests and give Socialists control of city hall. The Good Government League hoped that middle-class women would hesitate to vote for Harriman and socialism. But the choice wasn't between revolution or reaction. Socialists and good government reformers advocated similar platforms. What distinguished the two sides was solidarity with union economic goals and the reformers' distrust of them.

Otis and Chandler had a personal reason to fear a union-Socialist victory. As partners in a development company that was poised to benefit from the new Los Angeles aqueduct, the two men knew that a Socialist mayor and city council majority would wreck their plans for the thousands of dry acres they owned in the San Fernando Valley, not yet part of the city. Harriman had pledged to deliver Owens Valley water only to Los Angeles residents when the aqueduct was finished.

For publicity reasons, Harriman was chosen to head the McNamara legal defense team, but his focus was on the campaign for mayor and only occasionally on the trial, which Darrow, the rest of the defense team, and Gompers sought to delay until after Election Day in December. The drawn-out selection of jurors also concealed what Darrow (and perhaps Harriman) already knew—that James McNamara, burdened by guilt, had confessed his part in the bomb plot to Lincoln Steffens, a reform-minded magazine writer. But Darrow didn't know that prosecutors had secretly listened to the confession and to every conversation the McNamaras had with their defense team.

It was now a race between Election Day and the date the trial would start. It was a trial Darrow knew he would likely lose, and there is evidence that he (or others on the defense team) sought to bribe one or more of the members of the juror pool to guarantee a hung jury and a mistrial. Darrow, desperate to save the McNamaras from hanging, also joined in back-channel negotiations with

Harry Chandler of the *Times* with an offer to trade an end to existing strikes in exchange for lenient sentences for the McNamaras and suspension of the *Times*'s anti-union publicity campaign. Chandler agreed to begin negotiations with District Attorney John D. Fredericks on those terms. But Fredericks refused. Nothing short of full confessions by both brothers in open court was acceptable if James, the older brother, would be spared a death sentence and John be given a relatively short prison term. On December 1, only four days before the election, the McNamara brothers changed their pleas in open court to guilty. James McNamara admitted to having set the bomb that destroyed the Times Building on October 1, 1910. John McNamara admitted to having set the bomb that damaged the Llewellyn Iron Works on December 25.

Gompers was crushed by the news. "I am astounded, I am astounded," he told a reporter. "The McNamaras have betrayed labor."[22] Debs and the Socialist Party refused to condemn the McNamara brothers, blaming Otis, Chandler, and the Merchants and Manufacturers Association for creating a climate of anti-union terror. Darrow narrowly escaped conviction himself. He was indicted twice in 1912 for attempted bribery of McNamara jury members. Darrow was acquitted in one case and won a hung jury in the second. At least he was able to plead the case for labor justice that he had hoped to make for the McNamaras.

Support for Harriman and the union-Socialist slate did not disappear, despite the shock of the McNamara confessions, but on Election Day, many more westside voters turned out for Alexander and his slate of bankers, lawyers, and real estate salesmen. In some westside precincts, nearly all newly registered women had voted. Harriman trailed Alexander by thirty-four thousand votes, or 25 percent of the ballots cast.

In the aftermath of the bombing and the sensational trial, when those who had defended the McNamaras were proved to be gullible (if not dishonest), the alliance between Socialists and progressives reformers in Los Angeles was over, and any momentum the labor movement had gained was lost. The Merchants & Manufacturers Associations redoubled efforts to maintain the open-shop regime backed by the *Times*. Gompers and the American Federation of Labor abandoned union organizing in Los Angeles. Unions did not begin to show signs of new growth in Los Angeles until the 1950s. Progressives recoiled from socialist values to produce in the 1920s a technocratic city charter that still, even after significant revision in 1999, undercuts the democratic process in city government.

By the end of 1911, socialism and the Socialist Party were suspect, not only in Los Angeles, but also nationally. What might have become a broad coalition of union members and middle-class Socialists and moderate progressives failed to mature. Bombs and betrayals ended that possibility.

Kevin Starr: Interpreter of Dreams

Although entirely a Californian, Kevin Starr would probably have preferred to be known as a San Franciscan. The designation would have acknowledged the city he loved most for its ebullient creativity and its food and drink. Starr—historian, teacher, mentor, former city and state librarian, raconteur, and Catholic—was brilliant and winning in the way that San Francisco strove to be. But Starr, who died at seventy-six in January 2017, was larger in his embrace than San Francisco. His affections included Los Angeles, although some in his immense circle of friends wondered at his civic disloyalty. He even warmed up to Sacramento—at least its political part—and added it to the places where becoming Californian could have transcendent meaning.

Our state—of mind, of landscapes, of dreams—had been his defining subject, just as California had defined Starr, who endured abandonment in his childhood and poverty in his youth, who saw the state's post-war efflorescence into greatness, and who wondered where this life of his had come from. In a magisterial series of narrative histories, beginning with *Americans and the California Dream, 1850–1915*, Starr found provisional answers to his need to know what, in being Californian, he'd become. For those of us who know his books and shared his company, Starr illuminated all the ways in which the Californian experience spoke to and about American placemaking. California, in bounteous ways, was exceptional for Starr but not "the great exception," not so unique that its story offered America nothing but ironic entertainment.

Starr's loyalty to California has been criticized as boosterish, but that misinterprets what was essential to Starr: his faith. It was faith in the possibility that ordinary, imperfect lives might assemble from the raw materials of California a community of meaning in the twenty-first century, just as philosopher Josiah Royce had hoped for nineteenth-century California. It was faith in the possibility that popular democracy might sustain public habits of justice, reconciliation, and mutual support. It was faith in the purpose of writing and reading history, which I believe to be the formation of a moral imagination.

Starr accepted the convention that the idea of California would forever be connected to dreams, along with the implication that longing for meaning might be merely a dream, merely desire without substance or consequence. But Starr's use of "the dream"—as something that might justify desire—was his way of secularizing another faith: his belief in the Incarnation, in the mystery of the divine turned into our flesh or, as a title in his California history series puts it, in the realization of "material dreams." The manifestation of California as a place where longings might be assuaged and memories preserved, Starr imagined to be a kind of civil liturgy. That faith led him to constant engagement with Californians—as a teacher (most recently at USC), as an essayist in the *San Francisco Chronicle* and the *Los Angeles Times*, as the state librarian, and as an advisor to three California governors.

Starr believed in a California that was equally promise, commonwealth, and redemption, but California tested his faith. The state he grew up in—a state of big ambitions and even bigger public works—grew less convincing in the countercultural 1960s and after the 1989 Loma Prieta earthquake, the violence of the 1992 Rodney King civil unrest, the Northridge earthquake of 1994, and the hollowing out of the state's blue-collar industries after 1998. "California is everything and nothing at all," Starr wrote in the *San Francisco Chronicle* in 2003. "It is the cutting edge of the American dream—a utopia. But it could also become the paradigm of the dream lost—a nightmare dystopia."[23] Starr understood that nightmares have always accompanied dreamers.

In his introductory note to *Coast of Dreams: California on the Edge* (2005), Starr wrote that it would be "seductively easy [to] see California as one vast failed experiment. But if I succumbed to this temptation, I would not be seeing the full truth about California and its people." Starr still believed that binding "the shattered fragments of my neglected and incoherent youth" to the character of this place, "I could find in, with, and through California some measure of meaning."[24Winter] The tempered assertion of "some measure" characterized Starr's balance. He saw in the habits of Californians some meaning that was worth conserving and some memories—both painful and bright—that Californians shouldn't forget.

In all, Starr published more than a dozen books, including *Continental Ambitions: Roman Catholics in North America: The Colonial Experience* (2016), which he'd intended to be the start of a new series. Erudite, graceful, and accessible, his books took shape, he once said, as naturally as "a form of breathing." There was a spirit in that breath. There was conviction also, both political and moral, along with humor and a Shakespearean insight into the follies and grandeurs, the crimes and heroisms, of exemplary Californians. He didn't think storytelling—mere storytelling to critics—was work too humble for a historian.

Without Kevin Starr now, we must consider the meaning of California and measure our distance from the dream's realization ourselves.

Many years ago, Kevin Starr reviewed my attempts to find the meaning of my life in the Lakewood I know. He was very generous with his praise. We later shared public platforms, op-ed pages, drinks, and stories. His kindnesses to me are beyond numbering. I saw him last in October 2016, as I waited to speak to a student colloquium at the University of Southern California. He was full of conversation as he always was. It's my loss and a loss to Californians that his conversation ended too soon.

Huell Howser: At Home Everywhere

That name—*Huell*—made it easy to parody the Tennessee drawl he declined to straighten out into the Los Angeles broadcast standard. His on-camera gusts of wonderment at all things great and small were equally made for caricature, but he wouldn't change that either. It took strength of character to remain the Huell Howser we still watch on public television.

His death in 2013 was treated (at least by some) like the passing of a beloved uncle—the uncle who never married but who sent the best birthday gifts, the one who would go with you on the scariest carnival ride, and the one whose life at the end seemed to have too many blank pages. After his death, one commentator wrote of Huell Howser's circumspection. I thought of it as his wariness.

Huell Howser's biography was conventional enough: born in Gallatin, Tennessee, in 1945; graduation from high school; and afterward college and a degree. But he was keen to be more. He got an appointment as a Congressional page. He worked as an aide to Howard Baker's Senate campaign. After high school, he joined the Marine Corps reserves. At the University of Tennessee, where he was a history and political science major, he became a leader of anti-war protests. He once considered running for Congress.

Huell Howser had something he wanted to be and something he wanted to say. He usually overcame the impression he made of being big and sort of unformed. His presence was noticed, and he was offered a job at the Nashville NBC affiliate, where he did feature reporting in a style that pointed toward the programs he produced for public television twenty years later.

Despite the grin, he wasn't good ol' boy enough for Nashville where, according to a 2003 profile in *Los Angeles* magazine, Howser's reporting became increasingly critical of the city's indifference to its African American residents. Knowing that detail about him adds complexity to the Southern boyishness he portrayed.

After Nashville, he tried something similar for New York television, but the fit was wrong from the start. When he arrived in Los Angeles in 1981, he went back to the grind of feature reporting for the CBS affiliate with occasional interview segments for *Entertainment Tonight*. But that kind of television was a step back for Howser. It wasn't the gift he had for connecting with people who weren't celebrities. The clichés of entertainment reporting kept him from being—in his outsized, harmless way—intimate. There were hints that intimacy was a role he played. There are those blank pages and what appeared to be Howser's loneliness.

He volunteered at KCET in 1987 to produce short segments that weren't much different from the features he'd done in Nashville. But stripped down to minimal production values (often one continuous shot), the fit was finally right. By his warmth and joyous interest, Howser drew something—perhaps only a reflection of his apparent pleasure—from avocado farmers, minor bureaucrats, historical society docents, collectors of things, sellers of things, the endless explainers, and even the people who stood around gawking at this large, pink, and glowing man known for honking "Isn't that amazing!"

By 1990, Howser was a hugely successful public television personality. His shows grew to include *California's Gold, California's Golden Parks, California's Golden Coast, Our Neighborhoods,* and *Road Trip with Huell Howser.* He eventually appeared on virtually all the public television stations in California, as well as those in Hawaii, Nevada, and Oregon.

Howser was a smart businessman. He made money and he raised money for public TV. He was famous. He was satirized on *The Simpsons.* He was driven by his work.

His on-air relationships were intentionally brief. His amazement at the extraordinary hidden within the ordinary went only so far. But that was part of his project. Howser insisted that he wasn't a substitute for the viewers themselves, who ought to go into their own neighborhood fired with the belief that remarkable things resided there if only they experienced it with the same lack of prejudice that was Howser's best characteristic.

He was an evangelist of the everyday, but he also was a journalist who had a sophisticated understanding of what his kind of television could do. Howser believed in California, which was much larger than the California that tourists visit. He wanted his viewers to feel at home everywhere with an attachment that many find difficult to sustain. He leaned into his viewers—all head and mouth and loud yawp. He wanted you to like him, but he wanted more that you should like the places he went to and the people he talked to, all of them plump with the stories he drew from them.

At first, his audience was the demographic that historian Kevin Starr called the "folks"—plain people who had migrated to Los Angeles in the tens of thousands. The "folks" in Howser's audience radiated their pleasure back at Howser's televised presence, happy to go to a cat litter factory or a low-rider car show or a farm in the Central Valley or anywhere, as long as he was their guide. The "folks" were happy just to see a Californian so happy to be here. Howser's audience became as diverse demographically as public television's, although some part of this audience watched with irony the least ironic man on television. Howser preached the richness in everyday life that anyone should be able to see, particularly when the ordinary is viewed with joy. I don't know if the joy was a pose for him, but it's easy to see the subversion of expectations about California in Howser's happy demeanor.

His thousands of episodes will be around a long time, and any journalist who wants the same success will have to watch them to understand what Howser accomplished. I've heard it suggested that he no longer has a place in today's media ecology. If so, we've lost by his death what we need most—lessons on how to fall in love with the place where we are.

Shirley Savoy: The Button Lady

I went over to F&S Fabrics with a friend who was looking for material to reline a jacket and repair an heirloom coat. She also wanted to get new buttons for both. Naturally she went to F&S. The Button Lady works there. She works behind a long row of glass-topped showcases and in front of a towering wall of buttons sorted into narrow, covered cardboard boxes. The Button Lady has a system for classifying her buttons, and as I waited while she helped other seekers, I considered what her system might be. I never did figure out even the least of it.

F&S Fabrics has been on Pico Boulevard since 1956, currently spilling out into three locations within a few hundred feet of each other. The Button Lady has been behind the counter at the original corner location since early 1990, having been hired for her remarkable memory and her even more remarkable ability to make picking buttons an occasion for small-scale joy.

The Button Lady is Shirley Savoy, a name that would fit wonderfully on a 1950s movie theater marquee. Ms. Savoy is from the South, which you learn instantly from the music in her speech. She claims a near psychic ability to match button and buyer.

Ms. Savoy doesn't sell buttons, exactly. She has a conversation with the button seeker that almost always involves everyone who might be nearby. At the conclusion of this group discussion, it will turn out that a set of buttons has been sold. It will be a perfect set of buttons, because the button seeker and Ms. Savoy will have invested bits of plastic, wood, and plated metal with the glow of high style. They'll have done this together, the button seeker and Ms. Savoy, and when the tissue-wrapped package of buttons is taped up and put in a bag, the buyer will turn away from the counter still wreathed in some of that stylish glow.

Ms. Savoy has plenty of style to share, but it's important to come to her counter with the proper readiness. For one thing, be ready to slow down. Ms. Savoy will need some of your time to read what your garment lacks in buttons. It's a given that the buttons that came from the clothing manufacturer are entirely wrong. Ms. Savoy also needs time to read you. Your aspirations for the garment are important to her. And if you don't know what your aspirations are, Ms. Savoy's hands will play over her wall of button boxes, pulling down just one or two. And from them, she'll draw buttons to show you what your jacket or coat can hope to be.

After they agreed on the buttons for my friend's jacket and coat, Ms. Savoy had recommendations for lining material. She approved of the leopard print I tentatively suggested for the vintage camelhair. I beamed. She wavered on my friend's early choices to reline the new jacket. A silk floral print in colors of cream and old gold was handed around and Ms. Savoy pronounced it perfect. We all did.

. . .

That was in 2010. Ms. Savoy worked elsewhere in the Los Angeles fashion district when I last saw her in 2018. The boxes of buttons and the Button Lady's charm hadn't changed.

Signs and Wonders

Sentimentality for the commonplace is a defining characteristic of mature cities, which can be so heartless otherwise. When a corner bar closes, some locals get all weepy if the bar had been around longer than they have. That some Angelenos are getting sentimental over threatened landmarks signals something about Los Angeles but in the crazy way this city has of salting every good intention with irony.

The Hollywood sign is the current example. It's a genuine icon—blown up, shaken down, and incinerated in a string of disaster movies beginning with 1974's *Earthquake*. But the sign on the slope of Mt. Lee isn't the original. Put up in 1923 to boost sales in a suburban housing development, the original sign read "Hollywoodland." The "land" part was jettisoned when ownership of the deteriorating sign was transferred to the Hollywood Chamber of Commerce in 1949. The Hollywood sign continued to decay until 1978 when a number of Hollywood stars donated $27,000 each to replace its tattered sheet-metal letters and telephone pole armature with a sturdier but slightly smaller replica. The replacement was renovated in 2005 by the Hollywood Sign Trust. Protected by monitoring equipment to deter pranksters, who used to reletter the sign into configurations like HOLLYWeeD, the reworked sign stands for … well … what?

As a facsimile of two-thirds of the original (its remnant bits auctioned on eBay for $450,000 in 2005), the current Hollywood sign is shamelessly inauthentic. That makes it an ideal Los Angeles icon. There were worse alternatives. In 1988, a blue-ribbon commission of architects and community activists picked a design called Steel Cloud to be the West Coast's answer to the Eiffel Tower. Had it been built, Steel Cloud would have been a half-mile-long Brutalist train wreck of girders and struts hanging above the Hollywood Freeway as it passes through downtown. Outlying elements of the cloud would have linked the old plaza with First Street. The center portion would have been the width of the freeway. Into that space would have been set cafés and a movie theater.

Unlike the unlovable Steel Cloud, the Hollywood sign has become the people's monument, but much of the sign's hillside setting until 2010 was private land owned by Fox River Financial Resources, a Chicago investment firm. Bought in 2002 for $1.6 million, the 138-acre site, which was part of the estate of Howard Hughes, was listed for sale at more than $20 million in 2008. The

Chicago firm hoped to sell the site for mega-mansions of the sort favored by oil emirs and elderly rock stars. Although the sign itself wasn't at risk, its setting was. Pleas to city hall, fundraising by The Trust for Public Land, and large donations from celebrities (Hugh Hefner chipped in) succeeded in 2010 in acquiring nearly one hundred acres around the sign, which were added to nearby Griffith Park. For $12.5 million, the view of the sign was saved. Which meant that believers in the romance of Hollywood had protected the visual integrity of a remake of part of a real estate billboard. As they should have, despite the obvious incongruities. The public's regard for the Hollywood sign is such an amalgam of memories, false associations, blatant huckstering, and civic history that it's impossible to unmix them. Preservation of the sign's setting—or anything else of value in this city—preserves our delight in living here in all its garbled inauthenticity.

We've let so much of Los Angeles slip away in the undertow of progress, but the good news is that landmarks are everywhere and probably at the end of your street or around the corner. Take a look at the Million Article Thompson sign above a former hardware store on Vermont Avenue at 90th Street. It's a tower of girders and blue and orange metal panels (and neon, once) that even in its shabby disrepair asserts more about the brazen optimism of Los Angeles than almost anything I know. Or visit the bungalow court at 1428 South Bonnie Brae Ave. designed in the Egyptian Revival style by Edwin W. Willit in 1925 and looking as if a set from *The Mummy* had been relocated to be rented out to the star-struck. Or drive by the rows of Spanish Colonial houses on the lower tiers of Hollywood hillsides, dreaming of Andalusia. All of these images of Los Angeles—and the Hollywood sign too—materialize so much longing. It's longing that makes the fake landmarks of Los Angeles real.

Over Los Angeles

The former chief pilot of Lakewood's helicopter patrol program—begun in 1966 and among the first in the nation—told me about the perversity of helicopters. A plane with wings, he said, naturally wants to fly. It'll try to glide if the engine stalls. A helicopter doesn't glide. With the engine off, blades spinning in auto-rotation, a helicopter goes down. Helicopters don't actually want to fly.

Some irate Angeleños wish that helicopters didn't fly, at least not over their neighborhood. Homeowners and orchestra conductors (who've walked off the Hollywood Bowl stage in protest) are tired of the noisy company of tourist, pa-parazzo, news, and police helicopters, jet engines roaring, and blades thwack-ing the night air. Angry neighborhood associations have repeatedly petitioned the Federal Aviation Administration and their member of Congress to regulate helicopters out of their airspace.

The air/ground conflict is just another part of the familiar Los Angeles bait-and-switch. We're always being pitched one bright future and end up get-ting a darker, more troublesome one. Personal helicopters were promised in the 1950s, whisking commuters to downtown jobs and taking the family on a joyride to Palm Springs. Instead, the future turned out to be hedge fund billion-aires and Hollywood boldface names coptering over Los Angeles to avoid the gridlocked rest of us below.

We could have flown in relative comfort on Los Angeles Airways, which began scheduled helicopter flights to LAX in 1954 in a hulking, piston-pow-ered Sikorsky S-55. By mid-1955, LAA flew bigger and faster Sikorskys to twen-ty-five destinations in Southern California, including Hollywood, Disneyland, Newport Beach, and San Bernardino. The convenience turned deadly on May 22, 1968, when LAA Flight 841 crashed in Paramount with the loss of twen-ty-three lives. Three months later, Flight 417 crashed in Compton. Among the dead was the thirteen-year-old grandson of the airline's founder. Bad publicity, financial losses, and strikes brought down the company in 1970.

The LAA heliport next to Disneyland's Tomorrowland is gone, but you can still get to LAX by helicopter. Expect to pay a hefty fee to take flight from one of the many registered helipads in Los Angeles, some of them on the grounds of Brentwood mega-mansions. Having a helipad at home or on top of your bou-tique hotel is a sexy amenity if you're trying to unload a $60-million property or fill a $10,000-a-night suite.

Some of those helipads were required by law until 2014. The municipal fire code mandated a helicopter landing platform on all commercial buildings over seventy-five feet tall. Los Angeles was the only major American city with that regulation, which explains why the towers that crowd Bunker Hill all have boringly flat tops. Architects grumbled at the design limitation, but fire departments had invested heavily in an aerial future.

The Los Angeles Fire Department flies seven helicopters, all of them based at Station 114 next to Van Nuys Airport. The Los Angeles County Fire Department has access to an even larger fleet needed to cover the 4,084 inflammable square miles of the county's industrial parks, hillsides, mountains, and oceanfront. The LACFD Air Operations Section, with ten firefighting and rescue helicopters, flies from the Barton Heliport in Pacoima.

There are even more helicopters in the fleets of Los Angeles County law enforcement. The Sheriff's Department's Aero Bureau flies eighteen patrol and rescue helicopters from its base at Long Beach Airport. The Los Angeles Police Department flies nineteen helicopters—the nation's largest municipal airborne law enforcement operation—from the Hooper Heliport on top of the department's Piper Technical Center at the eastern edge of downtown (and apparently the largest rooftop airport in the world). The mascot of the LAPD Air Support Division is a glum looking vulture perched on a patrol car light bar.

The lazy circles a vulture makes over its future meal is a good metaphor for how a helicopter works a crime scene. What fires up the anger of Angelenos is a helicopter circling in a tight orbit overhead, generally at three or four hundred feet for better observation, and with the aid of million-candlepower searchlights at night. The lights, the engine noise, and the staccato beating of rotor blades biting into the sullen air infuriate the law abiding on the ground. A helicopter, lingering for twenty minutes or more above a neighborhood, sounds more like menace than protection.

Complaining to the FAA isn't going to change the flight plans of the county's law enforcement, rescue, and fire suppression helicopters. But complaints about media helicopters, traffic report helicopters, tour guide helicopters, and Hollywood helicopters have generated proposals to set altitude restrictions and designate "no fly" zones for commercial flights. There can be as many as fifty tour flights a day over Griffith Park to view the Hollywood sign on a summer weekend, often flying at altitudes of 500 feet or less. There is no traffic cop in the sky to run down and ticket helicopter scofflaws.

If the complainers want to pinpoint the moment when their misery began, the early afternoon of July 4, 1958 is the day and time. That's when the Telecopter—a Bell Model 47 rented by KTLA and fitted with a stripped-down version of the era's enormous TV camera—made the world's first broadcast flight. John D. Silva, chief engineer for KTLA, was the inventor of the TV 'copter. He risked his life for his invention.

During a test flight with Silva the day before the first broadcast, station engineers on Mount Wilson waiting for a signal reported that nothing was coming through. Silva suspected the problem was in the transmitter, told the pilot that he wasn't going to look down, and stepped out onto the helicopter's skid 1,500 feet over Hollywood. When he had jimmied open the transmitter housing, Silva found that one of its vacuum tubes had failed from heat and the helicopter's vibration. Back on the ground, he spent the night insulating and cushioning the transmitter; sixty-five years of car chases, celebrity weddings, disasters, riots, and freeway tie-ups followed.

The purpose of the Telecopter was simple, Silva told the Archive of American Television in 2002, "How can we beat the competition? Why, of course. If we could build a news mobile unit in a helicopter we could get over it all, get there first, avoid the traffic, and get to all the stories before anybody . . . . It'd be a wonderful thing."[1]

Helicopters were wonderful things once, in the future Los Angeles we thought we were getting. Admiring boys like me in 1957 watched Whirlybirds, a helicopter adventure series produced by Desilu and syndicated by Viacom. Kenneth Tobey and Craig Hill starred as pilots Chuck Martin and P.T. Moore, who flew their Bell Model 47 from a fictional California field that was played by the scrappy little San Fernando Airport. TV made the bug like Bell sort of glamorous and gave boys the idea that they could grow up to be dashing helicopter pilots. Some of those boys ended up piloting helicopter gunships. One of the lingering consequences of the Gulf, Iraq, and Afghan wars is a cadre of ex-military pilots looking for work and happy to fly helicopters for tour companies however much the sightseeing angers the earthbound. Zeroing in on the Hollywood sign or the backyard of a pop star for a moneyed tourist is safer than landing at the Bagram Air Base ever was.

There are risks because helicopters don't want to fly. Francis Gary Powers, famous as the pilot of the CIA spy plane shot down in 1960 as it passed over the Russian city of Sverdlovsk, returned from a Soviet prison to fly KNBC's updated version of a Telecopter. Powers and his cameraman were coming back from covering a brush fire in 1977 when their helicopter fatally slammed into the Sepulveda Dam Recreation Area. An as-yet unexplained failure in 2020 brought down the helicopter ferrying retired basketball star Kobe Bryant, his daughter Gianna, and six other passengers between airports in Orange and Ventura counties. The crash led to demands for improved helicopter safety equipment. There were 121 helicopter accidents in 2019, about the same as the year before.

I flew a few times in a small helicopter—essentially two seats and controls attached to rotors and an engine that looked as if it might have come from a lawnmower. It was a Hughes Model 300C, the Volkswagen of helicopters. I wasn't too worried, even though I knew that the helicopter didn't want to fly.

When I was up there, Lakewood was laid out like a three-dimensional map with toy cars and insignificant figures on foot. Some of them must have heard the helicopter clattering overhead, but none of them looked up, so used had they become to the city's surveilling eye.

Robert Winter: Revivalist

Angelenos are so ridiculously housed, complained novelist Nathanael West in *The Day of the Locust* (1939), that only dynamite would do to clean up the city's cockeyed architecture. Robert Winter thought otherwise. With fellow historian David Gebhard, Winter parsed the ways Los Angeles shelters itself and found most of them good. In *An Architectural Guidebook to Los Angeles,* Gebhard and Winter drew an opinionated and quirky mid-1960s map for finding a sense of place in a city that its critics presumed to be placeless. Their first, thin guidebook, covering mostly well-known architects and their buildings, evolved into the Bible of Los Angeles architecture. A sixth revision, completed with the assistance of Robert Inman, includes over 2,300 entries. It was published by Angel City Press in 2018, only a few months before Winter's death at ninety-four.

Winter, an Indianan whose degrees were from Dartmouth and Johns Hopkins, arrived in Los Angeles in 1956 to teach cultural history at UCLA. He expected to be disappointed. Instead, he was surprised and then beguiled by Los Angeles. Winter spent the next forty years in fascinated motorized *flânerie,* documenting the many ecologies of Southern California's architecture. He passionately adopted one of them—Pasadena's bohemian Arroyo Seco—becoming its exponent, sustaining a revival of its turn-of-the-century Arts and Crafts heritage, and eventually owning the Craftsman bungalow that master tile maker Ernest Batchelder built in 1909.

Winter shared his enthusiasms for the built environment, California culture, and the idea of Los Angeles with three decades of students at Occidental College in Eagle Rock before his retirement in 1994. Author and *Los Angeles Times* columnist Patt Morrison, one of Winter's students, found through his example how Los Angeles could be imaginatively inhabited as "a place whose unique standards and tastes were worthy and admirable and, yes, beautiful."[25]

Winter made a life's work of preservation, which USC historian William Deverell describes as "biographical recovery." Winter, he said, built up an interpretive framework for making Los Angeles legible, "something to lean against, agree with, or disagree with, but something that could be encountered."[26] In his books, essays, and monographs, Winter materialized a city that always threatens to dissolve into its dreams.

Finding Los Angeles

In the late 1970s, I used to go looking for Los Angeles with Michael Ward, an artist who has a passion for old buildings, any old buildings: industrial, domestic, and indeterminate. Michael had a camera. We'd meet on a Saturday morning in front of my house and drive with only the vaguest plan. We had looked through Michael's copy of the 1977 edition of Gebhard and Winter's guide. We knew where the iconic buildings were located—the Neutra and Schindler houses, the Wrights and the Green & Greens. Buildings that were scattered as solitary monuments separated by miles and miles of in-between.

Gebhard and Winter were smart and brave to make the claims they did about Los Angeles, that a different kind of modernism was given shape here, that Los Angeles had bred new forms for living and working, and that against all the complaints of a "formless and incoherent" city, it was as much a "real city" as New York or Chicago. That argument impressed Michael and me as a little beside the point.

After driving from one disconnected bit of named architecture to the next, it was the in-between that was entrancing. We drove in neighborhoods where the buildings themselves remembered—even if nothing and no one else did—the Egyptoid apartment court on Bonnie Brae, the Victorians of the city's first boom, Frogtown below Elysian Park, the bungalow neighborhoods of Long Beach (survivors of the 1933 earthquake), the Tiki-themed motels and dingbat apartments along Lakewood Boulevard where it turns into Rosemead, retail strips in Lynwood and Watts, Serb and Croatian blocks in San Pedro, and industrial Vernon, Cudahy, Commerce, and little towns like Bellflower, Artesia, Monrovia, Duarte, and La Verne.

Hundreds of 35mm photographs and hours of driving through the edges of a city of edges, through some neighborhoods we probably shouldn't have been in—two white guys in a white Pinto sharing a feeling for architectural survivors and the lesser histories of the city. On side streets and in marginal neighborhoods, conserved by neglect in the easy climate and too-bright sunlight, were the sheet metal gas stations, shingled or stuccoed houses, and Googie-style diners of the city's demotic commonplace—the mongrel architecture that binds the city, however loosely, together.

As his guides evolved, Winter made room for this ordinariness and its intimacy. "Bob was not a snob," Morrison notes. "Bob embraced Los Angeles not in spite of but because of its multiple esthetics, its ebullience, and confidence." It was not unlike the man himself, she thinks, who saw significance in the cityscape wherever he looked. Winter took Los Angeles seriously and examined its architecture closely for signs, not only of the city's utopian aspirations, but also for the fads and the prejudices that settled Angelenos in their separate enclaves. Housing insecurity and homelessness are in the new guidebook along with Richard Neutra and Frank Gehry.

By revealing the architectural heritage of Los Angeles, Winter inspired Angelenos to keep it. He helped draft Pasadena's historic preservation ordinance, supported the Los Angeles Conservancy, consulted in the making of a citywide survey of Los Angeles architecture, and served on the State Historical Resources Commission and the Los Angeles Cultural Heritage Board, where well-thumbed editions of the guidebook were the starting place for discussion. "Is it in the guide?" Winter remembered board members asking. He told them that the guide was just the personal feelings of "two guys" and not more than that.[27] But it was more. As Nathan Masters notes in the foreword to the new edition, "Inclusion has saved more than one building from demolition. Omission has also doomed some works of architecture . . . ."[28] The opinions of "two guys" have a cost, including incitements to nostalgia and gentrification.

Many Angelenos, however long their residence, remain wary sojourners in Los Angeles. Robert Winter fully inhabited the city, knowing its breadth, its romance, and its freedom. He saw the conversation that buildings have among themselves and wanted us to see it, too. He wanted Angelenos to see what they've made of Los Angeles and what Los Angeles was making of them.

Los Angeles Loves Wheels

Los Angeles loves chrome wheels on custom cars and polyurethane wheels on skateboards. Wheels over the asphalt or the concrete of any freeway or sidewalk if it leads away from where you are. Wheels are the fix for our need. The need—*the rush*—is momentum. Los Angeles moves or it isn't Los Angeles anymore.

Nothing is too good for wheels. There are at least 21,825 miles of roads, highways, and freeways in Los Angeles County. There aren't enough acres of parks in the city of Los Angeles, but there are acres and acres of parking lots.

Nothing is permitted to stop wheels unless it's more wheels. Angelenos, even if they've been here only a year or two, claim to remember a better time when the traffic wasn't as bad, and when driving was exhilarating and a promise that you could be in control if only of a car. Los Angeles is a city of joyrides, increasingly disappointed. The blues are played to the beat of tires slowly thumping over the concrete slabs of freeway lanes. No sound is more melancholy than that.

Angelenos will pretend to be in motion rather than be seen waiting, all of us making a rolling stop, making a right turn on red, making a lane change to get one car-length ahead. It's not about the cause for all that motion; it's only about movement. It seems to stand for something else. In *Play It as It Lays* (1970), Joan Didion's freeway-addicted Maria drives the way a dancer moves or a jazz player riffs on a melody. In Reyner Banham's *Los Angeles: The Architecture of Four Ecologies* (1971), driving the freeway writes the city into existence. It's not the destination; it's in being carried away.

I was made for wheels, but I don't drive. I would if I could, but that's another story. I'm detached from the second skin that surrounds drivers as they move in suave crowds, completely alone in their cars. I watch them from the curb, an exile from real Los Angeles. And when the urge to move overcomes me, when the longing that is Los Angeles takes me, I ride the bus or the subway just for the speed.

Los Angeles on wheels never feels like a place. We suffer disconnections, all of us in motion, because there's no still point that reveals where we are. That revelation would be the final gridlock, when the wheels would stop, and we step out of the car, get off the treadmill, dismount from the bike, and find ourselves at rest.

So Dense

We're more crowded than New York ... sort of. Whether the Los Angeles-Long Beach-Anaheim region is more densely settled than a place considered highly urbanized depends on where you draw the boundaries. Manhattan is more densely settled than downtown Los Angeles, but Los Angeles and Orange counties—as big as they are—are more densely urbanized than all the suburban and rural areas in the statistical region within and beyond the five boroughs of New York. (Of the top ten most densely urbanized areas in the nation, nine are in the West and seven of those are in California. California is the most urbanized state of all, with more than 95 percent of Californians living in "urbanized areas," as defined by the Census Bureau.)

The uniform density of Los Angeles (hedged around by the Census Bureau's methodology) runs counter to the perception that Angelenos have of their place, probably because Angelenos most often see their place through other people's eyes. If they could encounter their place without received preconceptions, they'd see that Los Angeles urbanism has taken a different form, and high densities coexist with suburbanization. Coastal Southern California wasn't urbanized through the piecemeal subdivision of freeholder farms, as was much of the East Coast and the Midwest, but through the planned development of miles-square tracts of ranchland originating in the Mexican land grants of the 1790s through the 1840s. When the ranchos passed from their Californio grantees into the hands of Yankee merchants in the 1860s and from them into the hands of San Francisco capitalists in the 1870s, the pattern of Southern California development was set: a large tract of land (not always contiguous to other tracts) would be improved as a unit and sold as acreage for farms and orchards and further broken down in the twentieth century into house lots. (A common residential lot size in Los Angeles was about five thousand square feet, almost the same area as the town lots parceled out by Spanish authorities when Los Angeles was founded in 1781).

After 1890, an almost continuous housing boom doubled the population of Los Angeles every decade, hiking the cost of land and making it easy to persuade newcomers that they didn't need (or couldn't afford) a house lot of an acre or two that was common in other parts of the country when suburban development moved into farmland. Developers in Los Angeles made fortunes by convincing buyers that they had acquired a whole landscape by owning just an eighth of an acre.

That land, unlike the East Coast, was (and is) subject to drought. Access to water in semi-arid Los Angeles has always been relatively difficult. Water delivery eventually required a substantial infrastructure of reservoirs, mains, and service lines. Many small lots spread those costs over more ratepayers who, in any case, couldn't afford to keep much more than their lawn and garden green. The scarcity of water and the costs of supply helped keep house lots small, but the reach of public and private water systems made it possible to have those small lots everywhere.

As they developed, former ranchos were connected by steam railways and dotted with farm towns platted along tracks laid down by the railways for their convenience and profit. Later, Pacific Electric trolleys began filling in the open land between existing towns. Freeway building after World War II replicated the pattern of in-fill development at ever greater distances from urban centers and their pre-war suburbs. By the end of the 1970s, Los Angeles had become more uniformly dense than comparable regions around the cities of the East Coast.

Today, we look at Los Angeles and see sprawl, as if 120 years of development had been an unreasoning imposition needing none of our imagination to comprehend what it is and why. That failure of imagination makes the density of Los Angeles appear paradoxical. But it's true. Los Angeles is thoroughly urban in its own way and just as broadly suburban.

I'm Dreaming of a Smoggy Christmas

The holiday weather outside wasn't frightful when I was eight. The days leading up to December 25 in 1956 had been in the mid-80s. Christmas sweltered at 86 degrees. All the Christmas cards that year had snowmen and sleigh rides and carolers bundled up against the frost, but outside my house, midwinter meant that our lawn had turned brown, leaves on the neighbor's tree had fallen, and the light of a low, southern sun glared through the smog.

1958 was just another year of temperatures above 80 degrees during Christmas week. Fog in the early mornings, accompanied by heavy smog later in the day, closed airports and shrouded freeways. The air in the Los Angeles basin and inland valleys became a 250-square-mile pool of ozone, nitrogen oxides, and molecule-sized bits of partially burned diesel fuel. Doctors warned of eye irritation, chest pains, nausea, and headache. Some warned of worse: chronic emphysema and lung cancer. I rode my Schwinn bike through hot, leaden air that forecast wildfires while car radios played the holiday songs of an alien America where Jack Frost nipped at the noses of walkers in a winter wonderland and folks dressed up like Eskimos to hear sleigh bells in the snow.

Let It Snow

Although boosters never speak of it, snow has fallen on Los Angeles (depending on what you mean by snow). Higher elevations in the city's foothills get something like thin slush from time to time. True snow fell on the flatlands where I live in 1949. During a three-day siege of storms that began on January 10, several inches fell. At first, a snowy Los Angeles was fun, despite the snow ball that went through the front window of Mrs. Frieda Deem in Pasadena. By the second day, snow, hail, and sleet tied up downtown streets and closed canyon passes with more than twenty cars trapped in Laurel Canyon alone. Snow (or something like it) reached cities as far south as San Diego. In Long Beach, the *Los Angeles Times* reported, "snow, rain, sleet, hail, thunder, and lightning succeeded one another" throughout the second night.[29] Snow fell on Catalina Island on the third day, dropping eight inches on Blackjack Peak.[30]

It's unlikely that snow like that will ever fall again. Paving over the basin in the years after 1949, as well as the mounting effects of climate change, will keep nighttime temperatures too high for Angelenos to wake up to a white Christmas. Los Angeles is now on average five degrees warmer than it was a century ago.[31]

Snow at Christmastime on the summits of the local mountains (when they could be seen through petrochemical byproducts) was a kind of theatrical backdrop to the sunny city I knew. It was like the fake snow in the movies, which was made of a sprayable mixture of fire extinguisher foam, sugar, and corn flakes. That formula, because it didn't crunch under the actor's feet, won a technical award from the Academy of Motion Picture Arts and Sciences in 1950.

When I was a boy, I understood snow as a special effect, but for those who come from snowed-in places, it's supposed to be a powerful instigator of memories. For Irving Berlin, a memory of snowy holidays produced the most successful Christmas song of all, selling well over 150 million copies after "White Christmas" was recorded by Bing Crosby in 1942. In the song's rarely heard introduction, there's a reason for the song's mood of reverie and loss: "The sun is shining, the grass is green/The orange and palm trees sway/There's never been such a day/In Beverly Hills, L.A./But it's December the 24th/And I'm longing to be up North." Johnny Mathis in "Christmas in the City of Angels" improbably sang, "When it's Christmas in the city of the angels the blue Pacific becomes the Sea of Galilee." "Christmas in Los Angeles," recorded by TV bandleader Lawrence Welk, may be the worst holiday song ever written. Mayor Tom Bradley made it the city's official Christmas song in 1981.

The snow-themed cards and the songs, the reruns of *It's a Wonderful Life* with acres of fake snow and the imposition of other winter holiday identifiers didn't fit my boyhood Los Angeles. I'd never seen chestnuts roasting on an open fire. I'd never seen a chestnut. Worse were awkward attempts to make a place for Angelenos around the Yule log of other people's memories. Surfin' Santa (San Diego's official representative of the holidays) and other hybrid seasonal avatars generated too much cognitive dissonance. If I want a simulation of a traditional holiday, I could attend the Winter Fest at the Orange County Fairgrounds in Costa Mesa. "Real snow" is blown in daily. Ice is even more uncommon than snow in Los Angeles, but you can skate on it through Christmas week at Pershing Square, onboard the Queen Mary in Long Beach, and in downtown Santa Monica where VIP cabanas are available in place of ice fishing cabins.

A Christmas tradition better fitted to the city's climate requires some walking. Popular in Mexico, the celebration of Las Posadas is a kind of pilgrimage done in imitation of the search Mary and Joseph are said to have made on the first Christmas Eve. Every night until December 24, you can join (or watch) a candlelight procession, with songs in and Spanish and English, that begins at the Avila adobe and continues among the historic buildings on Olvera Street.

I'll be hoping for an old-fashion Christmas this year—enough chill in the air to require a sweater, a quiet walk before an early dinner, kids on skateboards in the street, and colored lights strung in the palm trees. The smog (less thickly brown now) will be there, just like the Christmases I used to know.

Time and Again at Union Station

After three days of pageants and parades on Alameda Street with half-a-million spectators, Los Angeles Union Station opened on May 7, 1939. It was a Sunday. A man jumped from a window of a Pullman car to claim bragging rights as the first passenger to arrive. The first outbound ticket cost twenty-eight cents and took Mr. and Mrs. M.B. Sheets to Glendale.[32] The first child was lost and found. The first traveler to miss his train fell asleep in one of the throne-like chairs in the station waiting room beneath a painted ceiling with steel beams made to look like hewn wood.

Union Station was the last of the grand railroad gateways to be built in America. It was officially called the Los Angeles Union Passenger Terminal because it united in a single, forty-seven-acre complex, the Union Pacific, Southern Pacific, and Santa Fe railroads. It was built to frame an image of Los Angeles for tourists. Its construction razed a neighborhood that included Chinese herbalists, pacifist Russian Molokans, and refugees from the Mexican revolution.

Aerial photographs in 1939 show how big a footprint the railroads made in Los Angeles. The Cornfield, Bull Ring, and Taylor freight yards, along with their warehouses, repair shops, and stockyards, snaked up the Los Angeles River to the foot of Elysian Park. Nearly all that footprint will be gone soon, a large part of it to the greening of the Los Angeles River. Union Station remains but not as a relic. The station is a hub for rail and bus transit and a terminal for Amtrak and Metrolink trains. It will be even busier when the Regional Connector (linking subway and light rail lines) is finished, and Metro (the regional transportation agency) consolidates transfer points at the station. If Metro's plans are realized in full, more than a hundred thousand transit users, rail passengers, office workers, and casual visitors might pass through Union Station every day. I hope that some of them will stop and look around. Those who do will see a nearly perfect public space that was meant to be both monumental and deferential, designed to reassure as much as to impress.

Today's patient traveler will inevitably slip out of the everyday and into the station's memories of itself. All it takes is attention to patterns, vistas, shadows, and light to enable a timeslip through eighty years of family reunions and last farewells, the boredom of waiting travelers and the anticipations of those who came to Los Angeles. Travelers stepped down from their Pullman car or coach, walked through the long, echoing tunnel beneath the tracks, and entered the station. In the three or four minutes it took to walk past the waves of colored tile on the walls, Union Station would have had time enough to say, "You've come to Los Angeles where brilliant light is dominant, but see how it's tempered by this space, these fountains, and these flowering trees." The travelers' first experience of Los Angeles would have been this transformed brightness. Outside the station, Los Angeles sprawled and brawled and offered travelers the lure of endless self-invention, if they could stand it.

A Line Between

In Union Station, the city's power brokers projected the Los Angeles they wanted. It's in the vista through the elegant box of the entrance vestibule into the ticket concourse, soaring five stories high and with 115 feet of counters. It's in the landscaping outside—Chilean pepper trees, Amazonian jacarandas, and Mexican fan palms—intended to summon a vision of semi-tropical Los Angeles. It's in the station's high façade that faces the old plaza where Los Angeles began in 1781. Union Station was a line drawn from the colonial past to the "now" of 1939, between what had been superseded and its triumphant replacement. Among other things, the station was intended to be a concrete lesson about power.

In the war years between 1942 and 1945, a train passed through Union Station every fifteen minutes. Most carried outbound troops; some returned as war dead. As many as twenty military coffins passed through the baggage department each day. More coffins arrived from Korea in 1951 and from Vietnam in the following decades.

After months and miles of separation, war brides met their servicemen husbands in the arrivals lobby. Japanese American internees returning from an Arkansas relocation camp encountered four hundred Marines returning from the Pacific in 1946.

Movie stars Humphrey Bogart and Lauren Bacall were taken down the long tunnel to the train platforms, so were Errol Flynn, Kim Novak, Margaret O'Brien, and Virginia Mayo, who had her picture painted on the Super Chief en route to New York. Singers Mary Martin, Marian Anderson, and Elvis Presley arrived in the flash of news cameras, as did notables like Madame Chiang

Kai-shek, Lord and Lady Halifax, and Jim Thorpe and Ty Cobb. Convention-bound Shriners poured out of the station in 1950, as did Democratic Party delegates arriving in 1960.

The marble blocks in the floor of the waiting room are grooved from the tread of conventioneers, vacationers, aspiring starlets, and the unremarked mass of those embracing or abandoning Los Angeles. You can't put yourself in their shoes, but you can put yourself in the light they encountered. The shadows are the same. By a frequent quirk of the still air over downtown, shadows at Union Station are usually sharp and deep, as if drawn with a ruler and inked in. The shadows are there by design—to give cool shelter in the long arcades, to provide contrast to the white of the walls, and movement to the static mass of the building. John and Donald Parkinson, the station's supervising architects, understood the light and shadows of Los Angeles. In the Parkinsons' concrete reverie of mingled historical styles, Union Station appears as if from an alternate history where Moorish craftsmen ornamented an Andalusian basilica with tile geometry, where Franciscan gardeners enclosed paradises of orange and olive trees, and where the brash confidence of American engineers made all of it bigger and better.

It's possible even now to step into that imaginary past. Transient light and dark make patterns on the Montana travertine walls, marking local time without reference to the schedules on which trains and buses run. There are durable patterns in the 75,000 square feet of cement, marble, and linoleum floors, on the faience wainscoting, on the tiled benches and doorway surrounds, and even in the brick parquetry of patio walkways. Patterns in tile and stone hybridize at Union Station, partly Hispano-Moresque and partly Mexican, Native American, and Hollywood art deco. Pale rosettes on a blue background punctuate the walls of the ticket concourse. A zigzagging design in ochre, burnt sienna, brown, and yellow continues to jazz up what had been the arrivals lobby. Eight-pointed stars repeat in the grill over the entrance vestibule on Alameda Street and throughout the station. There are quartets of parrots on the walls of the former Harvey House restaurant and Mexican leather stitching on the booths. The restaurant floor is a block-long Navajo rug in white, terra cotta, and black linoleum, designed (as all the retail spaces at Union Station were) by Mary Colter, Southern Pacific's architect of station interiors.

Somewhere between aesthetics and religion is the idea that a pattern of simple forms repeating over a surface can be a metaphor for the orderliness of a knowable world. The benches, arches, doorways, walks, and walls and floors of Union Station are beautifully patterned and continue that confession of faith to those who pass by.

For the city builders of Los Angeles, a romantic past was supposed to blend with an easeful present on the way to a triumphant, machine-age tomorrow, exactly as the architecture of Union Station said. Left out of the design were other figures—mostly people of color—who were given no place in that consoling synthesis. Their claims on what Los Angeles should become weren't satisfied by the eclecticism of Union Station or by the tourist destinations of New Chinatown and Olvera Street or the granite acropolis that eventually rose on Bunker Hill. Today, unticketed visitors aren't welcome to rest in the station's supremely comfortable waiting room chairs. The homeless people who drift across Alameda Street on cold nights aren't wanted either.

One of the most beautiful public spaces in the city risks becoming much less public as Metro seeks to maximize income. Metro holds six million square feet of development entitlements that could turn the station and its grounds into the privatized foyer for office towers and blocks of condominiums.

We have arrived at the tomorrow that Union Station dreamed of, although the future didn't turn out the way the city's power brokers thought it would. Among the many things Union Station is today—glamorous symbol of Depression-era optimism, movie character actor, and marketable real estate—it's also a working time machine. For Angelenos who enter and pause, Union Station can take them back to the materials--illusory and real--from which Los Angeles was made and permit these time travelers to reflect on who we were and what we could be.

Thom Andersen: Looking Back

Thom Andersen's *Los Angeles Plays Itself*—a film essay on the image of Los Angeles in the movies—was finally released on disc in 2014. After a decade in the underground of bootlegged videotapes, Andersen's documentary was available to ordinary Angelenos. It should be required viewing for anyone who wonders why it's been so hard for so many to love this town. The misrepresentations of Los Angeles on film have sometimes been cruel and sometimes merely expedient, but mostly hallucinatory.

"Although Los Angeles has appeared in more films than any other city," Andersen has said, "I believe that it has not been well served by these films.... It happens that many filmmakers working in Los Angeles don't appreciate the city, and very few of them understand much about it, but their failures in depicting it may have more profound causes."[33] Identifying these failures of representation is Andersen's purpose, carried out in scores of clips from the silent era through 2001 accompanied by the methodical, mordant voice of narrator Encke King.

I met Andersen not long after *Los Angeles Plays Itself* had progressed from a lecture for CalArts students to something Andersen calls a "city symphony in reverse." He sent me a VHS copy of his documentary. I wrote him a fan letter.

Los Angeles and Los-Angeles-in-film are different places and not just in the displacements Angelenos wryly note when, at the movies or on television, familiar locations miles apart are shown as if around the block from one another. Disconnection is ingrained in the way the movies see Los Angeles, its inauthenticity contrasted with New York realities. When moviemaking became centered in Los Angeles, Andersen believes, "a lot of the people who were part of it were expatriates from New York and they romanticized it in the movies. And then it represented an ideal of the city, an ideal to which Los Angeles could never live up. ... Los Angeles was, for these New Yorkers, a kind of a joke of a city."[34]

Robert Towne's *Chinatown* (1974) sums up the difficulties of seeing Los Angeles in the movies. By the end of *Chinatown*, the city has been shown to be a sinister fake, screening an abyss of otherness, its image dwindling to a landscape seen in the rearview mirror of a car fleeing a crime scene. *Chinatown*'s fable of murder, greed, incest, and hydrology insists that in Los Angeles, we're only along for the ride. The antidote was supposed to be *500 Days of Summer* (2009), in which observing downtown Los Angeles—not a car chase—is a frame for encountering the city. The Joseph Gordon-Levitt and Zooey Deschanel characters sit on a park bench in one memorable scene and talk romantically about architecture. But *500 Days of Summer* was an anomaly in the performances of Los Angeles and hasn't the traction of *Chinatown*. We have *L.A. Confidential* (1997), *The Long Goodbye* (1973), *Blade Runner* (1982), and *The Day of the Locust* (1975) to reinforce the preferred image of self-deluding Los Angeles. The movies look at the city and see a sinister emptiness where decisions are made by fools or cunning manipulators, and where no one who isn't pulling the strings knows anything.

As Andersen has noted elsewhere, only privileged observers make the city we see in the movies. They're nearly all male. They're mostly white and middle class. Hardly any of them have been refugees or been poor. As a result, Andersen doesn't see the Los Angeles he knows in the city that filmmakers show him. Andersen thinks Los Angeles isn't photogenic. Perhaps he meant that the city on film didn't shamelessly appeal to sentiment the way New York on film often does. Maybe he meant that the character of Los Angeles couldn't be caught by a camera's roving. Los Angeles as played by Los Angeles looks garish or uncanny or horrific on film. Rarely does it look touching or like a place where anyone sober would want to live. *Los Angeles Plays Itself* is Andersen's explanation of why the more we see that Los Angeles on screen, the more we long for another.

The Death of Riley

My suburb sold itself into existence as The City of Tomorrow Today at the start of the second decade of aerospace Los Angeles. The end of Lakewood's tomorrow is down the street from where I live. The buildings where the future had been made, in the form of Douglas DC jetliners, stood not far from my house. Those buildings are gone now. The work those buildings stood for is gone too. No one assembles jetliners in Los Ángeles anymore.

Douglas began the post-World War II era as the largest aircraft manufacturing employer in California. But Douglas wasn't alone. By 1965, fifteen of the twenty-five largest aerospace companies in the nation were concentrated in Los Angeles County. Most were in a north-south industrial belt that ran from El Segundo to Long Beach and another that ran east-west from the San Gabriel Valley to Downey and Lakewood. From the 1960s to the end of the Vietnam War, defense and aerospace manufacturing in Los Angeles County employed more than 250,000 workers. As late as 1990, these industries employed more than 130,000 countywide. That was more than half the state's entire aerospace workforce.

It wasn't only DC-7s that the workers of my neighborhoods riveted together. The image of the men who were building the future also was fabricated here. At the start of the new age of aerospace, the image was Chester A. Riley, the hero of *The Life of Riley*, a long-running series of comedies that began in 1941 as a vehicle for Groucho Marx. The original program was called, with the blackest of Groucho Marxist irony, *The Flotsam Family*. Recast with William Bendix as the eponymous Riley, *The Life of Riley* radio series became a popular motion picture and then (after a false start with Jackie Gleeson) one of early television's most successful situation comedies, originally broadcast between 1953 and 1958 and rerun for many years after. Riley's exclamation of baffled indignation—"What a revoltin' development this is!"—was a catchphrase of the period.

A harmless, big-hearted lug, Chester Riley was aerospace flotsam, adrift with his nuclear family in a landscape of tract houses that was meant to be Hawthorne or Lawndale or Torrance. Riley became the prototype—the proof of concept—for television's Ralph Kramden, Fred Flintstone, Archie Bunker, and more recent working stiffs. Today, with greater irony, Riley's successor as a model technical worker is two-dimensional Homer Simpson.

Many of my neighbors worked at the Douglas plant in Long Beach. Many of them wore Riley's work uniform of khaki shirt and pants, not much different from the military uniforms most of my neighbors had worn. In the unlikely event any of them thought they were the heroes of a "the greatest generation," they had only to look to hapless Riley.

Riley lacked one characteristic of the aerospace age in Los Angeles. William Bendix was a wonderful character actor, but when he opened his mouth, it was the accents of Brooklyn that came out. To be true to life, Riley should have spoken with the twang of Oklahoma, Texas, Tennessee, Arkansas, or Missouri. In the first year of the war, between 30 and 50 percent of new employees at Southern California's aircraft plants came from these states.

Tom Treanor, a *Los Angeles Times* staff writer, wrote about young aircraft workers in "The Home Front," his weekly column about everyday life in wartime Los Angeles. They were from "Iowa, Texas, Oklahoma, Kansas, Nebraska, Missouri, and Arkansas," according to A.G. Bahl, who was the credit manager of a department store on Pico Boulevard. Did they come to Los Angeles just for the jobs, Treanor asked. "A good many of them" was the answer. "They'd get a jalopy, drive to California, come into the store for new spark plugs and tires, get a job, marry, take a house, and buy a stove."[35] Ralph Smith, a personnel manager at Vultee Aircraft in Downey, thought the boys from cities tended to spend their money. The country boys saved it. "Many of them plan to go back to the farm with their boomtime cash," Treanor supposed. That didn't happen. Aerospace migrants were already filling the cities of Huntington Park, El Monte, Bell Gardens, and other blue-collar communities along the Los Angeles River that eventually became the workshops of the Cold War. In 1950, they began buying houses in Lakewood with the money they saved working at Douglas, North American, or Consolidated.

Some of the men and women in my neighborhood had lived part of their childhood on the outskirts of Central Valley farm towns in camps provided by the Farm Security Administration. Some had lived in tar-paper shacks in the oil fields around Bakersfield. Many had been the first in their family to graduate from high school. Most learned to hide their twangs and drawls. They would reappear after a few drinks among the couples my parents invited over to watch television or play cards. They never lost their appreciation for the climate, however. It expressed itself in the fruit trees they planted in their backyards. Plums, apricots, oranges, nectarines, and pomegranates in absurd profusion were shared over fences in paper bags saved from the grocery store. Aerospace workers gave suburban Los Angeles a distinctive culture with its own music and food preferences, as well as its own politics and racial antagonisms. They resisted public housing and integrated neighborhoods and anything that would unsettle the charmed pattern of their new suburban lives. *Billboard* magazine, in describing their preference for the country-western music that specialized in the laments of men jilted by life, called them "khaki and overalled Okies." Today, it's hard to say how much remains of that distinctive amalgam of hope and resentment, now that "country" culture has blended into the generality of Los Angeles.

I grew up among "khaki and overalled Okies" and saw them whipsawed by cycles of boom and bust in aerospace. I watched Douglas workers go out on strikes that frightened their wives and threatened marriages and mortgages. I listened to their complaints about the men who supervised them at Douglas, an organization that seemed to be composed of dense layers of managers in short-sleeve, white shirts who had a disturbing inability to manage.

Embedded in aerospace Los Angeles were contradictory images of work and its meaning. Over at Douglas, ordinary men like Riley riveted together large parts of the tomorrow they believed had come with their tract house and crabgrass lawn. And other men managed only to threaten assembly-line Rileys with obscure regulations or cajole them into serving a Cold War mission that was unclear even to the white-shirted men with clipboards. Douglas Aircraft had nothing else to offer, least of all the meaning of work.

The work itself evaporated in the rounds of reductions that cut the Douglas workforce by nearly thirty thousand between 1990 and 1994. In the end, the managers in white shirts were as befuddled as the laid-off Rileys in khaki. Tomorrow, it turned out, didn't see much difference between the manager's clipboard and Riley's rivet gun. And when the future finally arrived without Douglas or any of the other aerospace giants, the future had no need of Riley or his bosses.

Aerospace workers had once gathered at places like Price's Foothill Club in Long Beach and the Palomino in North Hollywood to dance, drink, and listen to country-western bands. Price's Foothill went from Billy Mize and The Tennesseans to salsa and reggaetón and then went dark. After switching to rock and funk in the 1980s, the Palomino closed. KZLA, once the dominant country music station in Los Angeles, abandoned the format. "We apologize for any inconvenience this may cause," was the station's last web posting.

Tom Hatten: Rascals and Stooges

Sheriff John (John Rovick) is dead. So is Engineer Bill (Bill Stulla), Skipper Frank (Frank Herman), and now Tom Hatten whose stage name, if he ever had one, didn't stick. Afternoon television in mid-century Los Angeles was crowded with genial hosts in costumes who recycled old cartoons and comedy shorts to boys and girls sitting squarely in front of the family's black-and-white television set. I was one who sat too close to the screen.

The clowns, puppeteers, ventriloquists, and slapstick comics—an entire vaudeville troupe—fascinated kids like me by replaying the humor, pathos, and sly absurdism of the early twentieth century as conceived by animators Max and Dave Fleischer (*Popeye the Sailor*) and filmmakers Hal Roach (*Our Gang/ The Little Rascals*) and Mack Sennett (*Laurel and Hardy*). The violence and evils of those years were there, either taken for granted (like racism and sexism) or fractured into satire (of class inequality and fascism). Crudity wasn't a problem. There was plenty of room in the afternoon for the burlesque of Pinky Lee or Soupy Sales, for the anarchy of *The Three Stooges* (presented by Don Lamond, son-in-law to "Stooge" Larry Fine), or the surreality of watching Bill and John and Tom frame low comedy from the 1930s for children who had been born after 1946.

The dissonance was stark in Tom Hatten's show. Hatten was a smiling, youthful man in a deckhand's work clothes who taught youngsters a brief lesson in freehand drawing in between screening Depression-era Popeye cartoons. What were we in our suburban living rooms to make of Popeye's dockside slum with its greasy spoons, its saloons, its down-and-out residents, their cheap entertainments, and their almost incoherent speech? What translation did we have for their catchphrases? For the topical jokes whose references we could hardly know? Or for the wrongs of that time, refracted into comedy by Popeye, Bluto, and Olive Oyl?

For those of us who watched the detritus of the past's fads, fears, and aspirations, some of the lessons directed at us were intended. The sheriff, the engineer, and the sailor joined hands with parents and teachers in support of values that we were told were essential: kindness, generosity, deference to authority, and cheerfulness. But the sheriff, the engineer and the sailor were mistaken that this is all they taught. When we turned off the television set, our present reappeared, full of mid-century impatience for tomorrow to arrive tainted by anxiety. Our parents wanted us to live in that tomorrow as if it were newly made and better than the past. We watched Popeye, the Stooges and the Rascals and learned that tomorrow was implicated in its past. We saw history repeating itself with endings that weren't always harmless. The cartoons and comedy shorts told us that our future would be hilarious, undomesticated, and brutal. We soon found they were only partly right.

E. Manchester Boddy: Camellias and 'Commies'

There are few places in Los Angeles that are as historically layered as Descanso Gardens in La Cañada-Flintridge. It was part of the colonial-era Verdugo rancho. It holds tragic Japanese American memories. And it became the home of one of the most controversial figures in Los Angele history. A walk beneath the old-growth oaks and among roses, camellias, lilacs, and wildflowers is to be half lost in the California dream of abundance and cultivated beauty. It's jarring then, to recall that the comfortable house overlooking the wide slope of the gardens had been a place where the rough-and-tumble, mid-century politics of Los Angeles was made.

The house and gardens belonged to E. Manchester Boddy, newspaper publisher, commercial nurseryman, popular author, unsuccessful politician, and ultimately a loser in the contest to decide the future of Los Angeles. Boddy's estate was the foundation of the county-owned Descanso Gardens, greatly enlarged since the land was purchased in 1953. Boddy himself is almost forgotten, although both his camellias and his politics are part of how Los Angeles came to be what it is.

Mass Appeal

Boddy, a World War I veteran, was among the many self-made men whose trajectory through Los Angeles in the first half of the twentieth century was sudden and colorful. He had a salesman's gifts, Hollywood good looks, and a charisma that inspired confidence. He came west with his wife in 1920 for his health, headed the textbook subsidiary of the *Los Angeles Times*, and in 1926 (with only $750 of his own money) acquired the failing *Los Angeles Illustrated Daily News*. He had no experience running a newspaper.

The city's major dailies in 1926 were the rival *Los Angeles Times*, run by the Chandler family, and the *Los Angeles Examiner*, begun by Hearst in 1903. Other, smaller papers, ignored by prestige advertisers, struggled to connect with readers. Some papers were tabloids printed on a skimpier sheet than the big dailies, often on tinted paper, usually with lots of illustrations tending toward beauty queens, gory accidents, gangsters, and prominent people behaving badly. Read as entertainment by an expanding class of working men and women, many recently literate in English, the tabloids and their columnists typically gave the news a crusading spin.

The *Los Angeles Illustrated Daily News* had tried the same format without the sex and violence. It didn't work, went three million dollars in debt, and went bankrupt. But with Boddy as its new publisher and renamed the *Daily News*, the paper seemed to get the formula right, mixing in enough scandal and supplying enough violence. "The trick," Boddy said, "is to realize that the editorship of a newspaper is an elective office. The voters vote for you every day. If they don't put their nickels in the box, you're out."[36] On the peach-colored pages of the *Daily News*, Boddy cheerfully attacked the notoriously corrupt politicians at city hall and by implication the *Los Angeles Times* that actively defended them. Boddy's paper tied the equally corrupt Los Angeles Police Department to the rackets shielding prostitution, bootleg liquor, and gambling. The LAPD responded to criticism with intimidation, which pleased Boddy even more.

Personally, Boddy preferred the Republican politics of Herbert Hoover, but as the Depression worsened after 1930, he declared his paper to be Democratic, largely because his readers were. They were working people and shopkeepers, ethnically diverse and rarely noticed by the middle-class *Los Angeles Times*. Boddy took the anxieties and hopes of his readers seriously. As he told KCET's Ralph Story in 1964:

> Primarily, I think the *Daily News* appealed to the masses who craved a philosophy of life in their daily newspaper. An interpretation of what was going on in the world, what was going on in the United States. Why they couldn't get a job. Why they couldn't pay their bills on time, and that sort of thing. So we brought home, from the very beginning, a message to a large class of Los Angeles citizenship.[37]

Boddy's editorials discussed radical solutions to the economic crisis of the 1930s, including Francis Townsend's plan that the federal government give two hundred dollars a month to every citizen over sixty and the Ham 'n' Eggs plan that would get a thirty dollar check to the elderly every Thursday. Boddy also promoted Technocracy, a utopian movement that would have turned government over to scientists and engineers. Boddy eventually became a supporter of President Roosevelt's less radical New Deal. The *Daily News* was said to be the only paper on the west coast to display the National Recovery Act's blue eagle on its nameplate or to devote so many column inches defending New Deal programs. Fortunately, statewide Democratic victories in 1936 gave Boddy's paper additional political clout. Boddy didn't create a Democratic landslide in California that year, but the *Daily News* helped propel it.

In his editorials, Boddy insightfully analyzed the rise of Nazi aggression, the entry of the United States into World War II, and Roosevelt's alliance with Stalin and the Soviet Union. Of the war years, columnist Jack Smith later wrote, "It may be that few of us were perfectly sober when we put the Daily News to bed, but it was a wonderful paper, full of humor, youthful energy, good writing, and irreverence."[38] The paper's liberal bent contrasted sharply with the *Times*' rightwing editorial policy.

In the years after 1945, the paper began to align itself with the increasing political and cultural conservatism of Los Angeles. Boddy, who had been labeled a leftist in the 1930s, now worried in print about big government and the supposed threat of big unions.

Camellias

Boddy purchased the land that is now Descanso Gardens in 1937 and commissioned "architect to the stars" James E. Dolena to design a gracious home. From almost every window of its twenty-two rooms were vistas of the 165 acres that Boddy called Rancho del Descanso. The house was the setting for Boddy's lavish summer parties where much of his politicking was done.

Boddy, already an enthusiastic amateur horticulturist, took advantage of the wartime internment of Japanese Americans to buy the stock of nurseries owned by F.M. Uyematsu and the Yoshimura family when they were rounded up and sent to government camps. Boddy's sketchy business records leave his dealings with Uyematsu and the Yoshimuras unclear, although later accounts say he paid a fair price. Boddy was now the owner of sixty to eighty thousand camellia shrubs and became a major supplier of camellia blossoms to florists. He later began an experimental nursery for hybridizing new varieties of roses and lilacs. Boddy, his critics said, paid more attention to his flowers than his newspaper.

Boddy had grown tired of being a newspaper publisher and he'd begun to believe his own ballyhoo. In 1950, he ran for the US Senate in both the Democratic and Republican primaries (a practice California permitted). He opposed

Democratic Congresswoman Helen Gahagan Douglas and Republican Congressman Richard Nixon. It was a virulent campaign, charged with Cold War anxieties. Gahagan Douglas, a New Deal liberal, was smeared as a Soviet sympathizer in advertisements that appeared in the *Daily News* and the other Los Angeles papers. "Pink right down to her underwear" was the sneering, misogynistic charge. Boddy turned out to be a weak candidate, seemingly unconcerned with the demands of a modern political campaign. He ran a distant second in primaries that Gehagan Douglas and Nixon won. Nixon went on to characterize Gahagan Douglas as "the pink lady" and win the Senate seat that pointed him toward the White House.

Los Angeles in 1950 was markedly different from the city of 1930. It was more conservative and even then more polarized. The *Daily News* was still successful, but not successful enough. The paper depended on refinancing the loans that kept it going. As the *New York Times* noted, Boddy hadn't bought the paper on a shoestring; he'd bought it on a "borrowed shoestring." Kept on a short leash by investors who had interests in other Los Angeles papers, Boddy could no longer afford to be a crusading champion of working men and women. Nor did he have the spirit to carry on as one. Having made himself so thoroughly a figure of pre-war Los Angeles, he had no place in the post-war city.

Boddy got out of the newspaper business in 1952. In 1953, he sold Rancho del Descanso to the county for nearly $1.2 million and moved half of his camellia collection to northern San Diego County. In early December 1954, the *Los Angeles Times* purchased the debt-ridden *Daily News*, merged it with the afternoon *Mirror*, and fired the paper's unionized employees, leaving them jobless only days before Christmas.

Boddy didn't think much of the *Daily News* in his retirement. He suggested to Ralph Story that Descanso Gardens alone would preserve his contributions to the making of Los Angeles. It hasn't. Boddy is a Wikipedia entry, a chapter in the history of Los Angeles newspapers, and a footnote to the career of Richard Nixon. A walk through the rooms of his house, where his rise and fall are displayed, is a pilgrimage to a nearly forgotten shrine. Like many newspapermen in the West, Boddy had stirred up a half-formed town by trying to find his place in it. He had charmed his readers until he didn't. He had tried to shape a political movement and misjudged what others were making of it. Boddy died in 1967 at seventy-five in Pasadena and far from his camellias.

Don't Be Lonesome

Susan J. Matt, in *Homesickness: An American History*, calls out the least understood quality of Los Angeles when, after World War I, the city took in thousands of mostly Midwestern migrants. Matt quotes Carey McWilliams's bleak observation that the city he chronicled in *Southern California Country: An Island on the Land* suffered an "aching loneliness—the really terrible loneliness—that for years has been so clearly apparent in the streets and parks, the boarding houses and hotels, the cafeterias, and 'lonely clubs' of Los Angeles."[39]

Lonely clubs? In fact, there were several membership clubs for lonely people on the West Coast from the turn of the century through the 1940s, but Los Angeles seems to have had even more need to answer the "aching loneliness" of friendless newcomers. "There are 80,000 lonely persons in Los Angeles," the operator of one lonely club told the *Los Angeles Times* in 1933. "And I know there are hundreds of thousands more—forlorn widows and widowers, divorced people (disillusioned but still trusting they'll find someone congenial), elderly bachelors and the women we used to call 'old maids,' and younger people who are shy or who have come to town recently and want to find friends."[40]

The Lonesome Club of Los Angeles was one of the most successful. The club offered two evenings a week of polite conversation, card playing, amateur musicals, sing-alongs, and dancing. The club's ads promised:

> We'll sing the sweet old songs together. Learn and dance the beautiful old-time dances together, play together, laugh together, be good fellows together, each in his or her own way, making fun for all. Talk and write to each other, hike, picnic, excursion together, and so find in each other playmates, work fellows, chums.

Times reporter Alma Whitaker looked in on the club in 1921, shortly after it opened, and found members to be modest, genteel men and women, mostly past middle age, but also a few younger men who were, as she noted,

> [t]he kind that have home ties back in some small town, and who enjoy the society of the older folks, and get as much pleasure out of dancing with "somebody's mother," who is lonesome here, too, as with some frisky little fashion plate.[41]

It's likely that the members of the Lonesome Club were among the "joiners" who went to Aimee Semple McPherson's colorful services at the Angelus Temple in Echo Park or to a lecture on New Thought at Theosophy Hall near USC or to one of the state picnics in summer that brought out thousands to reminisce about back home in Iowa, Ohio, or Indiana.

The Lonesome Club's founder welcomed them all. He was M.A. Hatch of Minneapolis, a sometime doctor who had come to Los Angeles (like many, then and now) to reinvent himself after a troubled past. The Minneapolis *Star Tribune* reported in December 1915 that Hatch had been arrested for performing "illegal operations" at his home. Arrested again for manslaughter after another botched abortion, Hatch was tried twice but not convicted. Another death resulted in a conviction. While on bail and awaiting the outcome of an appeal that proved unsuccessful, Hatch found his office assistant—and chief defense witness—dead. Esther Peterson died of chloroform poisoning at Hatch's medical offices, although the circumstances of her suicide were so odd that Hatch was briefly held on suspicion of her murder.

Hatch ultimately served time in state prison. Like so many others looking for a second chance, he came to Los Angeles after his release. As he waited for his wife and son to join him, Hatch turned his own loneliness into a business proposition. He placed ads in newspapers and magazines offering dance lessons Monday and Thursday evenings with a social hour after the dance program for anyone looking for companionship. "Stranger, Don't be Lonesome!" the ads urged, "Bring a lonesome friend." The first ad brought thirteen replies. Subsequent ads drew more replies, each with the one dollar Lonesome Club membership fee. Lonesome Club members grew to more than three hundred by the end of 1921 and eventually to twenty thousand by the end of the 1920s. Not only were dues-paying members welcome, but anyone presentable could request a day pass (fifty cents for men, thirty-five cents for women). Dancing was the chief attraction. "At the first note of the music," wrote Lucile Marsh in 1935, "everybody turned full attention to dancing. It kept up until twelve o'clock, when most of the guests bid each other goodnight and went their own separate ways rejoicing."[42] Marriage was the occasional result.

Despite the high-mindedness of the management and the ordinariness of the clientele, there was something unsettling about the lonely clubs of Los Angeles. In 1933, Paramount produced *Strictly Personal* (subtitled "Adventures in a Lonely Club") that was billed as:

[the] inside story . . . of a subject about which the average American knows little and suspects less. The production finds real drama in the lives of these lonely folk, among whom are spinsters; widows craving the companionship which Fate has denied them; young girls who have no other means for meeting attractive young men; well-meaning bachelors, and others who use sentiment as a device for increasing their fortunes via the temporary matrimonial route.[43]

Waves of migrants coming to Los Angeles made good money for Hatch and his wife, who continually moved the growing membership of the Lonesome Club to a succession of larger rooms and finally to its own building downtown. The Lonesome Club Ballroom, designed in 1931 by Los Angeles architect Alec Curlett, was headlined by the Lonesome Club Orchestra (one of the grimmest names for a dance band). Performances were so popular that they were broadcast.

But Hatch had died by then, his health broken by the murder of his son in 1927 during a failed holdup of the club's receipts at the Hatches' bungalow (the modest house still stands, looking a little forlorn in Google Streetview). The Lonesome Club continued under his wife's direction through the 1930s until the elderly no longer danced and the young found wives or husbands. The Lonesome Club, the dance band, and its ballroom are gone.

Becoming Homeless

Bodies

The man was dead.[44] His body was on the sidewalk a few steps from Wilshire Boulevard, near the Vermont/Wilshire stop of the Red Line subway. He was a block from where an emergency shelter was to be set up. The neighborhood protested. The shelter hadn't opened.

The woman was sleeping under a tractor-trailer on Rosecrans Avenue in Santa Fe Springs.[45] The driver returned to his rig and drove off. The driver was unaware. The woman was crushed.

The man was living in his Mustang on Branford Street in Pacoima.[46] His car was hit by a speeding pickup truck. The Mustang overturned. The man died. The driver of the truck fled on foot.

The woman had been living on the street until she was found dead in a yard in Angelino Heights.[47] The coroner's report listed the cause of death as "effects of hanging, fentanyl, methamphetamine, and heroin."

The man was sleeping on the sidewalk near the 7th/Flower Metro station. He was beaten to death with a baseball bat. Another man was sleeping at the corner of Wilshire Boulevard and Flower Street. He was beaten to death a few minutes later.[48] That night and over the following days, seven sleeping men were attacked; three died.

The man—a musician—was camped on the sidewalk near Sixth Street and San Pedro Avenue.[49] That night, someone set his tent on fire. The man died of his burns. The day before, another man nearby had been beaten to death with a metal pole.

The man was slumped on a bench between Grand Avenue and Hope Street, apparently asleep.[50] A dark backpack was next to him. A younger man walked up, bent over the man, stabbed him repeatedly, and walked away with the backpack.

The man lay in an alley in Mission Hills. His neck had been broken.[51] Officials said he was a homeless person but provided no further details.

If I could give these homeless men and women their names, to hold them in your memory, I would. But the news accounts were mostly anonymous, and if a name was finally known, it wasn't called out in the tallies of the murdered.

In 2019, more than one thousand men and women living on the streets died in Los Angeles County; 806 died in 2017; 720 died in 2016. Between 2013 and the end of 2019, more than 5,600 died.[52] They died from heart disease, pneumonia, diabetes, cancer, cirrhosis, and bacterial infections. They died from overdoses, alcohol, drowning, and suicide. In mid-winter, they died from the cold. In mid-summer, they died from the heat. They died when hit by cars, when struck by assailants with bolt cutters and bats, and when beaten with boot heels and fists. They died when comfortable people like me looked away.

In 2020, those who sleep on the street and camp in waste places continued to be set on fire, to be run down, to die.

Statistics

On a typical day in 2020, an estimated 41,300 men, women, and children were without a home in the city of Los Angeles, an increase of about 14 percent over 2019. Another 25,200 were homeless in Los Angeles County. Of the 66,500 total, an estimated forty-five thousand were on the street when night fell. In 2019, 16,529 of them slept in vans, RVs, or cars. 11,086 were in tents or under tarps and plastic sheeting. 5,280 were children. Thirty-four percent were African American.[53] As many as eighty-three thousand county residents were without a home at some point in 2019. Thirty-seven thousand of them were on the street for the first time, but many more had been on the street for at least a year.

You're more likely to become homeless if you're male and not in a stable relationship. About 31 percent of homeless Angelenos are women. You're most likely to be homeless if you're a person of color; 67 percent of the homeless are Latinx or African American.[54] Not all homeless Angelenos are addicts, and they're not all insane. They've not just arrived here either; according to some measures, about 80 percent of the homeless have lived in Los Angeles County at least five years, and most have lived here ten. They are not that different from me, except they have no home.

The Young Man

I first saw the young man sitting at one of the tables on the plaza next to Lakewood City Hall. He was neatly dressed, although the coat he wore was too heavy for the warm day. He had a laptop and was looking at something on the screen. He had a backpack or a messenger bag by him. I passed by. I said nothing. He said nothing to me—an unremarkable encounter in a public place, except for his mismatch of coat and season. The young man was tall and seemed strongly built. I thought he might be Asian or Samoan or possibly Afro-Asian.

I saw him again, in nearly the same seat at the same table, the following day, dressed as before and watching or working at his laptop. I saw him two or three days later. He was sitting on one of the concrete bollards that line the street-facing edge of the city hall plaza. His bag was next to him. He was speaking into a cell phone. He was dressed as before.

Infrequent, silent meetings outside city hall went on for months, the young man either sitting at one of the tables on the plaza or on one of the bollards nearby, looking into the screen of his laptop or his cell phone. He wore the same clothes, but I may have only imagined that. He became a familiar figure in a familiar setting: the big young man with the laptop and cell phone. He was sometimes there when I walked past city hall on my way to mass on Sunday mornings, sometimes there when I left city hall in the late afternoons. He seemed to come from a place where ordinary life went on. And from there, wherever it might be, he came to this place to sit alone under the sycamore trees next to city hall.

His coat eventually matched the season, but now he no longer had his laptop. I still saw him from time to time with his cell phone. Eventually, the cell phone was gone, as was his backpack. He pulled a soft-sided, rolling suitcase instead.

I occasionally passed him on the sidewalk on Clark Avenue as I walked to city hall. He had begun to shuffle. I nodded hello as I passed; he didn't notice. I said hello once or twice, to which he smiled but said nothing. Once, I heard him angrily talking to himself, but not loudly. One afternoon, when it had begun to rain, I saw him sitting on one of the concrete bollards. He didn't have an umbrella or raincoat. I walked over to him with cash in hand. I told him he might want to get a room for the night out of the rain. He silently refused the money with a shake of his head and a smile. I didn't offer him money again.

The young man fell into ruin like an abandoned house. His bag and rolling suitcase were gone. He pushed an orange shopping cart from Home Depot that held a folded sleeping bag, some spare clothing, loose papers, and a small cardboard box. Later, he pushed a gray cart from Best Buy that held even less. Eventually, the cart held only a sleeping bag. Eventually, without a shopping cart, he carried the sleeping bag draped over his shoulders.

He slept some nights in the lightwell of a small office building near city hall. The alcove of the lightwell is partially screened from the sidewalk and the street. When nights stayed hot, he slept out in the open.

He sometimes talked to himself with abrupt gestures, as if haranguing someone. He turned away from eye contact as I passed him on the sidewalk. He seemed to have nothing now but shoes, a shirt, and pants.

It is July 26, 2019, as I write this. I've seen the young man on Clark Avenue for years. To my shame, I've done nothing to end his homelessness, done nothing at all beyond feeble gestures.

Enough

I don't know why the young man became homeless. I know how. He lost his home. He may have, like many who are nearly homeless in Los Angeles, spent more than half of his income on rent, and then the rent went up. It doesn't take much. In a 2017 survey of Los Angeles County renters, an increase of just five percent a month would push them into homelessness.[55] Maybe he had been one missed rent check, one major auto repair, one lingering illness, one false step away from eviction. Between 2010 and 2018, landlords filed 505,924 formal proceedings in Superior Court to evict tenants. Landlords may have made twice as many evictions "informally."[56]

The average one-bedroom apartment in Los Angeles rented for $1,707 a month at the start of 2019. The rental on a two-bedroom apartment was $2,181.[57] Of those made newly homeless in 2018, 53 percent were without a home because they no longer had a job or not enough of one to pay that much in rent.[58] It takes at least $100,000 a year to live in relative comfort in Los Angeles. The median household income in Los Angeles is $60,197.[59] At that level, affordable rent is about $1,400 a month. There are one-bedroom units at that rent for $1,400 in Los Angeles County, but not enough of them or where the jobs are or within reasonable commuting distance.

A lost job, a broken relationship, a rent increase, or worsening mental health may have put the young man on the street. The ragged safety net of county social services didn't catch him before he arrived on Clark Avenue. The lack of supportive services kept him there while everything he brought with him—a laptop, a cell phone, a rolling suitcase, and finally his human dignity—was taken from him.

When I was growing up in post-war Lakewood, life was about having enough (despite the slur that suburban lives were about wanting too much). For this young man, Lakewood meant not having enough. For want of only enough, he was without a home and a part of the defining tragedy of today's Los Angeles.

Solutions

In 2017, county voters approved Measure H, which added a quarter-percent county sales tax to generate about $350 million a year for homeless services during the measure's ten-year term. In 2016, voters in the city of Los Angeles passed Proposition HHH, a $1.2 billion bond measure to provide two thousand more shelter beds and build seven thousand units of housing with on-site health services, job training, and drug and alcohol treatment.[60] Apart from permanent and transitional housing, the city has plans for motel conversions, trailer camps, mobile showers and bathrooms, and safe parking lots for homeless Angelenos who sleep in their cars.[61]

More shelters, motel rooms, and safe parking lots change the location of homelessness, but don't end the tragedy. Those living on the street will be housed but still homeless. The solution to permanent homelessness is having a permanent home.

Countywide, of the 58,936 without a home in January 2018, only 21,631 were housed. But that was 23 percent more than in 2017 and twice the number housed in 2014.[62] And yet the number of people living in shelters, in vehicles, and on the street in Los Angeles County increased by 12 percent between 2017 and the start of 2019.[63] Even as more of those without a home receive housing support or find permanent housing, the number of homeless Angelenos goes up. The number goes up because housing policy is fundamentally broken.

Gentrification

It's hard to build permanent homes for the working poor who are at risk of becoming homeless. Los Angeles County had $700 million to spend on affordable housing in 2008. In 2018, the county had just $210 million. And even when funded, developers of affordable housing face restrictive zoning laws, environmental lawsuits, and NIMBYist homeowners. As a result, the deficit of affordable housing for low-income renters in Los Angeles County is at least five hundred thousand units.[64]

Squeezed by rent increases nearing 40 percent since 2000, the working poor in Los Angeles can't afford to live in neighborhoods that once had a place for them. Angelenos who make about double the county's median income can. They can rent a minimalist loft in a former single-room-occupancy hotel that had been remade to satisfy urban desires.[65] They can follow coffee houses and art galleries into bungalow neighborhoods that previously made a place for immigrant families.[66] Gentrification is another precursor to homelessness.

Becoming

Los Angeles has always been a place of becoming—becoming a movie star, a celebrity, a success—although most of these desires are never met. We learn to live in our city of regrets. And if we are housed in Los Angeles but are morally homeless, we still have the consolations of our things. I don't know what the young man who sleeps on Clark Avenue wants. He probably didn't want to sleep under the portico of the drive-through bank next to city hall. I know he didn't want to become homeless and to have nothing.

Death Rate

Deaths among the homeless residents of Los Angeles County doubled between 2013 and 2019. The number increased from 536 to more than one thousand. The death rate, which takes into account increases in the population of homeless Angelenos, also increased.[07]

I've not seen the young man who lived on Clark Avenue for some time, and I wonder what has happened to him.

La Virgen

Her formal title—Nuestra Señora de Guadalupe—is almost superfluous. As La Virgen, she appears everywhere in the diaspora of *mexicanidad* ("Mexican-ness"), slipping through border fences and evading ICE patrols. She waits on stucco walls, above shop counters and at roadside shrines, eyes downcast in an attitude of expectation, to receive appeals in Spanish, Spanglish, English, and the polyglot of languages that has always been the voice of Los Angeles. If ever a city needed a mediator between its citizens and their terrors—flood, earthquake, wildfire, civil strife, loneliness—it's Los Angeles. In a city repeatedly destroyed in the popular imagination, the Virgin remains, even when she's a faded turquoise outline framed by the countersigns of taggers.

She is supposed to have first appeared to Juan Diego on the hill of Tepeyac near Mexico City on December 12, 1531. Miracles were said to have happened after, including the appearance of her image on Juan Diego's cloak when he opened it before the astonished bishop of Mexico City. The greater miracle? She never abandoned those who trafficked her on shop walls, in barrios, and housing projects, in church sanctuaries, and tattoo studios.

Nearly everything we take to be Los Angeles was brought here from somewhere else, and most of that was undocumented. The migrant Virgin is true to our origin as exiles.

Patroness of the displaced, she has become the still point of Los Angeles. *"No estoy yo aquí que soy tu madre?"* ("Am I not here, I, your mother?") she reminded a perplexed Juan Diego in the story of her apparitions. She's with us too. Mother of the garment worker. Mother of the abused, the unemployed, and the homeless. Mother of the fallen away; it doesn't matter fallen from what. She regards her children's lack of faith as temporary; only their need is perpetual.

A city that manufactures images for sale has been given one without a price tag. Los Angeles needs the Virgin, her attentive silence, her modesty, and her blended identities. A human face like hers, reflecting multitudes, replaces the masks of indifference that have allowed grievances to breed into violence or despair in Los Angeles.

She who gave Juan Diego a sign—roses in December—takes in everything of the city. No particular belief is required at her shrines, only a longing to be reconciled. The Virgin was present as an indigenous world was ending and as a mestizo one was beginning on the hill of Tepeyac. She's equally present as Los Angeles seeks a way through its own uncertainties of purpose and mixtures of ethnicities from which something new is being shaped.

For the hopeful and fearful of Los Angeles, the Virgin promises to give a sign of her presence: a community that could earn our love.

PART 3

You Are Always Somewhere

"LOS ANGELES ISN'T A CITY, it's deprivation."[1] complained artist and critic Eleanor Antin, summing up the frustrations of all those who do not see past the hedonism, nostalgia, and regret that otherwise subdue a sense of place in this city. There is a remedy. Gradually, often imperceptibly, and sometimes contrary to original intentions, through the interplay of memory and the material world, Los Angeles can become an authentic place. Against over-hyped images of an extraordinary, unattainable, and ultimately disappointing city, are the familiar landmarks of its gridded neighborhoods and the overlapping communities that give the experience of Los Angeles scale and value.

The stories I tell myself about my own neighborhood don't describe a perfect place. They only illustrate my preference for ordinariness and help me resist the subordination of everyday life. These stories acknowledge that placemaking is a collaborative work and possibly redemptive. A sense of place assembled from "orange trees, the sun shining, freeways, and Chicano car stylings" isn't emptied of significance by familiarity. The maintenance and narration of memory give access to an affective landscape that is immanent, emergent, and in a state of latent intensity. Humble materials (as I hope the stories here show) have shaped what my imagination could make from the welter of the commonplace.

The stubborn facticity of the ordinary, however enigmatic it appears at first, never lacks traces of the sensuous matter of what is being lived. To be present in body and imagination, with wonder and forgiveness always ready, I knit the local into a world.

To Be Pedestrian

Walkers see ordinary—even humble—vistas opening at a pace that lets encounters occur unbidden. You can be distracted by daydreams or sorrow while walking a suburban sidewalk, but then a bird call, the rattle of the wind in a nearly leafless tree, or the sight again of some pattern in the streetscape will momentarily unfold your self-absorption, and a poem might be made. Walking is supposed to be progress. It can be stillness, too.

Asylum Street

Wallace Stevens (1879–1955) walked to work. He lived in Hartford, Connecticut, where he was a corporate executive for the Hartford Accident & Indemnity Company. A fellow executive later recalled that Stevens was respected by his colleagues, but he also was feared, if only a little. Stevens walked from his white, two-story house at 118 Westerly Terrace to his office each workday, turning down offers of a lift from other insurance men driving to work. It was a substantial walk of nearly two-and-a-half miles each way, most of it on a long, straight section of Asylum Street.

Stevens murmured to himself in rhythms and rhymes as he walked. Mornings, before he turned to work at his office, he wrote down the lines he'd considered at a walker's pace, including parts of "Man with the Blue Guitar," the "Disillusionment of Ten O'clock," "The Emperor of Ice-Cream" and "Thirteen Ways of Looking at a Blackbird."

Stevens was a successful businessman, an unhappy husband, and a difficult poet who won the Pulitzer Prize in the last year of his life. He thought having an everyday sort of career was important. He thought that walking was important. It's important to the pieces you're reading. To be pedestrian is important.

Peripheral

Unfortunately for pedestrians, Los Angeles is a good place to be killed while walking. According to statistics reported by the National Highway Traffic Safety Administration in 2017, Los Angeles was first among big cities in the number of pedestrians killed by vehicles, with 116 fatalities. (The number in 2016 was 130.)[2] Phoenix recorded ninety-eight pedestrian deaths. New York was third with ninety-five. Given the smaller population of the city of Los Angeles, a walker is almost three times more likely to be killed on the streets (and sidewalks) of Los Angeles than in New York. Pedestrian deaths are 16 percent of all traffic fatalities nationally. But in Los Angeles, 45 percent of all accident fatalities in 2017 were pedestrians.

When I watch you in your car, your SUV, your 4x4 pickup, from where I stand waiting for the light to change to cross the intersection of Clark Avenue and South Street, you, wrapped in your second skin of plastic and metal, seem oblivious. I, who cannot drive, am remote. I'm not even at the periphery of your gaze, stepping into the intersection as you turn into the crosswalk without looking.

Another Equinox

The seasons changed early on Friday morning. The northern hemisphere passed from summer to autumn through another equinox of equal night and day. Although summer-like days can be common this time of year in Los Angeles, the September equinox means we've begun another fall. I noticed that the crape myrtles along the street have suddenly lost all their color. The pastel reds and pinks of a few days ago are gone to rust and brown as if a switch had been thrown.

This morning (and all week), a thin, high fog stalled in the crowns of the bigger trees at the end of my block. The effect is to gray the light softly, and the limbs and leaves of the trees ahead were made unsharp, as if deceptively removed a little farther away.

I had to pause at the top of my porch steps (and so noticed the fog's effect on perspective), because an orb spider was making use of the bignonia vine over the steps. The spider and I faced each other through its web, which almost blocked my way. I ducked around.

The first day of autumn had a different light, more oblique and if anything, slower than midsummer's light. Perhaps that light makes whole days in this season seem like an interminable afternoon.

Spiders, morning fog, and a slight adjustment in the light don't have the autumnal effect of leaves blazing into red and gold (although the maple in my yard has taken on some color). The fall here hasn't that spectacle. What fall does is shift the everyday into the spiral that winds down into the dark in December. There is wistfulness in our fall and no glory.

I felt a cold wind blowing up Clark Avenue from Alamitos Bay and thought glumly about buying a new raincoat.

October Lightning

The slow rumble of thunder woke me on Thursday just before dawn. For a few minutes, the wall behind my bed, facing a west window, flared, faded, and flared again. The thunder rolled away to the northeast. A scattering of rain fell. Rain in mid-October on the Los Angeles plain is a rarity. This is supposed to be a month of aridity and hot Santa Ana winds.

Lightning and thunder are even more unlikely. Among the weather miracles sold to tourists and newcomers at the turn of the twentieth century was a "lightning free" Los Angeles. Supposedly, the region's warm, dry atmosphere made electrical storms, hailstorms, and tornadoes impossible. Compared to the Midwest from which most of the visitors and migrants came, the climate boosters were nearly right.

Childhood memory is a poor witness, but I hardly ever saw lightning or heard thunder as a boy. Years went by, it seemed, before the flash and boom of an electrical storm would blow up the Los Angeles River or come down from the mountains behind Pasadena and Monrovia. None of those encounters was anything like the long sieges of lightning and thunder in other parts of the country.

I can remember once, at ten or eleven years old, standing in the driveway of my house and seeing a filament of lightning appear overhead and hearing—perhaps imagining it—the sizzle of its passing. Had lightning been more familiar, I might have been more afraid.

Thursday's storm passed away before I left my house. There was a wash of rain on the sidewalk and semicircles of dry concrete where the tree canopy gave shelter. The clouds to the east were the indifferent color called CBS Gray, although the sun was already cresting the clouds' edges. The sun was intensely bright in the clean air, and suddenly it was too hot for a jacket and too cool for just shirtsleeves.

Everything in that light was distinct, insistent in its being there, sufficient to itself, like a room full of people who know they're important. The very last of the rain, in streaks that seemed yards apart, fell into and out of that light. The drops were brighter than the sky.

The odors that come with rain after a long dryness lingered halfway down the block before the rising heat evaporated them. I smelled the asphalt's astringent wetness, a memory of my elementary school playground. I smelled the oily duff lying under the eucalyptus trees, medicinal and bracing. There was the smell of the dust, faintly sweet, that the rain had vaulted into the air.

There were pea-sized snails out on the sidewalk, rasping calcium from the concrete to make bigger shells. Two crows cursed me from the wire that strings together the streetlights. I looked at them and they at me. They were unimpressed.

In my conceit, I'm always at the still center. In reality, the storm moves on. The dust breathes a momentary sweetness, and it's carried away. A crow follows, flying north.

Neighborhood. Night.

The months of winter have begun when, waking in the morning or walking home in the late afternoon, my day opens and ends in the dark. Although it isn't exactly dark. There's hardly true darkness out-of-doors in the Los Angeles basin, so much brightness pools on sidewalks from the regularly spaced streetlights, and almost as much ambient light reverberates back from even the least cloudy sky.

The city has been trimming the eucalyptus trees along South Street. The contractor doing the work left a bin the size of a freight car on the service road at the end of my block. When I crossed the boulevard returning home yesterday evening, I could see that the bin was filled to the top, dark branches above the yellow rim of the bin. I could smell the cut limbs and crushed eucalyptus leaves—a sharp scent as enveloping as a blanket. The scent followed me almost to my porch steps.

There's a streetlight on the strip of grass next to my neighbor's driveway that lights the porch, in fact the entire front of my house. Most of the city's lighting is its own, but in my older neighborhood, the streetlights are Edison-owned. The company recently replaced the original metal poles from the 1950s with concrete ones. I vaguely remember when the original poles were installed. I thought then that the new streetlight would help my father find his way when he walked home at night from the bus stop on Lakewood Boulevard, about a quarter of a mile away. He worked in downtown Los Angeles, and it took him well over an hour (and two buses) to get home. The streetlight is the marker I still use to tell an Uber driver which house is mine on a street of houses that seem similar in the almost dark.

My walk from home and back again would be dark except for all the light the city—and all of us—give away. I'm grateful for the gift.

December Silence

I got up at five on Sunday morning and left my house in the dark of the longest night of the year. Restless, with a project for the city to finish on deadline, I thought I'd get to early mass at St. Cyprian's, a forty-five-minute walk away.

Suburban streets like mine are never silent. But this morning—perhaps because of the recent cold or because night and dawn were poised at that hour—the street was quiet in the still air. I heard the click-click-click of a dog's paws on the sidewalk and the muffled rattle of its leash long before I could see either the dog or its owner. He materialized out of the shadow of a Chinese elm. The man and I exchanged unexpected good mornings.

The city recently repaved the highway bordering my neighborhood with rubberized asphalt concrete. The rubber came from tens of thousands of discarded tires, ground up and blended with the asphalt concrete mix. The effect of having rubber in the roadway was even more quiet. The noise of the few cars that passed as I turned the corner at the end of my block faded away noticeably.

The walk buttons at the intersection where I cross have been replaced. These now make a loud, slow tock-tock-tock for the benefit of those whose vision is impaired. I heard the sound from a block away, like the ticking of an enormous clock. When activated, the walk button announces in a mechanical male voice that the pedestrian signal has changed: "WALK SIGNAL IS ON! WALK SIGNAL IS ON!" The voice echoed over the empty intersection.

Part of my walk parallels a city park. Halfway across the park is a basketball court where, on most Sunday mornings, a pick-up game is underway. This morning, although it was nearly full dark with only a sliver of dawn in the east, someone was bouncing a basketball on the concrete court. Each bounce was a crisp smack on the concrete.

A customized, mid-1960s Cadillac convertible rumbled past with thumping bass notes from the sound system. Either the end of a long night of cruising or an early start to a custom car show.

The street trees are finally dropping their leaves, and in the stillness, the fall of one dry leaf striking another leaf clinging to a lower branch produced a click followed by a pause until another, lower leaf was struck—click and pause and click again—until the falling leaf struck the litter of leaves on the lawn with the same clear sound. Lifetimes were in those pauses, the nearly finished year in the tick-tick-tick of leaf fall.

There Will Come Soft Rains

The rain began about 7:15 on February morning. The light in my bedroom changed suddenly from pale yellow to gray-green, and the aluminum awnings over the front windows began to ping with the first drops. As the band of rain passed, the awnings rattled steadily, like someone shaking dice in a metal box. I got out my raincoat and umbrella.

It's a folding umbrella, but not one of those that opens to the size of a hand-kerchief and only good for one to two trips from the nearest parking place to the nearest doorway until the umbrella is forgotten under the front seat of the car. I have a hiker's umbrella, sturdy in a stiff wind and almost big enough for two to walk under.

The raincoat is a Burberry, bought when I went to London in 1984. It's missing buttons and it's as filthy as un-dry-cleaned years of rain and walking can make it. It seems to have lost most of its waterproofing, so much that the back of my hand in the raincoat's left pocket is wet when I reach city hall. When the rain sheers at an angle, the drops run down the front of the raincoat to drip off the hem onto the wetter and wetter knees of my trousers.

The rain came down hard at 7:45 a.m., backed by the rising wind. The drops that fell in the gutter made intersecting concentric circles in the water running to the storm drain opening at the end of the block. The wind, blowing from the west, was behind me when I turned the corner of my block, and the umbrella shook a little as the wind filled it. The cars on South Street hissed by. The rain gave them a characteristic shrillness. The sounds were loud enough for a noticeable Doppler effect, the pitch of the sounds higher as cars approached and falling lower as they moved past. The noise of its tires made even a meek Prius seem aggressive.

Some of the morning's rain was settling into the aquifers north and east of Lakewood that feed the Central Groundwater Basin. I'll drink that water one day. Some of it, nearer to my house, was running away into Coyote Creek and the San Gabriel and Los Angeles rivers and directly into the sea.

The rain mostly blew out by 8:30 a.m., leaving a question behind: to fold or not fold my umbrella. Walking with an open umbrella when it's not raining seems conspicuously foolish. But what if it's nearly not raining? Only half foolish?

Cars drove by without their windshield wipers running. I folded my umbrella.

I Saw This Morning

I saw this morning a hawk some minutes after it had taken a mourning dove as I walked to Easter Sunday mass. The tableau on the lawn of city hall wasn't exactly a still life.

The dove had become some gray feathers in a circle and a flash of rose-pink meat on the bright grass. On seeing me, the little predator lifted away, gutted prey clutched in its talons, to the top of a nearly leafless sycamore. It's springtime but not yet in full. From a bare limb, the *Buteo jamaicensis* looked down. I hurried under the bird's gaze. Mass was about to begin. I had another ten minutes to walk.

At mass, the congregation recited the old Easter sequence with its question about an empty tomb: *Dic nobis Maria / Quid vidisti in via*? "Tell us, Mary, what did you see on your way?" And in another verse, an answer: *Mors et vita duello conflixere mirando.* "Death and life locked in strange combat."

The Greatest Gift

It's Mother's Day—a fraught holiday for motherless sons. I'm one of them, and I often feel incomplete because of what I lack. Nostalgia rarely serves me well, but I remember, when I was a boy, that my mother was the best cook in my neighborhood.

Sons often remember falsely that their mother's cooking was the best. But my mother's cooking, which was commonplace, actually was the best that could be found on my block. On the tract-house plains of South Gate, Downey, Long Beach, Lakewood, and Bellflower, meals reflected what memories you stubbornly held on to. And when my neighbors ate to remember, many of the memories were of loss. I lived among families who had experienced the Depression and had fled the Dust Bowl, who had gone through wartime rationing, and eaten too many meals that were only a substitute for going hungry.

Families in my neighborhood were fed, but many weren't sustained very well. Husbands often insisted on eating poorly because their own mothers could only cook poorly. Part of it was the exile of young wives in the newly made suburbs, far from their mothers and grandmothers. Wives had scraps from a half-remembered high school Home Economics course and what black-and-white television commercials said could be done with Cheez Whiz.

In my working-class suburb—The City of Tomorrow Today!—the future of food hadn't fully arrived. Maxwell House instant coffee (1946) had only just been introduced. Swanson sold frozen pot pies (1951) but not TV dinners (1954). Rice-a-Roni (1958), Carnation Instant Breakfast (1964) and Cool Whip (1965) were years away. Bigger grocery stores showcased an aisle of frozen food, but our Coldspot refrigerator had room in its freezer compartment for only one or two rectangular blocks of Birdseye peas. The Helms Bakery truck would come by with its smoothly sliding, glossy wood drawers of bread, pies, and cakes. So did a guy who had converted a used transit bus with shelves and a cooler to bring cigarettes, milk, and cereal to house-bound mothers. My mother knew people in Bellflower who raised chickens and sold the eggs to mom-and-pop grocery stores.

Shopping was mostly done on foot then, since most housewives either couldn't drive or didn't have a car. Hiram's and The Boys markets were at the distant end of my block across a boulevard and several smaller streets. Their vegetable and fruit displays followed the seasons. You could get some fresh foods only a few weeks a year. Heads of iceberg lettuce—the only kind available—dwindled in midwinter. Corn on the cob arrived in July. The Farmer John meat processor in Vernon pitched its products as "easternmost in quality" because the local beef had a poor reputation. There were times you couldn't get chicken, but you could get rabbit. Fresh fish was harder to find. In 1958, Cardinal McIntyre, in the weekly Catholic newspaper, recommended "tunies"—tuna hot dogs—for Lenten Fridays. My family agreed that "tunies," despite an ecclesiastical blessing, were inedible.

As a percentage of family income, food in the early 1950s was expensive. Still, on a $100-a-week paycheck, you could manage to feed a family. The results were hardly memorable if all you knew was Wonder Bread and margarine, a roast cooked black and hard, canned string beans, plenty of mashed potatoes, and strawberry Jell-O for dessert. My mother made nearly the same meal, but the roast beef was savory, the side dishes were respectable, and there was always a salad. It's as if my family and the families on my block ate on two different continents, the width of a dinner table apart.

My mother cooked plain food almost untouched by the recipes in the women's magazines she read or even in the 1943 edition of Irma Rombauer's *Joy of Cooking*, kept in the cabinet over the refrigerator. She preferred a baked potato to Rice-A-Roni and anything simple to anything that technologized either the food or the experience of eating. Breakfast was always two USDA Grade AA eggs fried in butter and served with two strips of overcooked bacon as my mother prepared her sons for school and a future of heart disease. It was the breakfast the Department of Agriculture recommended.

My mother cooked the same dinners in weekly rotation for decades, punctuated by the obligatory dinners for Thanksgiving, Christmas, and Easter, when she used her wedding silverware. It was rote cooking—measured out in cans of Hunt's tomato paste and pounds of stew meat—but my mother treated the ingredients with enough respect that they always seemed more than just nourishment. The boys who were my friends, tasting medium-rare roast beef for the first time, fell in love with my mother. It was strange how potent the effect of Lawry's Seasoned Salt was.

My family's food habits were unfamiliar in other ways. We ate together at seven p.m. or later. Everyone else in the neighborhood ate by 5:30 p.m. My parents went through a martini-before-dinner phase when my sophisticated uncle

Arthur lived with us. My mother and father drank red wine with the spaghetti and meat sauce my mother made on Saturdays (the sauce to be served on Monday over more spaghetti and always tasting even better). My family ate out, too, and it seems to me that we might have eaten out more often than our neighbors. We ate at local places—at the Clock coffee shop, Clifton's Cafeteria, and Hody's Family Restaurant in Lakewood Center, caramel and tangerine stucco on the outside and walnut veneer and red vinyl in the half-dark interior. It was one of many Googie-style restaurants designed by Wayne McAllister. Hody's had counter service and carhops on roller skates. It wasn't exactly middle class.

I remember best the dried seahorses and starfish entombed in the plastic dividers that separated the booths in the dining room and the horrific face of the clown mask that was the menu for kids. I have almost no memory of the food, except for the intense tomato redness of the salad dressing. It was astringent and yet seemed sweet, like our lives then.

We hardly noticed, but all around us was an extravagance of food. Backyard trees in my neighborhood delivered fruit with casual overabundance. Only so much could be picked and eaten or shared or baked into a pie. Softball-sized peaches fell from the tree in my backyard. The winey smell of the fallen fruit in summer could be overwhelming. Those untended trees, with so much fruit, stood for what Los Angeles could mean to the refugees on my block from colder, harder places. All that wasted fruit was a promise that at least one hunger could be assuaged. If only we had known what was being put in front of us.

Transplants

My walk south on Clark Avenue used to pass a section bordered on both sides of the street by pines, which always looked to me like templates for the fluted Ionic columns that once fronted Roman temples and American banks. When Lakewood houses were sold, each house had a tree planted in a strip of lawn along the street. The Clark Avenue pines were more than forty years old when most of them were cut down by the city. They had grown too large to keep in company with the sidewalk and adjacent curb.

A few of the trees—four or five—still remain on the grounds of Mayfair Park. The pines, like all the trees in the park, are non-native flora, deliberate transplants from someone's memories to the rectangle of former pasture that had preceded the park.

The pines in Mayfair Park persist in the company of another transplant. About fifteen years ago, I began to encounter an occasional squirrel (*Sciurus niger*) on my walk to city hall. The adaptable squirrels are among the most recent of at least twenty-two non-native mammals now making the Los Angeles basin their home. The squirrels joined house sparrows, European starlings, and crows as tenants in my neighborhood. Sparrows and starlings were set free in the nineteenth century by misguided bird fanciers who wanted American skies to look more English. Crows brought themselves. Even the garden snails that traverse sidewalks in spring don't belong here. The snails came to Los Angeles as a side dish for nostalgic Basques. Possums supposedly arrived as a food animal for Southern immigrants with a taste for game.

The immigrant squirrels went from Midwest forests to local tables to Los Angeles parks around the start of the twentieth century. The squirrels of Clark Avenue are native to the eastern half of the continent, and a subspecies is common along the Mississippi and its branches between Illinois and Tennessee. Beginning in the late 1880s, waves of migrants came from those borderlands to Los Angeles. The ancestors of the squirrels on Clark Avenue, by some accounts, arrived in 1904 in the company of aging Civil War veterans who came to live at the Sawtelle Veterans Home at the edge of what is now Westwood Village in Los Angeles. Whether to animate the landscape or make squirrel stew, the veterans set squirrels loose on the grounds of the home. The squirrels were in the walnut orchard north of the veterans' home soon after. They were in Santa Monica shortly after that. By 1910, the squirrels were in San Pedro, a distance of twenty-five miles. By the 1930s, they were in Ventura, almost fifty miles away. Bringing squirrels to California is now illegal, and deliberate relocation of squirrels is prohibited.

Studies had previously suggested that immigrant squirrels were disinterested in the suburban flatlands of southeast Los Angeles County, which had been, it was thought, so thoroughly domesticated. The suburbs turned out instead to be full of wild possibilities. Squirrel pioneers—perhaps brought to Long Beach by homesick Tennesseans working in defense plants in the 1940s—eventually made their way to the grounds of Long Beach City College and from there to Mayfair Park. Eventually, the squirrels and I encountered each other along Clark Avenue.

They and other small lives in the backyard ecology of my neighborhood have evoked predators. Coyotes lope through power line rights-of-way. Hawks are now residents of my street. In season, a pair furiously defends a nest in a row of street trees near my house.

Residents of Los Angeles have become used to this unexpected wilding. The squirrels share with raccoons, possums, and skunks a tolerance for human-managed landscapes, an eclectic diet, and a certain wanderlust. Like possums, the squirrels use overhead utility lines to travel outside their home range, relatively safe from cats, dogs, and the cars that are the primary causes of their mortality. Oddly, the wire highways bring more of this nature into older, working-class suburbs than into affluent ones where utility lines are almost always underground.

As suburban transplants, squirrels suffer from the cyclical drought conditions that climate change is worsening in Southern California. The acorns, eucalyptus buds, and pine nuts that form the squirrel diet are dependent on rainfall. Squirrels under stress are subject to periodic plagues of mange caused by mites.

I have some sympathy for the squirrels that moved into my neighborhood. I know they bedevil gardeners with their foraging. Some would prefer that the squirrels had been kept in their place, just as there had been those who tried to keep Dust Bowl migrants, with a taste for squirrel stew, in their place. Squirrels and other migrants are here anyway. I think that hunger made the suburbs of Los Angeles. That hunger is not yet satisfied.

Designed for Living

I look at sidewalks a lot. Miserable eyesight makes the far-away a muddle better ignored. Miserable depth perception makes the up-close a zone of potential missteps. What I'm walking on occupies me.

Like much of the everyday, the sidewalk's plainness conceals a history, not just of its being there at all (a product of suburban convictions) but also the decisions that determined the sidewalk's four-foot width and its transverse stress grooves that give a warning clickity-clack when skateboards overtake me from behind.

The sidewalk I'm on might have been the result of dispassionate calculations having nothing to do with design, but that would make all sidewalks as uniform as a two-by-four. Even the most utilitarian of things is lifted from the mechanical by the hands that shaped it. Variation within a formula implies creative choices.

Someone designed the curb along the street as well, its wall canted a few degrees away from vertical. The speckled white and gray aggregate concrete of the streetlight (designed in 1912 in Los Angeles by someone at the Marbelite Corporation of America) begins with a stepped base (sort of Doric Moderne) and ends with a cannonball finial. The column of the streetlight sprouts the ubiquitous "cobra head" light fixture (first introduced in 1957).

Every bit of the landscape in my constricted field of view has been given shape. The cross-hatched ridges that cover a wide service grate to prevent walkers from slipping on its potentially slick surface are repeated in miniature on the five-inch-diameter cover of a sprinkler control. The one is iron and at least sixty years old. The other is green plastic installed last year.

None of these things is beautiful. (Very little is beautiful here.) But each of these things is marked by the application of hands. As I go on my way, monuments of the imagination are at my feet.

Lost and Found

I walked through the Lakewood Sheriff's Station parking lot and noticed, lying on an eroded patch of asphalt, a rosary. I picked it up. It was made of olive wood.

I thought at first that the rosary was broken, perhaps run over by a car pulling out of the station or it had been lost because the cord tying the beads into groups of ten had become undone.

Because even a broken, discarded rosary means something to me, however tenuous, I planned to dispose of it respectfully. But the string of beads in my hand was undamaged. I turned over its cross. It was stamped in blurred black ink, not all the letters complete, with the rosary's place of origin: Jerusalem. A tourist's memento or more likely something shipped from a Gaza factory and bought in a Catholic articles shop for five or six dollars.

I thought for a moment of all the reasons why someone might be holding a rosary in the parking lot of a sheriff's station and why the rosary might then fall from someone's hand, unnoticed.

The parking lot was deserted. If I had stepped into the station to find a deputy to take this bit of lost-and-found, I might have waited for some time. I might have had an awkward conversation about why I brought so trivial a thing as a string of olive wood beads into the station for safekeeping. I might have felt the flinch of otherness that Catholics sometimes feel when small matters of their faith leak into the non-Catholic world.

A rosary is a counting device for a sequence of recurring prayers. It's a recursive loop entered and left through the crucifix that's appended to the string of beads. A rosary measures the repetition of a petition—"pray for us now and at the hour of our death"—said as a blunt imperative.

A rosary like this one, that might be carried in a pocket or a purse or worn around the neck as a fashion statement or magical charm, is a miniature. A full rosary is fifteen groups of ten beads (each group of ten beads is called a decade). If you had gone to a Catholic elementary school in the 1950s, the nun in her burka-like black habit would have had a fifteen-decade rosary drawn through the wide belt at her waist. The rattle and click of wooden rosary beads against each other and against the edge of a student's desk are a permanent sense memory for former Catholic school kids who are now in their late sixties.

I was going to take the rosary I'd found and I went some yards farther when, thinking better of it, I turned back. Someone's memories were encoded in this rosary, perhaps needing to be recovered.

There is a row of thick pillars, about four feet tall, spaced evenly along the walkway in front of the sheriff's station. The pillars are decorative enough, but their purpose is to stop a terrorist's car from being driven through the station's entrance. The pillars are an inconspicuous part of our permanent emergency. I put the rosary on top of the pillar nearest the parking stall where I had found it.

The following morning, I walked through the parking lot. The rosary was gone. The loop of need, as I saw it, was mended.

Steel and the Men

A line of cars was pulled up at the curb at Mayfair Park on Sunday morning. I walked by them on my way to early mass at St. Cyprian's farther down the street. The men (they were all men) stood on the sidewalk casually dressed in Hawaiian shirts and chino shorts, waiting while registration tables for the Chamber of Commerce car show were set up. The men stepped aside to let me pass. I took a long look at their cars, at their old American steel.

The men were mostly in their fifties, a little young to have known these cars when the cars were new. Perhaps an older brother or their father had owned a green '53 Pontiac Chieftain or bronze-and-cream '56 Chevrolet Bel-Air or a red '59 Ford Galaxie like the ones lined up on Clark Avenue. The newer cars had been customized, and the older ones had been restored to a degree of finish that Detroit had never shipped.

Many men in the suburb where I live did some backyard auto mechanics in their teens or later worked in a machine shop or an aerospace plant. These men are like my older brother. He fixed bikes as a boy and then lawn mowers before taking up Volkswagens at seventeen, turning VW belly pans into dune buggies, which he sold—one after the other. I was strong-armed into helping him and became, purely out of boredom with bleeding brakes, a passable mechanic's helper. (Ironically, I'm not able to drive.)

When my brother and I were young, we would ride our bikes to the car lots in Bellflower to linger around the new models and page through glossy sales brochures. The salesman tolerated us, knowing that we would return one day, older and eager to buy. At least my brother did. But the showrooms for Packard, DeSoto, Studebaker, and Nash were gone before our desires could be answered in vinyl and chrome. Oldsmobile and Pontiac are gone, too, but iconic models of each brand were in line to enter the annual car show that day. One owner, holding a spray bottle, was buffing a patch of the hood that only he could see was imperfectly waxed.

It's not just nostalgia that brings these men and their cars together, although that's most of it. I'm reminded of Susan Faludi's *Stiffed: The Betrayal of the American Man* (1999) and the argument she makes that something has become broken in the relationship of men to the work they do. Those cars waiting on Clark Avenue can be fixed by anyone with a set of socket wrenches, feeler gauges, and a timing light, along with modest mechanical skills and a copy of the right Chilton auto repair manual. It's still possible for these men to master a great, shining, and breathing thing with their own hands even if they master nothing else about their lives.

A passerby isn't permitted to touch these deuce coupes, the Impalas and Fairlanes, the customized muscle cars. And so I hurried on, only my gaze lingering.

An Elm and Time

The man down the block has taken out the tree that had been in his front yard for as long as I can remember. It was a Chinese elm and had grown tall and drooping under the negligent care of a long-ago homeowner. The original tree was cut down to a stump by the next homeowner, only to resurrect itself as multiple shoots a year later. Over the next few years, those shoots grew into trunks as thick as a man's arm. Cut down again by the current resident, the elm renewed itself once again as a bundle of willowy branches and a bushy crown high enough to arch over the sidewalk again.

The weeping branches, their cascade of jagged leaves, the slim trunks that sprouted from the stump, and the stump itself are entirely gone now. The corner of my block that had been defined, at least for me, by this persistent tree is now undefined. Each time I round the corner, the tree in my memory drips steadily in the rain, or spider webs, precisely at eye level, span the gaps in the branches through which I had to pass. It was an annoying tree some of the time, but I miss it.

Chinese elms are a graceful tree when mature, although they have a tendency to quirky shapes. They used to be a common street tree in Southern California. But it's fallen out of favor now because the roots can heave the sidewalk, and the tree drops its leaves in winter and small, winged fruit in the fall.

We often speak of the velocity of everyday life, and yet so much stays the same from year to year. The patience of the everyday interests me, not its speed. My neighbor had good reasons, I suppose, to remove his dogged elm from his front yard, uprooting a marker of my days. Nothing has taken its place yet.

Home Again

I've been back home since January. That's not to say that I strayed from the house where I was born or the town in which I still live. It's not a building that I've had to return to but the home I imagined almost thirty years ago when I began writing *Holy Land: A Suburban Memoir*. I went back because I'd been asked to draft a screenplay that would, I suppose, translate the experience of reading *Holy Land* into something like a film. I didn't expect the writing assignment to be such a troubling return.

I've had the privilege of reading from *Holy Land* and discussing it with audiences of all sorts since the book was published in 1995. Third-grade students at the school down the block and graduate students from Minnesota have heard me tell what my boyhood was like and what aquifers are and why ordinary places like mine matter. Every audience has taken my performance at face value, and they've asked good questions (mostly the same ones). But it's been a performance. I play the part of the man who wrote that book, as an actor who can read its lines with feeling and get a laugh with the jokes. But the author of *Holy Land* isn't me. He's become a character, although I play him with some skill.

The inauthenticity doesn't distress me. My book is hardly mine anymore but the property of anyone who reads it. I'm acquainted with the author, but he's like someone I knew in college. He's familiar and so are his quirks, but I haven't spent much time with him in years.

Until recently, that is. Turning my text into narration and the occasional enacted scene turned me back to my home of thirty years ago and into *Holy Land*. I became that long-ago interpreter of myself again or as near to him as it's possible now. It wasn't easy or particularly satisfying, but I did learn some things.

What angered him, it turns out, still angers me, particularly how ordinariness is held in such contempt. What he loved then I find I love even more now, and I'm grateful. His grief, also thankfully, is less to me, but it was still painful to see him grieve again as a result of adapting his thoughts to film and finding other means to show his sorrow.

His remedy for his life then was his book. It was his argument, too, and his apology for what he thought, by most measures, had been a badly spent life.

My life is still badly spent, but I've become more simple-minded since then, partly by way of having written *Holy Land.* That's been his consolation to me.

I can't imagine what the production company will do with my screenplay. It's far odder than his memoir. I wonder what he'd think if he knew that I've plagiarized his story.

I've Got You Under My Skin

It's a good day. The summer monsoon has pushed thunderstorms into the high desert, and there's a risk of flash floods in the foothills above the city. The inversion layer is down to 600 feet, clamping a lid overhead as featureless and solid seeming as a sheet of concrete. Visibility is ten or fifteen gray miles into nothingness. Los Angeles is marooned in its air. Still, it's a good day.

The Air Quality Management District's online monitor says particulate pollution is only moderate; ozone levels are low. The air quality index is only just beginning to peak into the range of "unhealthful for sensitive groups" in the San Fernando and San Gabriel valleys. Some people may begin to feel a familiar catch in the back of their throat.

Sixty years before, when I was ten and spent every summer day outside with a pack of other kids in my baby-boomer neighborhood, the breaths I drew with such urgency contained some of the highest levels of air pollution ever measured in the Los Angeles basin. The bright sun overhead cooked together gritty particulates from diesel trucks, nitrogen oxide from manufacturing plants, carbon monoxide from car exhaust, sulfur dioxide from oil-fired furnaces, and stray hydrocarbons evaporating from solvents and degreasers, household paints, and gasoline. Epidemiological studies in 1959 would show an extra 1,200 fatalities in mid-August 1955, mostly among the elderly and chronically sick. Ground-level ozone concentrations rose in the still air on each of those summer days, topping at 0.68 parts per million (or more than six times the federal health standard).

Boys hurrying down the block to catch the Helm's Bakery truck couldn't see the ozone. It's not a color in the palette of smog. It's a transparent, highly reactive gas refined in sunlight from volatile hydrocarbons and auto exhaust. For many adults, at 0.02 parts per million (the current AQMD "stage 1" alert level), ozone can sting the eyes and tinge each breath with pain. At higher concentrations, people wheeze and develop a headache. Some cough. Some feel lightheaded. Running in that air for thirty minutes, according to the American Lung Association, was like smoking a pack of cigarettes.

Little kids, oddly enough, were said not to experience adverse reactions, or they didn't report them to the district's researchers because that's what kids born into smog imagined the summer air was supposed to smell like, like a combination of spot remover and a gas station (and not an entirely unpleasant smell).

I didn't pay attention to what I couldn't see in the air of a mid-1950s August. Maybe my throat was scratchy, but my mom was a heavy smoker then, and I felt the effects of that far more. I don't remember my eyes watering. I've mostly forgotten what breathing unmitigated smog felt like, but my body hasn't. I still bear the marks of those afternoons in my lungs and heart and arteries. The marks were made even after responsible adults knew what caused the air to turn the color of a fresh bruise, knew what air pollution could do to boys like me, and knew how to prevent at least some of it from happening.

The first breath I took in 1948 was of already troubled air. Its quality had been declining steadily since 1919 when the region's non-agricultural economy began to hum, and new waves of infatuated migrants arrived in Los Angeles to begin enjoying health and happiness in what they had been told was a land of sunshine. They had taken the usual bait and switch. Oil refining, tire manufacturing, aircraft assembly, automaking, and shipbuilding were giving sleepy Los Angeles a business-like air that made the place something more than a retirement home for Hoosiers and Buckeyes. By 1935, Los Angeles (with Firestone, Goodyear, and Goodrich plants) was second to Akron in tire production and (with GM, Chrysler, Ford, and Studebaker), second to Detroit in auto assembly.

Industrialization improved Los Angeles—so much improvement that the decline was obvious in the city's extraordinary qualities of light and air, which everyone in the previous thirty years had remarked on and had helped bring filmmakers from New York in 1915. By 1948, noirish Los Angeles—the shrouded city that always cheated on its lovers—was already painted in the colors of smog: sunsets that ran from peach to dried blood, daylight that shaded from urine to adobe.

The smog had rolled in with smokestack industrialization, giving good jobs with real benefits to people like my parents. They bought cars. They bought houses. They lived better through chemistry, a lot of it extraordinarily polluting. Their sons and daughters ran laughing through prosperous, smoggy afternoons that their parents had helped to make by wanting some of the good things of a new kind of working-class life. And as their children filled their lungs, each breath multiplied their lifetime risk of heart disease, chronic emphysema, and lung cancer (among the reasons not to be nostalgic about a 1950s childhood in Los Angeles).

Boys and girls playing in the park near my house today—children running as hard as they can in the clearer light—will nevertheless carry traces of today's air pollution all their lives. Their burden of risk, I hope, will be lighter than mine because parents and politicians finally made hard choices. Air quality in Los Angeles is better today, but advocates fear that momentum to make it safer has stalled, now that the air seems clear even in summer. And some nerves are rattled by the greater changes that will have to be made in transportation and power generation so that future breaths will be taken in Los Angeles with air that won't frighten us.

When I stood on the knob of Signal Hill, twenty-five miles south of Los Angeles, in early 2017. I saw, as in a bright panorama, Catalina Island, the Palos Verdes hills, the Santa Monica Mountains, the huddled towers of downtown Los Angeles, and the San Gabriel and the San Bernardino mountains until, after turning almost a full circle, I saw the Santa Ana Mountains and the coast-line stretching away to the south in the silver light. It no longer hurt to breathe. It no longer hurt to see. Yes, particulate pollution in the basin is no better and probably worse. Risk is in every breath. Still, I drank in the air and thought that it was a better day.

Every Day Is Arbor Day

Arbor Day is in April on a date chosen because it promises spring somewhere that's not Los Angeles. In my neighborhood, every day is Arbor Day. I walk about a mile from my house to the basement cubicle at city hall, where I'm sorting out Lakewood's history. In that more-than-a-mile, I pass trees that came here from five continents and perhaps a dozen climatic zones.

The crape myrtles on my street are blooming now, from garnet red to bubblegum pink. Like many cities, Lakewood has been replacing older street trees with crape myrtles. They're slow-growing, don't lift sidewalks and curbs, and look pretty while in flower. But no street tree is perfect. Given human nature, there'll always be someone who has a grudge against the tree their street has been assigned. Having a representative of nature at your curb—even as tamed as a city-maintained tree—is too much for some. Abuse, neglect, and instances of tree killing follow.

My neighborhood is older than the rest of Lakewood, so my block doesn't have a uniform treescape. Homeowners over the decades have planted their own version of the perfect tree, probably based on the way the tree looked in a five-gallon can at the nursery. Those trees, now grown old, haven't worked out well, buckling concrete and bulging roots into the roadway asphalt. A pair of misplaced magnolias rise tall and column-straight at one house down the block. The city will have to come one day and saw them down.

At the end of the block, on the long parkway panel that separates the service road from the highway, the boles of the eucalyptus trees are turning from pale green to gray. The trunks of the trees are as sleekly curvy as a Maillol nude.

The jacarandas on the north side of the service road have begun to drop their blue flowers; a few freshly fallen pop under my step. These trees will bloom again in the fall, although with less exuberance, which makes the many who hate jacarandas for the mess they make even more outraged. Sometimes beauty is unendurable.

The trees were migrants, as nearly all my neighbors are. We charm or infuriate one another until each of us—the trees and we who sojourn here—reach our limit, is cut down, and is carried away. Until then, we might hope to imitate the inoffensive crape myrtle—kindly, mostly fitted to its place, and flowering generously in its season.

History Turning Into Nature

Tumbleweeds

When I was a boy, although I was surrounded by square miles of tract houses, tumbleweeds would appear on my street in the fall, blown from the Edison right-of-way beyond Ashworth Street or from decrepit pastures in Dairy Valley (soon to be subdivided and renamed Cerritos). The wind-driven tumbleweeds brought a cliché of the Old West rolled into my neighborhood to fetch up against a front yard fence or skitter across South Street in the slanting afternoon light. I expected to hear the Sons of the Pioneers in mournful harmony sing of being "lonely but free" drifting along with the tumbling tumbleweeds.

According to the *Los Angeles Times*, tumbleweeds have grown to become an "infestation" in this drought year. Homeowners in valley and foothill neighborhoods are supposed to be under siege from weeds. "There is an established brush-clearance program in place, and we expect homeowners to maintain defensible space around their property year-round," Kevin Johnson, assistant chief of the Los Angeles County Fire Department's Forestry Division, told the *Times* in 2014. The weeds are "tumbling kindling."[3]

Tumbleweeds—also called Russian thistle—are immigrants. They appeared in the late 1870s in South Dakota, according to some accounts, and in North Dakota and Nebraska by 1880, rolling every autumn before the prevailing winds until tumbleweeds grew wherever overgrazed range and exhausted farmland made a place for them. By 1885, tumbleweeds had reached California, became naturalized, and opportunistically crowded out native plants.

The tumbleweed's short history has turned into our nature. And like so much of that nature, we're anxious about losing control of it. Part of our concern may be how ephemeral, insubstantial, knocked together, and easily knocked down Los Angeles seems. A place with a tumbleweed in place of a heart.

Bees

A good breeze was blowing from the south this morning. Where I live, south is the direction to the sea. It was cool after hot days that seemed to kill any sign of life in my neighborhood. The possums and feral cats had lain low. Even the jays, mockingbirds, and crows went missing.

Sunday was the first true day of our temporary autumn that lasts until the hot, dry Santa Ana winds begin with the smell of adobe dust and jasmine. This day, hummingbirds made aggressive, tack-tack-tack calls overhead, warning off interlopers with the sound of tiny machine guns. Bees were at work in the blossoms of the Brazilian pepper trees that remain on my street.

The peppers—the oldest trees on the block—produce thousands of tiny yellow blooms that are mostly hidden in the tree canopy. Wild bees find them, though, and work them hard with a sound that was unusually loud on an otherwise quiet morning. The urgency of the bees had shaken down spent flowers in a steady rain that ringed each tree with a circle of pale yellow. The falling debris littering the sidewalk shows my footsteps and those of an earlier walker who had dropped advertising circulars on driveway aprons.

I was comforted by the bees after so many warnings of their disappearance, even though the flowers the bees shook down had to be brushed repeatedly from my hair.

The eucalyptus trees at the end of my block wore new bark that was turning a pale tan. In a few months, the color will turn to brown, and the bark will loosen. Strips of it will blow into the front yards of the houses opposite. Eucalyptus trees shed throughout the year, dropping bark, oily leaves, and sometimes whole branches. They're protectors and perpetrators of an ecology of fire in their native Australia. In alien Southern California, homeowners expect fire to come with the wind.

Memory

As histories turn into nature, a kind of intelligence emerges within the felt space each of us inhabits. We have a capacity for this awareness, mapped on the brain's hippocampus by aptly named "place cells." The mapping is done with the aid of a class of memory molecules we share with rats, fruit flies, and even snails. Other brain structures—called "grid cells"—seem to provide a framework for integrating motion with position. Rats have that framework too. With this apparatus—subtly joined to brain centers for pleasure and avoidance—we navigate a space of sense and imagination in which ambient nature, recollection, and habit are integrated.

I walk every day, without a companion or electronic media. I listen to what's in the air, not broadcast over it. It's not strenuous walking, which makes it more like purposeful loafing. I walk because I can't drive. My walking is a means to an end, but between my front door and my destination is an experience in nature that is so palpable that I'm sometimes stopped by it.

I walk while the thumbnail curve of the waning moon rides brightly in and out of the arms of the sycamores, maples, and liquidambars that line some blocks near my home. They had been planted with bureaucratic efficiency in front of each house. Contingent nature has taken this plan and twisted it, and the trees are no longer just instances of a scheme. Each tree is itself—bent or straight, thick or slim—and each is different in every season.

I have to see the clearing evening sky, when it's broken by clouds after a day of rain, to know something of a world that has nothing to do with me but is continuously and subtly being made around me. When I stop in the middle of the sidewalk at dusk and pivot slowly to take in the whole sky above the rooflines, I also know that the wheeling contrast of the lighter clouds against the blue-black sky is an artifact of the reflected glare of the basin's tens of thousands of streetlights.

No less beautiful is the drawn-out, two-note call, repeated from yard to yard, of mourning doves, or the way their startled flight from front lawns begins with a clap, like a folding chair being closed, and the piping whistle of air through their wings that diminishes as the birds ascend. The doves rise up into light that is suspended like a luminous substance, a local atmospheric phenomenon caused by sunlight scattering from particles of granite eroded from the San Gabriel Mountains.

Walking is a burden when the wind slants rain under the edge of the umbrella, and I'm cold and wet. The cold is relative—generally no worse than 45 degrees in the wide swale between the San Gabriel and Los Angeles rivers—but I still have to clench my cold fingers into fists and jam them into my coat pockets. Then spring jolts the street into a weedy exuberance until the breathless glare of summer.

Some of us look for a place in nature. We travel great distances or take risks getting closer to it. Some of us seek to demonstrate how superior that world is to the one I pass through. I walk two or three miles every day, and I never leave nature's city.

PART 4

A Feeling for Landscape

ANGELENOS ARE INCESSANT TIME TRAVELERS. They reach into the past daily and bring up ghost shores (*The Well Brought Up Silt*) and histories of disturbance (*Lessons from the Gold Rush*). They make use of a durable past (*A Traveler Comes to a Bridge*) but rarely take notice (*Souvenirs*). Too often, we brush the past away (*Dust to Dust*). Attention is necessary (*Everything Visible*) even to see the past mislaid in plain sight.

Most often, we fail to see how nature and Los Angeles are interleaved in re-curring cycles that span oceans (*Nothing but Blue Skies*) and an acre of vacant lot (*Strangers in a Strange Land*). Wilderness prophets warned us, but I believe that intimacy with the compromised nature we have isn't betrayal of a purer faith (*Muir Centennial*). The gifts of the natural world are even in a neighbor-hood park (*Sharing Eden*). It's true that Los Angeles is a lost paradise. Because of that, it's more truly my home (*Emparadised*).

The Well Brought Up Silt

The well at the edge of the strip mall brought up silt finer than talcum powder and pearly gray as it dried. The well fed directly into the city's water distribution system (after a protective dose of disinfectant), so early risers in the adjacent neighborhood were the first to call the city. The water from their taps had run that morning with a milky sheen.

The well was taken out of service and left to pump into the street for a while. The gutter along the north side of the street half filled with silt drifts that were wave riffled.

Later, the well was abandoned, a lengthy process closely regulated to prevent contamination of the aquifer from which the well had drawn. The bore of the well, in which a submersible pump hung, had originally been drilled to irrigate the hay fields and truck farms that once covered what is now a grid of streets and houses.

Much older are the buried landscapes the well penetrated. The bands of aquifers under my town flow with water that is years or decades old, contained between layers of gravel, rock, and clay that are tens of thousands of years older. What happened thousands of years ago is still here if you go down deep enough. A winter's flood, a slowly dying lake, a retreating ocean shoreline—these facts are inscribed on the invisible landscape below.

The silt that glistened briefly in the gutter that morning, until it dried and drifted in pale wisps, had been buried by gravel and mud from the eroding mountains above the Los Angeles Basin. The silt had lain there, filtering the runoff of long ago winter rains and snowmelt, until the pump drew it up. Pumping had collapsed a dune of wind-blown dust at the margin of a long-ago desert or disturbed the bank of a vanished creek. The city's well was a time machine, let down into the past to draw up water to wash the bodies and slake the thirsts of today. The silt that clogged the city's well showed that we are in the past as much as in the present. We hadn't expected such durability or that every glass and bath is filled with history.

Lessons from the Gold Rush

In 2013, Governor Jerry Brown told the California Chamber of Commerce:

> [T]he Gold Rush was the best stimulus program ever invented; 300,000 people came from every country in the world, got a shovel and pick, and started picking. They got billions into the economy. The Federal Reserve didn't even exist. The federal government wasn't even heard from, so far away. They dug and they got gold; they spent it and more and more people came and they haven't stopped.[1]

There are layers of irony in the governor's ode to digging and getting in the mid-nineteenth century. Californians remain, 170 years later, inheritors of the Gold Rush. As taxpayers, we've inherited the uncalculated costs of cleaning up the poisoned tailings of mining sites like New Almaden, said to have been the world's largest mercury mine. Mercury was used to amalgamate the flecks of gold sluiced from the Sierra foothills by hydraulic mining. We've also inherited the badlands that hydraulic mining produced. More than a hundred years after that destructive form of mining was outlawed for its environmental impacts, Gold Country badlands leach heavy metals into California's streams and lakes. And we've inherited an uncounted number of other abandoned mining sites. An estimated 47,000 discarded mines litter the state's deserts and foothills. At least 5,700 of them are assumed to be environmental hazards, many of them in Southern California. Once remote, many of these abandoned sites are now at the fringe residential development in places like San Bernardino and Riverside counties.

As Californians so often have, we build on the poisoned tailings of an earlier boomtime.

But toxic mines and altered landscapes aren't all that we've inherited from the Gold Rush. Among the Gold Rush tailings are habits that began with the first gold strike on the American River in 1849. As Gray Brechin and Robert Dawson pointed out in *Farewell, Promised Land: Waking from the California Dream* (1999), the disastrous environmental history of California has been an epic bender from which Californians haven't fully recovered. Lured by an intoxicating image of El Dorado, too many Californians today are still attached to the certainty that everything here might be easily gained and with so few consequences.

Thomas Swain was there in 1850 and saw the effects of the Gold Rush as they happened. Writing in 1851, Swain lamented, "The people have been to each other as strangers in a strange land . . . . Their hearts have been left at home."[2] Few hearts had changed when, fifty years later, Frank Norris wrote *The Octopus: A Story of California* (1901). "[These Californians] had no love for the land," Norris wrote.

> They were not attached to the soil. They worked their ranches as a quarter of a century before they had worked their mines. To get all there was out of the land, to squeeze it dry, to exhaust it, seemed their policy. They did not care.[3]

The lessons of the Gold Rush should inform us each time we turn again to wring all that we can out of the land of California.

In 2019, with a new governor, came new calls to weaken or administratively bypass the California Environmental Quality Act. We're poised again to earn Thomas Swain's reproach that Californians

> . . . have considered that, as this is but a temporary stopping place for them, they have not been called upon to do anything for California but all for themselves.[4]

A Traveler Comes to a Bridge

As the traveler starts to cross, one foot is still earthbound; empty space is beneath the other. The next step requires trust. The traveler is uplifted less by steel or masonry and more by invisible forces kept in balance with the void waiting below. A bridge seems static, but every footfall must be absorbed, its effects distributed by tension or resisted by compression. A bridge responds. Its span springs to each step in order to be unmoved.

The traveler is unimpressed by the daring that permits a walk above the earth. The traveler prefers to see a gesture, a symbol, a poetic vault from known to unknown. But a bridge also is faithfulness and constraint. Mid-span, the traveler can't veer off to wander the green bank of the river below. The traveler can't choose a new path of desire. No meanderings on a bridge. The traveler can only depart from one place and return to another. A bridge is the exposed space between. There's no refuge there. A traveler in flight can only run back to what was feared or run toward whatever is hoped.

But this traveler pauses, leans against the parapet and takes in the elevated view. A bridge affords perspective but also detachment. What happens below a bridge happens without the traveler's intervention. Water flows or trains pass or cars make their way. Standing on a bridge, more than the traveler is suspended. Daydreams wait on a bridge. So are nightmares of vertigo, of falling, and suicide. The bridge itself is vulnerable if the forces that keep it standing shift. Every bridge is uneasy. If a bridge falls, what had seemed a trivial gap becomes a barrier again, and the two places the bridge assembled disconnect. Overcome a bridge, and communities at both ends are estranged. A bridge is a promise that a riven world can be more whole.

The traveler knows only the upper half of the bridge. Unlike most structures, bridges have an above and an underneath that are intimately joined yet separate places. The footloose traveler above could abandon the bridge's flow and settle below with others who have given up a destination, a trajectory that's imposed on those overhead. Instead of supports, the uprights, struts, and parabolas carrying the bridge deck could be the traveler's shelter. The traveler could exchange a vista for the intimacy of an encampment.

Instead, the attractive force of the opposite end of the bridge—its constant offer of novelty—leads the traveler on a path perpendicular to the possibilities under the traveler's feet. The bridge has taken the traveler to an encounter only to take the traveler from it.

One long glance

It's mid-October 1877, and you're looking west from the white bluff of Boyle Heights to opposite bluffs backlit by an autumn sunset. A panorama of green shadows—vines and fruit trees in apple-pie order—fills the valley below, tessellated by farm roads and a rail line that has bound Los Angeles only recently to the rest of America. North of you, between the mesa of East Los Angeles and the lip of Reservoir Ravine, is a gap. The Los Angeles River runs through it. Sycamores and laurels step down to the stream. Willows and tule reeds touch the water. Herons wade for fingerling trout and the toads that will give Frogtown its nickname one day. South of the gap, the Los Angeles River is slower, wider, braiding, making and unmaking gravel islands, and wandering into and out of orchards and vineyards and finally out of anyone's caring.

The falling light strikes the cupola of the high school on Poundcake Hill opposite. It strikes the gilt cross on the Cathedral of Saint Vibiana and the tower of the county courthouse. The river's valley is filling with the night. The 136 gas streetlights of the city are being lit. Still in sight are the three bridges that finger across the river: a railroad trestle northward and the Aliso Street bridge southward. Between them, a slab-sided, pitch-roofed, wooden bridge lit with kerosene lamps stolidly crosses at the river's narrowest point. No one calls it the Macy Street bridge. It's just the "covered bridge." From the crest of Boyle Heights, all of this is visible—bridges, gap, river, roads—even the loom of Catalina Island, like a band of fog on the southern horizon.

It's near the end of the time when Los Angeles can be taken in one long glance.

Yesterday's storm

It's February 16, 1887. Looking south from the trestle of the Southern Pacific Railroad, every river crossing except for the covered bridge has been damaged by yesterday's storm. The trestle of the Los Angeles and San Gabriel Valley Railroad stands, but a hundred feet of its western approach have washed away. The eastern end of the Downey Avenue bridge went into "a howling chasm" when the riverbank was undermined. The foot of the Aliso Street bridge disappeared. Streetcar track "still attached to the western stump of the . . . bridge, trails disconsolately down the river." Gaps, with the river running through, separate the western and eastern ends of the First Street bridge from the river bank. Although the storm passed early this morning, the "hoarse roar of the river, audible all over the city," continues to frighten residents.[5]

They had good reason. The river had flooded in 1782, 1811, 1814, 1825, 1851, and 1861. After the flood of 1867, water lay over the Cahuenga Valley for days, with the hills of west Los Angeles like islands in a sea. Flooding in 1876, 1884, and 1886 (with several deaths) began efforts to confine the river to an "official bed," which is only some lines drawn on a map.

Annihilated distance

Looking north from the First Street bridge, a reporter for the *Los Angeles Times* pauses on December 4, 1891 in his streetcar tour of Los Angeles. Beyond him is Boyle Heights "on a high mesa which terminates in a bluff, at the foot of which the river formerly ran." This, he tells his readers, is the city's most "airy and healthy residence section." Elevation, he says, is important from "a hygienic point of view." The heights are doubly hygienic because residents are safely across the river from the tenements of Sonoratown and Chinatown and the immigrant Italian and Basque neighborhoods around the old plaza.

The reporter has one regret as his tour of the city ends (and he'll not be the last to feel it). "Much of Los Angeles is almost a *terra incognita* to many of our residents, in spite of the fact that rapid and frequent transit has to a great extent annihilated distance."

A new span

From the deck of the new Fourth Street viaduct on January 12, 1905, the members of the city council's bridge committee, here to approve the work, can see the trees of Hollenbeck Park and the houses along Boyle Avenue at the crest of the heights. At the committeemen's feet is unbuilt acreage ready to be developed, now that the carriageway of the new viaduct connects Boyle Heights to the city's manufacturing district on the west bank of the river.

It had taken ten years of political maneuvering by Isaac Van Nuys, Moses

Sherman, James Lankershim, William Workman, and other men with a stake in real estate to engineer the viaduct's construction. Workman, former mayor and now city treasurer, often reminded the bridge committee that the river lacked a crossing between First and Seventh streets, a distance of a mile, and that those who live on the heights and farther east "were of necessity greatly inconvenienced." The lack of a bridge inconvenienced Workman. The sale of his fifty-five acres of floodplain at the foot of Boyle Heights depended on having a bridge. Workman depended on the sale of his property to wipe out years of debt.

It had taken some weeks of city council politics to get construction of the viaduct started. The sale of municipal bonds in 1903 had raised $100,000, not enough to repair old bridges and build a new one. The municipal engineer advised city councilmen to spend the bond revenue only on bridge repairs. He was skeptical of the proposed Fourth Street viaduct. "It winds around like a snake, and I doubt if it would be satisfactory if finished," he complained. The councilmen traded votes, cut funding for bridge repairs, and overruled the engineer.

It had taken the J.D. Mercereau Company seven months to build the viaduct. The footings of the western end lay at Santa Fe Street, followed by two hundred feet of wood trestle connecting to five wood and steel spans over the railroad tracks on the west bank, three hundred feet of steel truss to cross the river, and another five hundred feet of wooden trestle over more tracks to reach the edge of Boyle Heights where Workman's acreage waited to be developed.

The Fourth Street viaduct is two thousand feet long. It has a six-foot-wide footpath for pedestrians, who now have an easy walk of slightly more than a mile from Boyle Heights to reach the depots, warehouses, and factories that crowd the western bank of the river. The viaduct has a twenty-foot-wide carriageway for farm wagons but increasingly for motorcars.[6] (The Tourist, the first automobile to be manufactured in Los Angeles, is popular; 2,692 were built between 1902 and 1910.) The new span is paralleled a few feet away by its twin—the Los Angeles Traction Company's steel truss bridge erected in 1898. The spindly supports and thin girders of the two bridges are emblems of an unpretentious, readymade aesthetic.

Beneath the traceries of steel, the river sprawls. Dry most of the year, the riverbed is a tumult of sand ridges and gravel flats, some of them mined to make concrete for the tall buildings that have begun to crowd Broadway. The eastern side of the riverbed is a dump where the city's garbage and trash are hauled, some of it to be set afire, the rest to be rooted through by hogs that belong to a Mr. Clemmons. He sells the fattened hogs to the city's abattoirs. Butchers sell the pork as "the finest corn-fed."[7]

Elimination of ugliness

"The public demands a harmonious and graceful design," Louis Huot reminded readers of *Architect and Engineer* magazine in 1933.[8] Huot is a member of the city's Department of Public Works under Chief Engineer of Bridges Merrill Butler. (Butler oversaw the engineering of six river crossings between 1924 and 1932.) Huot designed the ornamental features of the bridges the city is building;[9] and the only public he finds demanding is the city's Municipal Art Commission. The commissioners' goal is "to work for the gradual elimination of ugliness";[10] and the wood trestles and girder trusses over the Los Angeles River are "about as ugly as they can be."[11] The commissioners feel that a better Los Angeles can be summoned through architecture. City Engineer John A. Griffin agreed. The character of the bridges his department will build "will be such as to excite comment from visitors who enter and leave Los Angeles," Griffin told the city council in 1923. The bridges will "raise the status of Los Angeles as an enterprising, properly developed city."[12]

It's an extraordinary epoch for Los Angeles, defined by bridges. The *Los Angeles Times*, the Automobile Club of Southern California and the railroads persuaded voters (many of them new motorists) that replacing narrow trestle bridges will relieve traffic congestion and give the city monuments to its ambitions. With bonds approved, eleven river crossings are built: Ninth Street in 1925, Macy Street and Franklin Avenue in 1926, Fletcher Drive in 1927, Fourth Street over Lorena Street and Spring Street in 1928, Glendale-Hyperion in 1929 and now the Fourth Street viaduct, begun in 1930 and finished two months ahead of schedule. (Still to come will be bridges at Washington Boulevard in 1931, Sixth Street in 1932, Figueroa Street in 1937 and Riverside Drive in 1938.)

They were designed for an accelerating city. "These bridges, especially over a stream of this character, should seem as little like bridges . . . and as much as possible like improved bits of street," landscape architect Charles Mulford Robinson had told the city council.[13] They should be "conformable to the automobile which it carries across the chasm," according to Huot. The bridges of Los Angeles will be horizontal monuments for a horizontal city.

The material of ambition—of enterprise and speed—is steel-reinforced concrete in arches, spandrels, and bridge decks, and in the pylons, parapets, light standards, brackets, and balusters that decorate the roadways. Mixed on-site, the concrete is poured into temporary wood forms held up by wood frames called falsework. Smoothed, the concrete will look like finished limestone. In less visible parts, the concrete will be left untouched. After the concrete has set, the impression of the rough forms will remain. The knots and grain of the wood will still be visible, a permanent shadow.

Huot's design vocabulary comes from imperial Rome, Renaissance Italy and Spain, and the Paris of Louis Napoleon. Nearly all the new bridges are variations on the classical tradition, except for the Fourth Street viaduct, where the design is Gothic Revival.[14]

Degrees of disorientation

"What nature divided has been brought together," David Faries of the Los Angeles Traffic Association tells the women of the Hollenbeck Ebell Club, who are waiting on July 30, 1931 for the speeches dedicating the Fourth Street viaduct to end.[15] A locomotive whistle interrupts him. The Playgrounds Department band waits to play "Sidewalks of New York" with its refrain about "east side, west side, all around the town." Officials from the three railroads that pass under the new viaduct are next to speak, happy now that the last wood and girder bridge over their tracks is gone. Celebratory banners hang from the catenary wires that support the electrical cables powering the streetcars that share the roadway with motorists. Dedication day is overcast and hot.

Nature's divide, for Faries, means the Los Angeles River, bracketed with levees but not yet bound in concrete, still hummocked with sand mounds but no longer the city dump.

The marginal river is the least of the bridge's concerns. Most of the 2,700-foot length of viaduct from Molino Street on the west to Anderson Street at the foot of Boyle Heights was designed to elevate traffic above two industrial roadways and braids of rail lines leading to repair shops, freight yards, and passenger terminals. The actual river crossing, supported on graceful, open-spandrel arches, is only 254 feet long.

As the city engineer in 1903 had warned, the new viaduct snakes across rails and roads and the river. It's split in two at its western end and bends as it reaches what had been William Workman's fifty-five acres. Seen from the air, the viaduct appears uncertain about its start and uneasy about where it must end. Fourth Street on the west side of the river angles southeast, conforming to the thirty-six degrees of disorientation from north and south in the original colonial street grid. Fourth Street on the heights side angles northeast. The two ends of Fourth Street, offset where they should face each other across the river, can't be made to line up, as if the western and eastern parts of Los Angeles were never meant to be in one city.

The viaduct's sinuous geometry can't overcome the racial politics keeping the halves of Los Angeles separate. A report sent to the board of the Federal Home Loan Bank explains why. Boyle Heights "is a 'melting pot' area and is literally honeycombed with diverse and subversive racial elements. It is hazardous residential territory."[16] In 1939, federal housing surveyors, as a warning to lenders, redlined the racially mixed heights.

There is a long flight of steps that takes pedestrians up from Santa Fe Avenue to a streetcar stop where the western end of the viaduct splits to drop one leg down to Mateo Street while the other leg runs farther west and north. After the dedication ceremonies, streetcar passengers will wait at the stop in the middle of the roadway, in a rectangle painted on the new asphalt. Motorcars will pass on either side while streetcar passengers stand within the outline of the "safety zone." The speed limit for motorcars is twenty-five miles an hour.[17]

The streetcar fare is seven cents.[18] 1931 is the second full year of the Depression, and not all workmen have seven cents. Many will continue to walk from Boyle Heights to jobs in the rail yards, factories, and warehouses between First and Sixth streets. When those men, lucky to still have a job, return in the evening, some might pause and rest on one of the small concrete benches that Louis Huot placed on either side of several of the light standards that spire from the bridge parapet's railing. The weary men probably no longer notice, in the fading golden light, the decorative elements that Huot had cast in concrete.

Yahrzeit

Evergreen Cemetery is at the end of the streetcar line that the Fourth Street viaduct carries over the river. The streetcar route is Main Street to Third Street, east to Traction Avenue, south on Merrick Street, another turn at Fourth Street, across the river to Fresno Street in Boyle Heights, north to First Street, and then a stop at the cemetery gates. The dead could take this way by chartered streetcar; two had been specially designed to carry a coffin, screened by a stained-glass panel, while mourners sat beyond. More recently, automobile corteges cross the river and turn off Fourth Street to Evergreen Avenue and the cemetery.

The new bridges Merrill Butler and his engineers have built north of Fourth Street allude to imperial grandeur, confirming with reinforced concrete that the westward course of empire had arrived triumphantly in Los Angeles. The style of the Fourth Street viaduct is different. The pylons at each end of the bridge span look like memorial cenotaphs. Their lancet openings suggest the entrance to a nave. The columns of the light standards, which also support the catenary lines that power the streetcars, rise above an acanthus-leaf capital to taper like the finals atop a medieval cathedral. They lead the eye heavenward. The frames of the streetlight lanterns are crowned with a final that could be mistaken for a cross. The parapets lining the viaduct are decorated with alternating equilateral triangles. Each is pierced by an opening in the form of a trefoil; its three-part shape represents stylized leaves of clover. Both the triangles and trefoils are reminders of the three-in-one of the Christian Trinity.

The Fourth Street viaduct crosses the Los Angeles River with a pastiche of ecclesiastical architecture and Christian iconography suitable, Huot must have thought, for a bridge that bore the dead. Gothic Revival details inspire somber recollection, although these aren't the memories of the Jews of Boyle Heights. Years later, did their sons and daughters, returning at the yahrzeit, notice that the bridge to Mount Zion Cemetery and the Home of Peace was marked by remembrances of English cathedrals?

The mourner crossing to Evergreen Cemetery by streetcar and the businessman bound for Montebello or Whittier by automobile see one bridge. The train passenger below the viaduct sees a regular pattern overhead of arching ribs, uprights connecting the bridge's deck to the arches and cross members joining the pairs of arches to each other. Above is historical decoration. Below is structure without a past, beautiful in its economical management of invisible forces.

There is something else to see, perhaps best seen by the occasional pedestrian. Nearly every outward-facing surface of the viaduct, above and below in the penetrating light of Los Angeles, is patterned with areas of sun-struck brightness and panels of knife-edged shadow.

In the moving light, if the pedestrian lingers, the surface of the concrete moves too, projections dripping shadows, moldings shedding darkness over plain surfaces, incised grooves stacking alternating white and black bars, all of it declaring the three dimensions of pillar, pilaster, corbel, and column. The Fourth Street viaduct, gleaming in the sunlight, is a bright thing for a city that wishes to be only white, yet it comes alive in the absence of its whiteness.

Dislocation and indifference

Empty in mid-October 2017 except for a stream of processed wastewater in the low-flow slot perfectly centered in its concrete floor, the Los Angeles River passes beneath the almost level deck of the Fourth Street viaduct. Belvederes, set into the arches of its sentinel pylons, overlook an engineered void. In the months with no rain, under a sky the color of dried urine, the river and the viaduct are mirrors of Angeleno desire.

Evergreen Cemetery is the furthest the city extended eastward across the Boyle Heights mesa. The ambitions of Los Angeles weren't in the modest houses and two-story shops along Fourth Street as it rose to the crest of the bluff. The future was westward, away from the threat of flooding and beyond the historical claims the old plaza made or the ethnic pluralism of Boyle Heights. East of the river is where the city housed its lepers and syphilitics, where its orphans were asylumed and where the city sent its aged and infirm. East is where the city sent its dead, not just to Evergreen Cemetery but also to the Odd Fellows and Masonic cemeteries and to the cemeteries (segregated by prejudice and theology), for Catholics, Serbians, Chinese, and Jews, and where the city's abandoned dead are still cremated and buried in a mass grave as each year ends.

In the 1950s, the California Department of Transportation, taking advantage of the effects of racial redlining, began cutting rights-of-way along the bluff that Mexican residents in the 1830s had called, because of its white face, the *Paradón Blanco*.[19]

Freeways replaced rows of wood-frame houses where Russians, Italians, Japanese, Latinx, and Jews had lived together and left for work together across the Fourth Street viaduct. The immigrant heights became a tangle of six freeways by the mid-1960s with their attendant air pollution and childhood asthma. Affluent Laurel Canyon, Beverly Hills, and Malibu were spared the freeways proposed for them.

The families of Boyle Heights remember the freeways' dislocation and the civic indifference behind it. The community resents a second displacement that has begun with what they see as aggressive gentrification. When real estate speculators arrive from downtown, they come by way of the Fourth Street viaduct.

Functionally obsolete

The Fourth Street viaduct bears a city's desires across railroad tracks, across access roads, across the blank surface of the river channel, and across time. Some are desires Angelenos may not recognize today or want anymore. But the viaduct cannot do otherwise, so well made was it with skill and an eye toward the effect of its repeating elements of arch and trefoil, pylon, and spire, light and shadow. These elements, which framed the city's aspirations for the future in 1931, are still available today for a city crowded with new anxieties about tomorrow. The contained river below and the stylish viaduct above were intended to be monuments of Anglo triumph over nature and space. These are compromised achievements today and need thoughtful translation.

A traveler comes to the Fourth Street viaduct and finds an articulate framework suspended between its past and the traveler's future. The number of pedestrians is fewer now, and the riders waiting for streetcars are gone. A Metrolink train rumbles under one of the viaduct's arches. A tree, rooted within or under the roadway deck, tops the parapet where it crosses Santa Fe Avenue.

A homeless man is living on the belvedere that projects from the arch of the first pylon as the bridge prepares to leap east. A shopping cart and plastic sheeting make a barrier in front. The sidewalk here is five feet wide, and the footing is uneasy because the battered metal plates that provide access to conduits under the sidewalk are uneven. Pearly grit, thick enough to support a few shoots of grass, has gathered along the foot of the parapet as if a slow-moving river had passed overhead dropping its silt. The belvedere opposite stinks of urine. Its lanterns are missing glass panels, so only skeletal arches remain in the metal frame.

Time and the vandalism of indifference are at work on the viaduct every day, part of the pathos of the things in our lives. Yet an insulator for the vanished streetcar's electrical cables remains on the light standard next to the pylon, and a catenary holdfast over its arch endures as the viaduct's memories of itself, not yet fully erased. The banister under the traveler's hand has the feel of stone. The thread of water in the low-flow slot of the concrete channel below glints and murmurs. Some birds wheel overhead.

In 1998, the Fourth Street bridge was retrofitted to improve the lateral stability of its arches in an earthquake.[20] In 2014, the National Bridge Inventory of the Federal Highway Administration determined that the entire Fourth Street viaduct met the "minimum tolerable limits to be left in place as is," although the geometry of its roadway deck is "basically intolerable." The report added that the Fourth Street viaduct is "functionally obsolete.

Any traveler coming to a bride will tell you that crossing is risky.

Souvenirs

The other day, I crossed the cement apron that leads out of the alley behind the houses that face on to Clark Avenue. I'd crossed that alley entrance from the time I was a boy and through the thirty-two years I walked to work after my father's death, but this time a thin sheet of water, probably leaking from a backyard hose, spilled across the concrete. I noticed that there were names inscribed there, almost worn smooth. The loose water brought out the contrast in the faint letters.

I'm not inattentive. The aspects of the everyday interest me. Yet here were the marks of lives that had neighbored mine, but I had never seen them, would never have seen them except for the contingencies of that moment. I stopped. Children had written their names awkwardly in the wet concrete but with respect for each other. Their names didn't overlap. None were crossed through or roughed out.

The route that takes me past the alley hardly ever varies. The route is the same, but the walk is always different, and not just because the conditions of light and air and ambient sound are various. In the midst of the many things that persist are as many that I see for the first and last time. The shadows cast across the sidewalk every bright, returning day. The pattern of the leaves on the birch tree that leans over the sidewalk. The shining tracks of snails, gone by noon. The bloomed-out roses behind the chain-link fence that will be there only another day or two.

The names of the children have been in front of the alley for decades. They may be there until some upheaval bulldozes away my neighborhood. It strikes me that the names revealed through the ephemeral sheen of water aren't any more or any less durable than any other part of what touches me.

I used to seek permanence in marks like the children's names. I think now what I have is provisional. Enough stays the same to give me hope.

Dust to Dust

Los Angeles—a city of self-inflicted amnesia—may suffer another memory loss. Casa Adobe (also called the Johnson house) has been denied city landmark status, despite the advocacy of conservancies in Santa Monica and Los Angeles. The preservationists see Casa Adobe, located in Brentwood Park, as an early example of the Spanish Colonial Revival style. The Los Angeles Cultural Heritage Commission saw the house as a tear-down.

Casa Adobe failed a political test of preservation. But this house deserves to linger, if only in our imagination, for what it said about who we are and what we came from. Casa Adobe is a memory made of sun-dried mud—of adobe dug from the grounds of the house and formed into bricks by itinerant Mexican laborers in 1919. Harry and Olivia Johnson built their house of adobe because it connected them to something they longed for in Los Angeles. Harry Johnson sketched the plans himself. He sought construction advice from John Byers, a family member with no formal architectural training but with some knowledge of construction and who could communicate with the Mexican workmen. They formed the flat rectangles of adobe, left them to dry for a season and later mortared the bricks into courses. The workmen raised the rafters, laid the tile roof and returned to trowel stucco over the adobe walls they had put up the previous year.

The finished house was characteristically hybrid in form: a hacienda-style rectangle with single-story wings embracing an inner courtyard fronted by a two-story, Monterey-style central block. In its upper room, frescoes by Knud Merrild and Kai Gotzsche, two Danish student artists, covered the walls in a pattern of scrolls, figures, animals, and a Spanish galleon under full sail. The Johnsons never pretended that their house was authentic. The Spanish Colonial Revival style was always a reimagining.

Although not as well-known as George Washington Smith or Wallace Neff, John Byers had a career as an architect in Los Angeles and Santa Monica. He was noted for his mastery of the Spanish Colonial Revival style and his love of adobe as a building material. The house he helped the Johnsons build endured with alterations and some losses, none of them essential. The current owners paid $6.3 million for it and a nearly 20,000-square-foot lot. The new owners know what they have: a big lot in a golden ZIP code and a ninety-year-old house made of dried mud.

Building a house in Los Angeles or demolishing one raises the same question: How do we make our home here? The Johnsons answered, as did many of their contemporaries, with an uncomplicated house of light and shadow, stucco walls, and rooms that opened outward into gardens and patios that are like rooms themselves. Could anything be more indigenous than a house constructed of the local soil and built for owners yearning to materialize their Los Angeles dreams? Many Angelenos in 1919 hoped to possess a place where all of nature and all of domestic life might be bounded by a garden wall.

Between 1916 (the date of George Washington Smith's first Spanish Colonial Revival home) and the mid-1930s, the architects who worked in the style designed houses of astonishing sympathy and presence. They designed for a knowing clientele of businessmen and their wives who wanted modern conveniences, accommodation for their automobiles, access to outdoor amenities, and rooms that flattered their taste (but with an appealing modesty). Critics later dismissed these homes as nostalgic, but they were as much of the future as they seemed to be of the past. The houses are romantic, but they also were anticipatory answers to a question. How should Angelenos live as if they belonged here as much as the oak trees and the sun-browned hills?

Casa Adobe is an inquiry into this problem and a response. The Johnsons sought a perfect confluence of setting and dwelling that would shield them from the new century's addictions to speed and anxiety. Human-scaled, in touch with the landscape, and narratively coherent, this house still asks—even if we don't—why that aspiration was so important. Between its rise and devolution into mediocrity, the Spanish Colonial Revival gave Los Angeles a distinct architectural tradition, a habit of outdoor living, and a playfulness that signaled something new about domestic life. Like Casa Adobe, these houses were made for an Angeleno imagination.

In the texture of its stuccoed walls, in the peach and vermillion of its roof tiles and in the simple geometry of its elements, Casa Adobe embodies a purpose larger than shelter. "[T]he house is one of the greatest powers of integration for the thoughts, memories and dreams of mankind," French phenomenologist Gaston Bachelard wrote.[21] Every house, he believed, sets the template for a life. This house has one more purpose: to remember on our behalf. Casa Adobe is mestizo at its heart: an integration of distant Spain, present Mexico, something of Los Angeles sham, and something of the anonymous workmen who built it. The obvious touch of their calloused hands in the stucco around doorways and windows is the mark they made in time.

The demolition of Casa Adobe touches me, not because I want to believe that everything old is worth saving, but because everything we save from the bonfire of discarded memories makes us more whole. Push this house back into the mud from which the Johnsons brought it, and we lose another part of what Los Angeles hoped to be.

· · ·

We lost that part. The Casa Adobe was demolished in 2010.

Nothing but Blue Skies

Is Los Angeles the Land of Sunshine? You don't need a weatherman to tell you it isn't. The long-time Angeleno (here at least a year) knows the disappointment of waking to skies as gray as freshly poured concrete, of noons filtered through a vault of dirty milk glass and afternoons that play out in dullness until, as the day's cruelest gift, a florid sunset roars through a slit in the overcast in colors of magenta and gold. Let's drop any pretense about sunny Los Angeles. This is the place we've come to, and it's as much mediocre gray as superlative brilliance.

The climate people say we have two seasons in Los Angeles: wet and dry. But Angelenos know, depending on where they live, many more seasons. Right now in my neighborhood, it's the season of buyer's remorse. The city's shiny sales pitch had left out the dingier climatological details of May gray and June gloom. Spring and early summer in Los Angeles, according to the National Oceanic and Atmospheric Administration, deliver just eleven clear days in May and fourteen in June. That's an average. At Marina del Rey, there are only nine perfectly clear days in June. The definition of a clear or a cloudy day is subjective, but on even days described as partly cloudy, the daylight hours are at least half obscured.

The gray season is made in the Pacific Ocean. Cold currents rise close to shore; a persistent high-pressure zone farther west channels warmer air eastward; and the vortex of the Catalina Eddy fabricates fog from the interaction of cool water and warm air, As the inland valleys of Los Angeles heat up, the air over them rises, pulling gray skies on shore. Television weathercasters call this stuff the marine layer, although what they're talking about is a dome of fog.

The gray ambles over the beaches, flows up the former bed of the Los Angeles River through the western half of the city, takes possession of downtown, and stalls there under the same inversion layer that brews smog. On good days, the sun eventually burns through and illuminates a city that seems to have been forgotten by color. You could look on the bright side: grey skies are part of the air conditioning that helps make the coastal plain cooler than the inland valleys.

And it might be worse. Tourists at the turn of the twentieth century complained that a dull haze shrouded the charms of what had been advertised as a sunlit, Mediterranean city. Seasonal wetlands covered all the low ground of western Los Angeles in the nineteenth century, creating daytime "advection fog." It results when warm air crosses damp, cool ground in the same way the marine layer is created over cold water. Days are brighter today because the basin is much dryer than it was then.

But our season of gloom won't get any shorter unless the oscillating cycles of El Niños and La Niñas return to the pattern they had before 1998. According to Cal Tech oceanographer William Patzert and Steve LaDochy and Jeff Brown of Cal State Los Angeles, the 1980s and 1990s were years of endless summer in Los Angeles. The oscillation from maximally gloomy to generally sunny used to take about twenty-five years. Global warming is unsettling that pattern. We may have a long time to wait for the pure light that was promised us.

Everything Visible

The photographer John Humble lay on his back and pulled himself through a gap under the chain-link fence that imprisons the Los Angeles River. He was near the river's official beginning—two creeks engineered for this purpose. He retrieved the camera, tripod, and bag he'd already lowered over the fence. The barrier was there because the river was made for the transmission of billions of gallons of runoff when winter storms pile up against the nearby mountains. When it rains, the concrete channel fills quickly. In a few minutes, the water can be waist high and flowing faster than you can run.

Only a little water covered the concrete floor at the confluence point the day Humble walked up the riverbed with his equipment. No one saw him approach. The riverbed is typically deserted (although the city's homeless men and women camp beneath the bridges farther south). Humble positioned himself at the point where the inward curving walls of the river's tributaries intersect in a demonstration of pure Euclidean geometry and took a picture. It's a beautiful picture in its unnatural way.

Humble crossed other barriers to complete his series on the Los Angeles River. He waded through streams of wastewater. His big, view cameras were awkward to use. His prints have a gravity that recalls the heroic tradition of American landscape photography. What is indistinguishable on the freeway at seventy miles an hour acquires in his photographs a monumental identity.

Humble pictures the city of the commonplace where, he says, everything of its garbled inauthenticity is visible in the uniquely still air and particularizing light. Los Angeles ceased to be picturesque long ago. Diminished to the postcard iconography of palms-surf-freeway-Hollywood sign-mountain peak, the clichéd city of the tourist snapshot is now a concealing screen for the tragic and humanizing body of Los Angeles. When the screen is pulled back, as in Humble's photographs, the city appears to be, in geographer Jérôrme Monnet's words, "alien, troubling, menacing, and cut off."[22] But it's our failure of imagination that renders Los Angeles the city of our fears. Humble's assumption, he said in a 2007 interview, is that "my pictures come from me, not the city."[23]

Other photographers have passed through Los Angeles, notably Ed Ruscha and Robbert Flick. They turned over the work of imaging Los Angeles to their cameras, which repeated back in deadpan snapshots the weight of the city's unwanted banality. Ruscha has said of his photography collections that the books were exercises in filling up pages, calling into question the making of images and even the act of looking at them.

If the city reveals itself to those who never remember, who accept only its dystopian mythology, the image of Los Angeles seems to collapse into metaphors of ironic distance and the mechanical replication of enigmas. Los Angeles feels like absences: the absence of hierarchies and limits; of urban intensity; of a center; and for some, merely the absence of New York. And finally we're absent, wrapped in reveries of another Los Angeles that substitutes for the city we're busy forgetting.

Fixed in Humble's photographs is the conundrum of Los Angeles. All the city's hills are scaled with houses; all its rivers are concrete; the air overhead is a petrochemical byproduct; pavement extends to the horizon in every direction. And yet everywhere in Los Angeles are the complex natural systems in which Angelenos have always been participants. It might better be said that Angelenos since the 1880s have bound the city more—not less—to the consequences of flood, fire, tectonic forces, and drought. The elements of nature penetrate the city at every freeway off-ramp and on every block within the framework of its gridded streets. We who live here are embedded in a compromised nature. Just as Humble shows, our anxious place is by the side of the river's gleaming channel, emblem of our ruined paradise and now our home.

Muir Centennial

A hundred years after his death in Los Angeles in 1914, what is John Muir's place in the story of California? The answer is complicated. And controversial, as environmental historian Jon Christensen expected when he told the *Los Angeles Times* that "Muir's legacy has to go. It's just not useful anymore."[24]

Muir was an icon of California when I was a boy in the 1950s. He'd said what white, middle-class Californians wanted to be said about California, that the state was exceptional in its beauty, boundlessly generous in its gifts of Nature, and possibly redemptive. Muir himself was a model of becoming a Californian. He was the migrant who arrives as a seeker, is enraptured by the limitless California promise, and becomes a booster of all that California had given him. Muir's career in California was even a guarantee that distance from the cultural capitals of the East wasn't an insurmountable obstacle to renown. You could be famous for being a Californian.

Muir was celebrated as a lyrical spokesman for untrammeled Nature and its curative powers. He was a friend of presidents and an ally of Theodore Roosevelt in the early decades of the conservation movement. He fought for the protection of the Yosemite Valley as a national park (a battle he helped win) and for the preservation of the no-less-grand Hetch Hetchy Valley (a fight he lost).

Muir didn't turn conservation into national policy by himself, but he was among the best at explaining to middle-class Americans why wilderness conservation should be the goal of federal and state governments. Out of Muir's passionate defense of California's high country came the Sierra Club (which he joined in founding). The state's protected wilderness areas began with Muir, along with the parks that surround the redwoods and giant sequoias. It's no wonder that Muir achieved a kind of secular sainthood through his advocacy of an ethic that validated a spiritualized conception of wilderness.

The scope of nature's realm (and where we might be in it) were questions that lay behind Christensen's poke at Muir's legacy. Along with his UCLA colleague Glenn McDonald, who holds the John Muir Memorial Chair in Geography, Christensen feels boxed in by Muir's belief that California's landscapes can be reduced to three simple categories: Urban, Rural, and Nature.

For Muir, cities were necessary for commerce and industry. Rural farms produced food and raw materials. Above them stood Nature, literally higher in altitude and vastly higher in moral worth. Up there, Muir argued, the nerve-shattered businessmen of 1910 and factory owners of the smoke-stack industry could recover from the sickliness of urban life. They could put aside society's effete sensibilities in vigorous outdoor recreation. They could relearn manly self-reliance in order to continue, down below, the Darwinian struggle of progress. Muir's conception of wilderness mirrored the anxieties and urgencies of post-Civil War America. In twenty-first-century California, Christensen and McDonald argue, we should reject Muir's narrow categories and his conviction that redemptive Nature is segregated from where people work and live.

Muir's transcendent Nature doesn't seem necessary to many contemporary Californians or even very welcoming. Membership in the Sierra Club has declined, according to Christensen, and has grown older. A smaller proportion of Californians today trek into the forests Muir valued. Latino, African American, and Asian Californians look at Muir, Thoreau, Emerson, and other nineteenth-century apostles of a secular religion of wilderness and see few parallels in their own cultural practices. They don't often see anyone who looks like them in Muir's Nature. Diverse Californians no longer share a master narrative about Nature and how it is to be seen and appreciated.

For some of my neighbors in Lakewood, nature is what they grow in their backyard and put on their table as food. For me, nature is what's at my feet when I step off my front porch. For environmental historian Jenny Price, nature is present in the cup of organic coffee in your hand and in the bottle of mango whip body lotion in your bathroom.

Some environmentalists, in the spirit of Muir, believe that autonomous Nature should be valued above the nature that's implicated in my ordinariness. Nature with more than a fleeting human presence seems no nature at all. But from my perspective, no part of the landscape is privileged over any other solely by its relationship to the kind of nature that Muir preferred to worship. To decompose Californian landscapes into parts more or less worthy, as Muir once did, imposes human values to which uncaring Nature is indifferent. It's aesthetic privilege that separates the landscapes of California into moral categories and validates one of those categories by denying equal meaning to the others. Saintly exhortation is bracing, and historical advice can be useful, but Muir didn't see California as it was even in 1914, with its disregarded communities of color and its laboring poor. His vision traced mountain tops, not playgrounds for tenement children.

Muir heard the eloquence of the outdoors, as I think I do, but are there different natures or only one? The easy answer is that Muir could have his Nature on a mountain peak, miles from the things of everyday life, and I can have my nature on a suburban street with miles more of the same all around. But that might be the wrong answer. Astrophysicist Adam Frank is convinced that all lives are in contact with immanent Nature. "It's a conversation," he said, "expressed not in words but in the immediacy of experience and the poetry of the one, single now."[25] That is where the experience of sacredness abides wherever we are in the natural world.

Perhaps we should see nature from the perspective of the once tropical parrots that flock above my suburban street. They exalt loudly, ignoring differences. The willful parrots see nature as the place where they are.

Strangers in a Strange Land

I waited for a bus opposite the last bit of never-built-on land in my neighborhood. It seems odd that these four acres, out of the thousands that once stretched as far as the eye could see, are empty still. They're hardly what anyone might identify as natural.

Fierce, insistent piping came from the lot over the sound of traffic on the adjacent boulevard. In the middle of the lot, two pairs of shorebirds stood over nesting scrapes. I couldn't tell what sort of birds they were, a fault of bad eyesight. Whatever they were, the birds were out of place. They should have been, I suppose, at the gravelly margin of a beach, just above the highest tides of spring. The houses and hotels on the ocean edge of Long Beach have crowded out these birds. They were six or seven miles from the nearest beach. An unbuilt lot surrounded by houses and shops was the nearest equivalent.

The little birds skittered across the gravel, agitated by the presence of five or six crows a dozen feet away. One of the crows paced along the boundary of the little birds' fear, rose hardly a foot or two above the ground, and glided inward. A little bird ran to confront the crow and then half flew, half ran on a vector away from its scrape, piping shrilly, perhaps to lure the crow away. Another crow rose from the ground and glided over the spot where the little bird had stood.

The feints and dashes by the little birds and the crows' cooperative foraging continued, sometimes taking pairs of crows into the branches of a crape myrtle nearby. The shorebirds never went very high or far from their middle of the empty lot. Occasionally, the crows lifted off in a group, circled overhead, but settled again on the gravel.

Not much more happened while I waited for the bus. The crows eventually left, turned west over some eucalyptus trees, and roused fifteen or twenty more crows perched there. They took wing and turned into a vortex, looking like torn construction paper silhouetted against the yellowish sky. The piping of the shorebirds on the empty lot died away.

I can't say that the interaction of the crows and the little birds was natural or even part of Nature. I'm not sure that capital-N nature exists, except as an idea some observers say they see. On a patch of gravel the color of the full moon, something played out that had nothing to do with me. It had the quality of life and death for some of the participants. I found no metaphors in what had happened and kept only this insignificant memory.

Sharing Eden

Former USC librarian Lawrence Clark Powell remembered that his mother arrived in Los Angeles from "back East" around the turn of the twentieth century carrying her horticultural prize—a geranium.

The geranium was a tender plant where she came from, best kept in the parlor during winter to protect it from the cold. She held the geranium in its pot on her lap during the entire transcontinental train trip. And when she had stepped off the platform of the Arcade Station in wintertime Los Angeles, she saw geraniums in bloom everywhere. They were weeds in the empty lots of the half-rural city. In humiliation (and perhaps with some relief), she threw her pampered geranium away. You might say that we've been tossing out the geraniums ever since. All of Los Angeles is a kind of garden after all. Would anyone want more?

This is another of the paradoxes of this city, and it's among the reasons that Los Angeles is park poor. From the right perspective, the city's tens of thousands of suburban yards merge into a savanna of lawns and trees. Even in neighborhoods that some Angelenos won't drive though, roses scent the air, oranges hang in bright clusters from backyard trees, and ripe fruit drops to the ground uneaten. Nature appears available everywhere. Who needs to set aside a park in Eden?

The city of Los Angeles has roughly four acres of parkland per one thousand residents, considerably less than the nearly seven acres per one thousand available in other, equally dense cities. And those acres of open space in Los Angeles aren't equitably distributed. The five poorest of the city's fifteen city council districts have less than 20 percent of the parkland. Similar disparities affect crowded neighborhoods throughout Los Angeles County. Maywood, a working-class Latinx community, has slightly more than half an acre per one thousand population. Manhattan Beach, affluent and Anglo, has almost six acres. In wealthy Palos Verdes, one-quarter of the city is devoted to park-like open space. Across the county as a whole, forty-one of its 262 neighborhoods have less than one acre of park space per one thousand residents.

Los Angeles had a plan to give residents the public places they deserve. The plan was published in 1930 by the landscape design firm of Olmsted Brothers and the urban planner Harland Bartholomew. The Olmsted-Bartholomew plan (commissioned by civic activists, not by city government) would have framed Los Angeles with a ring of beaches, parks, and wetlands from the San Fernando Valley to San Pedro. It would have set aside at least seventy thousand acres of open space for public enjoyment. The plan was shelved for all the reasons that Los Angeles remains one of the most private of cities.

There are hopeful conversations underway today along the banks of the Los Angeles and San Gabriel rivers that frame how seeing nature differently will let us see a different Los Angeles. Although the conversations look back to the Olmsted-Bartholomew plan, parkland advocates shouldn't depend too much on the pathos of that narrative. As eloquent as the 1930 plan was, it imagined its green necklace of parks as a middle-class amenity. Its greenbelts were tree-lined parkways paralleling wide boulevards—a panorama for sightseeing from a car.

Although iconic among today's park advocates as the city's greatest missed opportunity, the Olmsted-Bartholomew plan also was a mirror of Anglo anxieties in a rapidly urbanizing city. The plan was quickly buried in the files, and the fabric of open space in Los Angeles remains tattered. Los Angeles parks and beaches don't connect if you don't have a car or the time to take public transit.

A shared place in nature is one definition of a park. It's also a lens for looking at an anxious city that won't rub shoulders with strangers, regards pedestrians and bike riders suspiciously, and can't imagine needing accessible, free, and public places that foster the promiscuous mixing of races and classes.

Liberating Places

The city's densest neighborhoods have needs that are more urgent than a conversation about the place of nature in Los Angeles, but the talk can't be set aside as untimely or worse, unnecessary. Wildfires combust from our failure to talk about nature in Los Angeles. Mudslides and flooding flow from it. Even the city's tendency to explode into communal violence has roots in our failure to be grounded in our nature, which is hardly ever imagined as this city's common place. Just sitting and talking to one another in a neighborhood park could do some Angelenos some good.

Among other things, and as important as soccer fields and basketball courts, parks alter time and space. Nothing in a proper park is for sale; nothing clamors for attention; nothing reminds you that you're late for something else; nothing is poised there to enrage or humiliate. There, the rhythms of your steps change. Your preoccupations recede. The trees spread more broadly, rise higher, and the light beneath them is different. It's in our human nature to long for these liberating places. The city's retail "groves" and "promenades" are unsatisfactory substitutes.

We can do better. We can move beyond a history of loss to envision the nature we have, which only requires a greater intimacy, like walking or biking a riverside trail, to begin to restore to us our shared nature.

Emparadised

Its American occupiers in the mid-nineteenth century thought Los Angeles was a place of not enough, specifically not enough trees. There was sunshine everywhere, but you couldn't make a barrel or a wagon out of it. As Jared Farmer points out in *Trees in Paradise* (2013):

> [A] landscape of "savannah and chaparral puzzled American settlers from eastern climes. They missed the shade, the green and the chatter of songbirds. Accustomed to bosky abundance—and habituated to unthrifty wood use—they desired lumber and firewood, lots of it.[26]

And as James C. Williams notes in *Energy and the Making of Modern California* (1997), lacking firewood and coal, Los Angeles didn't have the fuel to run a steam-driven economy, another reason why San Francisco led the state in manufacturing. Industrial development in Los Angeles lagged until 1892, when Edward Doheny and Charles Canfield brought in the first oil well in the Los Angeles City Field, setting off a petroleum boom and then an industrial one.

Farmer resurrects a word—emparadise—that California Governor George Perkins had used in 1881 to describe what American settlers were doing to the disappointing landscape of Los Angeles. They gradually "paradised" the city with what it lacked: trees for shade, construction, furniture, and firewood. Angelenos have been improving the place with trees ever since and with the appearance of extraordinary success. Farmer argues that:

> American settlers in the Far West wanted to "complete" a land blessed with exceptional sun and soil. By adding drought-tolerant trees from other parts of the world, California horticulturists succeeded in making grasslands wooded. . . . Dendrophiles called it "reclaiming" the "wastelands." . . . They forced grasslands and wetlands to metamorphose into fields, orchards and garden cities. As a result of rural and urban afforestation, the whole region contains more trees today than at any time since the late Pleistocene.[27]

The imperative to complete what had been left undone had racist overtones.

A treeless Los Angeles had been the fault of primitive Native Americans and idle Californios, said the city's Anglo ascendency. Planting a tree rooted Anglo wholesomeness in alien soil and redeemed the landscape from the failures of its former holders.

We carry on improving Los Angeles today, ever anxious to perfect what other improvers thought they had perfected. Given the mixed results, is it any wonder that emparadised Los Angeles leaves our desires unfulfilled? And yet as Marcel Proust mused, the real paradises are the ones you've lost.

Falling in Love

One must always maintain one's connection to the past and yet cease-
lessly pull away from it. To remain in touch with the past requires a
love of memory. To remain in touch with the past requires a constant
imaginative effort.
— Gaston Bachelard, *Fragments of a Poetics of Fire* (1988)

SOME YEARS AGO. I wrote an account of a place where redemption, carpen-
try, the Laws of the Indies, and a dead cocker spaniel figured in. The miscellany
that became *Holy Land: A Suburban Memoir* served as a description of the
place where I still live. It also was an apology for my life. I wondered then if that
was enough. I wonder still. I had begun with silent conversations during the
walk from my house to Lakewood City Hall and from city hall to my house, the
rhythm of each stride eliding into the rhythm of my thoughts. The conversations became an argument, initially over the folly of staying here and then the
folly of faith, of believing that so much ordinariness added up to anything. One
day, I found that I had argued myself into falling in love with the place where
I am, and I began to write about the civilizing power of having fallen in love.

A lover's gaze has a political outcome. Attention leads to awareness of potential obligations and ends in pragmatic sociability—a habit of give and take

across ideological, religious, gender, ethnic, and racial boundaries that grows into sympathy. As much as it's a source of wonder and delight, a sympathetic imagination is a tool that helps people trust one another and to be faithful to their trust. That faithfulness supports our efforts to make beloved communities and breed in them what author Sally Fitzgerald called "habits of being." One habit is a sense of place. Without it, Los Angeles dematerializes into a terrible abstraction.

The causes of placelessness can be found in our history—causes worth talking about, hence the pieces in this book. But standing against an abstracted Los Angeles (and its distractions) is my longing for the much-handled things I already have. Longing for what is present around me is the means by which I've written myself into this city and its mix of tragedies and joys, negotiating my way from a flawed private life to the flawed place that is Los Angeles.

When I first looked at Los Angeles, I saw the awful effects of what historian Norman Klein calls erasure. The leveling of the multi-ethnic neighborhood of Bunker Hill, for example, left behind a soulless corporate acropolis. Concreting the Los Angeles and San Gabriel rivers made nearly invisible the continuing presence of nature there and caused communities of color to be marginalized. Erasures of memory were the precondition for a half-century of failed policies that worsened conditions for the working poor, homeless Angelenos, and recent immigrants. In forgetting the conditions under which modern Los Angeles came to be, voters failed to understand why city and county government became so callous and remote. Disregard of a violent history of Los Angeles gave cover to decades of corruption and abuse in law enforcement. Willful amnesia legitimizes gentrification in Los Angeles neighborhoods today.

A question runs through *Becoming Los Angeles*: can awareness of the city's past be of any worth to us except as nostalgia or irony? Some Angelenos don't want any history at all. Some are content to be perennial tourists but never citizens. And other Angelenos see only a simulacrum as flimsy as a Hollywood set. If Los Angeles is imagined to be either a disappointing heaven or an unsatisfactory hell, then the city's representations may be seductive but they're just another entertainment, best witnessed while lightly sedated. But sometimes, as we see now, our experience of Los Angeles resonates with unexpected immediacy, and the image fabricated to enable forgetting falls away. Attunement makes it possible to reinhabit places abandoned by indifference and to dwell there critically and actively, sensing the continuity of the past and present, the nearby and global, the tangible and imagined. A sense of place will animate where we are—a somewhere and not a nowhere.

New interpreters, in their myriad identities, have begun to assemble a re-figured sense of place for Los Angeles, mapped out in common encounters and everyday practices. The city's new interpreters tell roughened, textured, thrown-together stories that feel like something. This is the kind of public speech I aspire to.

This book is how my sense of place has "insinuate[d] itself into the very heart of personal identity."[1]

I write about sacred and humanizing Los Angeles because I find myself there.

NOTES

KEY TO ABBREVIATIONS:
CLA: *Curbed Los Angeles*
LAH: *Los Angeles Herald*
LAT: *Los Angeles Times*
NPR: National Public Radio
NYT: *The New York Times*

PREFACE

1. Black Angelenos are slightly less than 8 percent of the county's population; they're at least 36 percent of the county's homeless men, women, and children. Of the nearly nine hundred Angelenos killed by police in Los Angeles County since 2000, 80 percent have been people of color. These disparities are rooted in the city's history, politics, economics, and society.
2. Simone Weil; edited by Siân Miles, *Simone Weil: An Anthology*, 212.

INTRODUCTION

1. Eric Avila, "Essaying Los Angeles," *The Cambridge Companion to the Literature of Los Angeles*, edited by Kevin R. McNamara, 179.
2. Megan Garvey, "Stem Cell HQ Won't Be in L.A," *LAT*, Apr 13, 2005, https://www.latimes.com/archives/la-xpm-2005-apr-13-me-stem13-story.html.
3. Kate Pickert, "Eric Garcetti Writes a New LA Story," *Time*, Mar 20, 2014, https://time.com/31924/eric-garcetti-writes-a-new-la-story.
4. Greg Hise, "Sixty Stories in Search of a City," *California History*, Vol. 83, No. 3, 2006, 8.
5. Michael Maltzan, "No More Play," *No More Play: Conversations on Urban Speculation in Los Angeles and Beyond*, edited by Jessica Varner.
6. Benjamin Schneider, "A Field Guide to California Urbanism," *The Urbanist*, Apr 2019, https://www.spur.org/publications/urbanist-article/2019-05-16/field-guide-california-urbanism.
7. Eric Monkkonen, "Community on the Edge," *The Long Term View: Community and Isolation*, Vol. 4, No. 2, Spring 1998, 27–33.
8. Doreen Massey, *Space, Place and Gender*, 146.
9. Kathleen Stewart, *Ordinary Affects*, 128.
10. A point made by David Rio in his introduction to *Beyond the Myth: New Perspectives on Western Texts*, .
11. David Ulin, *Sidewalking: Coming to Terms with Los Angeles*.
12. Neil Campbell, "Affective Critical Regionalism in D.J. Waldie's Suburban West," *Beyond the Myth*, 87–106.
13. Kathleen Stewart, "Cultural Poesis: The Generativity of Emergent Things," *The Sage Handbook of Qualitative Research (3rd edition)*, edited by Norman Denzin and Yvonna Lincoln, 1028.
14. Barry Lopez, "A Scary Abundance of Water," *LA Weekly*, Jan 9, 2002, https://www.laweekly.com/a-scary-abundance-of-water/.
15. Barry Lopez, "We are shaped by the sound of wind, the slant of sunlight," *High Country News*, Sep 14, 1998, https://www.hcn.org/issues/138/barry-lopez-we-are-shaped-by-the-sound-of-wind-the-slant-of-sunlight.

16. Ismail Muhammad, "Walking with the Ghosts of Black Los Angeles," *Freeman's*, Sep 20, 2019, https://lithub.com/walking-with-the-ghosts-of-black-los-angeles/.

17. Juhani Pallasmaa, *The Eyes of the Skin: Architecture and the Senses*, 43.

PART I

1. "Exterior postcard view of the Tomas Feliz adobe at Campo de Cahuenga in what is now North Hollywood, where John C. Fremont and Andres Pico signed the treaty ending the fighting of the Mexican American War in California on January 13, 1847." Security Pacific National Bank Collection, Los Angeles Public Library, https://tessa.lapl.org/cdm/singleitem/collection/photos/id/113605/rec/14.

2. Edwin Bryant, *What I Saw in California*, 866.

3. John C. Frémont, *Memoirs of My Life*, 600.

4. John M. Foster, et al., *Second Addendum Report: Archaeological and Historic Investigations at Campo De Cahuenga CA-LAN-1945H*, 23.

5. *Ramona* was serialized in the pages of *The Christian Union*, a popular religious weekly.

6. *Mestizo* identified Californians of mixed ethnic heritage. Californio was the self-identification of native-born Californians.

7. Chelsea Pearson, "'Call me a Californio': Translating Hemispheric Legacies in Helen Hunt Jackson, Don Antonio Coronel, and José Martí."

8. Helen Hunt Jackson, "Echoes in the City of the Angels," *Glimpses of California and the Missions*, 193.

9. Jackson, "Echoes," 194.

10. Harris Newmark failed to mention Antonio Coronel's missing English. Some later accounts of his life have Coronel checking the proof pages of *Ramona* before publication; other sources say Mariana did the proofing. Mariana was surely bi-lingual, so much so that her profile in *An Illustrated History of Los Angeles County, California* (1889) highlighted the benefit of her mixed heritage since "she speaks both the English and Spanish languages with equal facility."

11. "Echoes," 194.

12. Helen Hunt Jackson, letter dated November 8, 1883. *Through Ramona's Country*, edited by George Wharton James, 20.

13. Jackson, "Echoes," 177.

14. Phoebe S. Kropp, *California Vieja: Culture and Memory in a Modern American Place*, 45.

15. H.D. Barrows, "Antonio F. Coronel," *LAH*, Jun 10, 1894.

16. "Gladstone City. The Cream of the East San Gabriel Valley," *LAH*, Apr 22, 1887.

17. C.C. Baker, "The Rise and Fall of the City of Gladstone," *Annual Publications of the Historical Society of Southern California*, 1914, 191.

18. J.M. Guinn, "The Great Real Estate Boom of 1887," *Historical Society of Southern California*, 1890, 6.

19. Guinn, "The Great Real Estate Boom . . . ," 18.

20. Baker. "The Rise and Fall . . . ," 191.

21. Richard Henry Dana Jr, *Two Years Before the Mast*, 216.

22. Benjamin Cummings Truman, *Semi-tropical California: its Climate, Healthfulness, Productiveness, and Scenery*, 35.

23. James DeLong, *Southern California, A Book for the Million, Treating the Climate, Soils, Productions, General Resources, and Development of Semi-Tropical Southern California*, 5–6.

24. Elizabeth Logan, *Urbane Bouquets: A Floricultural History of California*, 49.

25. Charles Dudley Warner, *Our Italy*, 19–20.

26. R.W.C. Farnsworth, *Southern California Paradise*, 9.

27. Charles Nordhoff, *California: For Health, Pleasure, and Residence*, 11.

28. Truman, 34.

29. George Kress and Walter Lindley, *A History of the Medical Profession of Southern California*, 7.

30. Richard Requa, *Architectural Details, Spain and the Mediterranean*.

31. Nathanael West, *The Day of the Locust*, 3.

32. "Anything haywire is always most haywire in California," *Architectural Forum*, Aug 1935, 30.

33. In recent years, the indigenous people of the Los Angeles Basin have called themselves the Tongva, Gabrieleños, and Kizh (pronounced "keech"). Gabrieleños references Mission San Gabriel.

34. "In the Heart of Bungalow Land, Laurel Canyon," *LAH*, Mar 14, 1909.

35. *Los Angeles Examiner*, Feb 6, 1909. Quoted in "A Blueprint for Paradise," Laurel Canyon Association, 2015, https://www.laurelcanyon.org/blog.

36. "Bungalow Land in Laurel Canyon," *LAH*, May 16, 1909.

37. "People Pay for Costly Road to Eldridge's Land: Supervisor Revealed as Owner in Tract Most Benefited by Road to Nowhere'," *LAH*, Jul 21, 1910.

38. Advertisement for Bungalow Land, *LAT*, May 22, 1909.

39. *Analysis of Greater Alarm Operations, Laurel Canyon Brush Fire*, City of Los Angeles Fire Department, Sep 16, 1979, 1.

40. Lisa Robinson, "An Oral History of Laurel Canyon, the Sixties and Seventies Music Mecca," *Vanity Fair*, Mar 2015, 271.

41. Robinson, 271.

PART 2

1. "El gentilicio correcto de Los Angeles es angelino," *Dario Libre*, Feb 13, 2008. https://www.diariolibre.com/revista/el-gentilicio-correcto-de-los-angeles-es-angelino-GKDL4976.

2. H.L. Mencken, "The Advance of Municipal Onomastics," *The New Yorker*, Feb 8, 1936, 54.

3. *The American Language: A Preliminary Inquiry into the Development of English in the United States* went through multiple editions after its publication in 1919.

4. Robert D. Angus, "Place name morphology and the people of Los Angeles," *California Linguistic Notes*, vol. XXX no. 2, 2005.

5. Michel De Certeau and Pierre Mayol, *The Practice of Everyday Life: Volume 2: Living and Cooking*, Translated by Timothy Tomasik, 142–143.

6. Joan Didion, "On Morality," in *Slouching Towards Bethlehem*, 158.

7. Joan Didion, "Where I Was From," in *We Tell Ourselves Stories in Order to Live: Collected Nonfiction*, 973.

8. Didion, *Slouching . . .*, 176.

9. Didion, "*Where I Was . . .*," 974.

10. Didion. "*Where I Was . . .*," 113.

11. Gustavo Arellano, "My Dad, the Illegal Immigrant," *LAT*, Sep 14, 2008.

12. Lawrence Weschler, essay in exhibition catalog for "Hand Eye Heart: Watercolors of the East Yorkshire Landscape, Feb 26–Apr 2, 2005," 17.

13. William Faulkner, *Uncle Willy and Other Stories*, 300–301.

14. David Colker, "Building a 'Future' in 1948: A riddle and a single house launched 'American way of life' in Panorama City," *LAT*, Sep 4, 1999. https://www.latimes.com/archives/la-xpm-1999-sep-04-mn-6823-story.html.

15. Maria Konnikova, "Why Summer Makes Us Lazy," *The New Yorker*, Jul 22, 2013. https://www.newyorker.com/tech/elements/why-summer-makes-us-lazy.

16. Konnikova, "Why Summer . . . ."

17. Jeff Turrentine. "L.A. Takes the High Road," *Resilience*, 2013, this and all quotes from Turrentine in this essay are from the same source. https://www.resilience.org/stories/2013-06-11/l-a-takes-the-high-road/.

18. Errol Wayne Stevens, "Two Radicals and Their Los Angeles: Harrison Gray Otis and Job Harriman," *California History*, vol. 86, no. 3, 2009, 52.

19. Paul Greenstein, et al., *Bread and Hyacinths: The Rise and Fall of Utopian Los Angeles*, 29.

20. Cecilia Rasmussen, "A Socialist Who Almost Was Mayor." *LAT*, Oct 31, 1999.

21. Greenstein et al., 67.

22. Philip S. Foner. "The AFL in the Progressive Era, 1910–1915," in *History of the Labor Movement in the United States*. vol. 5 , 25–26.

23. Kevin Starr, "The Golden State has a rendezvous with destiny," *SF Gate*, Aug 3, 2003. https://www.sfgate.com/opinion/article/California-dreamin-The-Golden-State-has-a-2599066.php.

24. Kevin Starr, *Coast of Dreams: California on the Edge*, xii.

25. Email correspondence with the author, 2019.

26. Email correspondence with the author, 2019.

27. David Ulin, "The Revised 'Bible' of L.A. Architecture is out. Let it be your guide," *LAT*, Dec 7, 2018.

28. Nathan Masters, Foreword to *An Architectural Guidebook to Los Angeles: Fully Revised 6th Edition*, by David Gebhard and Robert Winter, edited Robert Inman, 10.

29. "Snow Falls for Third Night," *LAT*, Jan 12, 1949.

30. "Snow Cloaks Catalina with White Mantle," *LAT*, Jan 12, 1949.

31. Nathan Masters, "Why Doesn't It Snow in L.A. Anymore?" KCET, Dec 9, 2016. https://www.kcet.org/shows/lost-la/why-hasnt-it-snowed-in-los-angeles-since-1962.

32. "Union Station Service Starts," *LAT*, May 8, 1939.

33. Thom Andersen, "Get Out of the Car: A Commentary," *Czarabox*, 2017. http://czarabox.blogspot.com/2010/11/get-out-of-car-by-thom-andersen.html.

34. Andersen, "Get Out of the Car . . . ."

35. Tom Treanor, "The Home Front," *LAT*, Oct 20, 1941.

36. "Manchester Boddy Dies at 75," *NYT*, May 13, 1967.

37. *Ralph Story's Los Angeles*, episode 48, KNX-TV, Jan 19, 1965. http://www.riprense.com/Dailynewspagestory.htm.

38. Cecilia Rasmussen, "Descanso Gardens Blossomed Along With L.A. Newspaper," *LAT*, Jun 6, 2004.

39. Susan J. Matt, *Homesickness: An American History*, 185.

40. Mary June Burton, "Confessions of a Lonesome Club Operator," *LAT Sunday Magazine*, Jan 22, 1933.

41. Alma Whitaker, "Lonesome Ones Unite," *LAT*, Nov 27, 1921.

42. Lucile Marsh, "A Survey of Social Dance in America," *The Journal of Health and Physical Education*, vol. 6, no. 1, Jan 1935, 34.

43. "'Strictly Personal' Announced," *LAT*, May 2, 1933.

44. "Another Death on the Streets," *L.A. Taco* blog, Dec 31, 2018. https://www.lataco.com/another-death-on-the-streets-more-than-1200-homeless-people-died-in-los-angeles-in-2018/.

45. "Woman Found Dead," *Whittier Daily News*, Feb 27, 2018. https://www.whittierdailynews.com/2018/03/27/woman-found-dead-in-santa-fe-spring-parking-lot-may-have-been-hit-by-big-rig-coroner-says/.

46. "Man Asleep in Parked Car," CBS Los Angeles, Dec 9, 2018. https://losangeles.cbslocal.com/2018/12/09/pacoima-hit-and-run-fatal/.

47. "Homeless Woman Found Dead," *The Eastsider*, Dec 24, 2018. https://www.theeastsiderla.com/news/news_notes/homeless-woman-found-dead-in-angelino-heights-th-grader-s/article_93d034f8-a29a-54ac-af34-b718f7e8627a.html.

48. "Suspect in Baseball Bat Killings," *LAT*, Sep 25, 2018. https://www.latimes.com/local/lanow/la-me-ln-ramon-escobar-homeless-killings-20180925-story.html.

49. "Homeless Man Burned to Death," *LAT*, Aug 25, 2019. https://www.latimes.com/california/story/2019-08-27/homeless-man-burned-to-death-in-skid-row-area.

50. "Police Seek Public's Help," *LAT*, Dec 19, 2018. https://www.latimes.com/local/lanow/la-me-ln-lapd-stabbing-downtown-perez-20181219-story.html.

51. "Man Found Lying on Mission Hill Street," NBC Los Angeles, Jul 23, 2019. https://www.nbclosangeles.com/news/local/Mission-Hills-Mysterious-Death-man-found-dead-street-513101321.html.

52. "The Homeless are Dying in Record Numbers." *Kaiser Health News*, Apr 24, 2019. https://khn.org/news/the-homeless-are-dying-in-record-numbers-on-the-streets-of-l-a/.

53. "Greater Los Angeles Homeless Count." Los Angeles Homeless Services Authority, Jun 4, 2019. https://www.lahsa.org/news?article=557-2019-greater-los-angeles-homeless-count-results. Updated as of Jun 15, 2020.

54. Elijah Chiland, "2019 homeless count, by the numbers," *CLA*, Jun 4, 2019. https://la.curbed.com/2019/6/4/18652755/2019-homeless-count-los-angeles-numbers.

55. Bianca Baragan, "If rents rise 5%," *CLA*, Mar 8, 2017. https://la.curbed.com/2017/8/3/16089812/homeless-affordable-housing-rent-increase-la/comment/438750905.

56. Jenna Chandler, "New report underscores link between 'shocking' number of evictions, homelessness," *CLA*, Jun 10, 2019. https://la.curbed.com/2019/6/10/18659841/evictions-homelessness-rent-burden-los-angeles.

57. As of June 2019.

58. Elijah Chiland, "L.A. rents aren't budging in 2019," *CLA*, Feb 4, 2019. https://la.curbed.com/2019/2/4/18210857/los-angeles-rental-prices-2019-average.

59. "Los Angeles, California," *DataUSA*. https://datausa.io/profile/geo/los-angeles-ca/

60. "L.A. City Homeless Population Up 16 Percent." *City News Service*, Jun 4, 2019. https://www.kcet.org/shows/socal-connected/la-city-homeless-population-up-16-percent-garcetti-calls-it-heartbreaking.

61. Gail Holland, "Why L.A. County's homelessness crisis has been decades in the making," *LAT*, Jun 5, 2019. https://www.latimes.com/local/california/la-me-ln-homeless-housing-crisis-count-history-skid-row-20190605-story.html.

62. Doug Smith, "L.A. says it got 21,631 homeless people into housing," *LAT*, Jul 21, 2019. https://www.latimes.com/california/story/2019-07-20/homeless-permanent-housing-shelter-point-in-time-count.

63. "Why L.A. County's homelessness crisis," *LAT,* Jun 5, 2019. https://www.latimes.com/local/california/la-me-ln-homeless-housing-crisis-count-history-skid-row-20190605-story.html.

64. Elijah Chiland, "Report: LA needs 516,946 affordable homes," *CLA*, May 21, 2019, https://la.curbed.com/2019/5/21/18634232/los-angeles-affordable-housing-shortage-how-much-need.

65. Bianca Baragan, "Downtown's low-income Barclay Hotel," *CLA*, Jul 30, 2019, https://la.curbed.com/2019/7/30/20734560/downtown-barclay-hotel-boutique-renovation-relevant-group.

66. Rachel Monroe, "Meet the Residents of the Contested Territory of Boyle Heights." *California Sunday Magazine*, Nov 19, 2018, https://story.californiasunday.com/boyle-heights.

67. "Recent Trends in Mortality Rates," Center for Health Impact Evaluation, County of Los Angeles Public Health, Oct 2019, http://publichealth.lacounty.gov/chie/reports/HomelessMortality_CHIEBrief_Final.pdf.

PART 3

1. Eleanor Antin, "Reading Ruscha." *Art in America*, Nov–Dec 1973, 71.

2. "Traffic Safety Facts: Pedestrians," National Highway Traffic Safety Administration, Mar 2019. https://crashstats.nhtsa.dot.gov/Api/Public/ViewPublication/812681.

3. Louis Sahagun. "Drought Triggers Southern California Tumbleweed Infestation." *LAT*, Sep 24, 2014.

PART 4

1. Steven Harmon, "Gov. Jerry Brown has business people rolling in laughter," *The Mercury News*, May 22, 2013. https://www.mercurynews.com/2013/05/22/gov-jerry-brown-has-business-people-rolling-in-laughter/.

2. Robert Dawson and Gray Brechin, *Farewell, Promised Land: Waking from the California Dream*, xiv.

3. Frank Norris, *The Octopus: A Story of California*, 14.

4. Dawson and Brechin, xiv.

5. "The Storm. The Situation of Yesterday Fully Set Forth," *LAT*, Feb 18, 1887, 1.

6. City council's bridge committee, 2000 foot length: "Big Bridge Accepted," *LAT*, Jan 13, 1905. Bridge advocates, of necessity greatly inconvenienced: "More Interest in Los Angeles Real Estate." *LAH*, Nov 24, 1901. Not enough to repair, it winds around like a snake: "Calls It a Steal: Kern Fights for Fourth Street Bridge," *LAH*, Jul 19, 1903. Sale of land benefits Workman: "Bridge Street Tract Sold," *LAH*, Sep 20, 1903. Construction details: "Plans for Fourth Street Bridge." *LAH*, Oct 8, 1903. City council politics: "To Submit Plans for New Bridges," *LAH*, Jan 3,1904.

7. "City's Garbage Turned into the Pork We Eat," *LAT*, Jun 24, 1906.

8. Louis L. Huot, "Modern Lines Are Reflected in New Los Angeles Viaduct." *Architect and Engineer*, Oct 1933.

9. Stephen D. Mikesell, "The Los Angeles River Bridges: A Study in the Bridge as a Civic Monument," *Southern California Quarterly*, 68 no. 4 (Winter 1986), 365-386.

10. "Art Commission to Beautify City," *LAT*, Oct 31, 1903.

11. Charles Mulford Robinson "The City Beautiful: Suggestions," *Los Angeles, California*, Los Angeles Municipal Art Commission, 1909, 3.

12. City of Los Angeles Engineering Department, "Annual Report." City of Los Angeles, 1923, 30.

13. Robinson, 3.

14. Merrill Butler, "Architecture and Engineering Are Harmonized in Fourth St. Viaduct," *Southwest Builder and Contractor*, Aug 7, 1931, 50.

15. "Fourth Street Span Dedicated." *LAT*, Jul 31, 1931.

16. Home Owners Loan Corporation City Survey Files, "Area D-53, Los Angeles;" quoted by George Lipsitz in *Time Passages: Collective Memory and American Popular Culture*, 137.

17. Al Parmenter, "Change in Motor Law Goes in Effect Friday," *LAT*, Aug 9, 1931, 1.

18. Laurence M. Benedict, "No Review on Fares," *LAT*, Jan 7, 1930, 1.

19. George J. Sánchez, "What's Good for Boyle Heights Is Good for the Jews: Creating Multiracialism on the Eastside during the 1950s," *American Quarterly*, 56 no. 3, (Sep 2004), 634.

20. National Park Service, Historic American Engineering Record. *Fourth Street Viaduct, HAER No. CA-280*, (National Archives, Washington D.C., nd), 7.

21. Gaston Bachelard; translated by Maria Jolas, *The Poetics of Space*, 6.

22. Jérôme Monnet,"The Everyday Imagery of Space in Los Angeles," *Looking for Los Angeles: Architecture, Film, Photography, and the Urban Landscape*, edited by Charles Salas, et al., 304.

23. John Humble. "Shooting Los Angeles." *LAist* interview, Mar 23, 2007. http://www.laist.com/2007/03/23/shooting_los_angeles.php.

24. Louis Sahagun, "John Muir's legacy questioned as centennial of his death nears," *LAT*, Nov 13, 2014.

25. Adam Frank, "When Nature Speaks, Who Are You Hearing?" NPR, Apr 15, 2014. https://www.npr.org/sections/13.7/2014/04/15/302198431/when-nature-speaks-who-are-you-hearing.

26. Jared Farmer, *Trees in Paradise: A California History*, xxiii.

27. Farmer, xxiv.

AFTERWORD

1. Edward S. Casey. "Between Geography and Philosophy: What Does It Mean to Be in the Place-World?" *Annals of the Association of American Geographers*, vol. 91, no. 4, Dec 2001, 684.

BIBLIOGRAPHY

Abrahamson, Eric John. *Building Home: Howard F. Ahmanson and the Politics of the American Dream*. Berkeley: University of California Press, 2013.

Adamson, Paul, and Marty Arbunich. *Eichler: Modernism Rebuilds the American Dream*. Santa Barbara: Gibbs Smith, 2002.

Avila, Eric. "Essaying Los Angeles." Essay. In *The Cambridge Companion to the Literature of Los Angeles*, edited by Kevin R. McNamara. Cambridge: Cambridge University Press, 2010.

———. *Popular Culture in the Age of White Flight: Fear and Fantasy in Suburban Los Angeles*. Berkeley: University of California Press, 2006.

Bachelard, Gaston. *The Poetics of Space*. Boston: Beacon Press, 1969.

Banham, Reyner, and Joe Day. *Los Angeles: The Architecture of Four Ecologies*. Berkeley: University of California Press, 2009.

Barraclough, Laura R. *Making the San Fernando Valley: Rural Landscapes, Urban Development, and White Privilege*. Athens: University of Georgia Press, 2010.

Bartlett, Lanier, and Virginia Stivers Bartlett. *Los Angeles in 7 Days, Including Southern California*. New York: R.M. McBride, 1932.

Bottles, Scott L. *Los Angeles and the Automobile: The Making of the Modern City*. Berkeley: University of California Press, 1987.

Braudy, Leo. *The Hollywood Sign: Fantasy and Reality of an American Icon*. New Haven, Connecticut: Yale University Press, 2011.

Brodsly, David. *L.A. Freeway: An Appreciative Essay*. Berkeley: University of California Press, 1981.

Bryant, Edwin. *What I Saw in California*. New York: Appleton, 1849.

Campbell, Neil. "Affective Critical Regionalism in D.J. Waldie's Suburban West." *Beyond the Myth: New Perspectives in Western Texts* 48, no. 3 (2011): 87–106.

Certeau, Michel de, Luce Giard, and Pierre Mayol. *The Practice of Everyday Life: Volume 2: Living and Cooking*. Translated by Timothy Tomasik. Minneapolis: University of Minnesota Press, 1998.

Coleman, Wanda. *Native in a Strange Land: Trials and Tremors*. Santa Rosa, California: Black Sparrow Press, 1996.

Dana, Richard Henry. *Two Years Before the Mast*. Boston: Houghton Mifflin, 1911.

Davis, Mike. *City of Quartz: Excavating the Future in Los Angeles*. London: Verso, 1990.

———. *Ecology of Fear: Los Angeles and the Imagination of Disaster*. New York: Vintage Books, 1999.

Dawson, Robert, and Gray A. Brechin. *Farewell, Promised Land: Waking from the California Dream*. Berkeley: University of California Press, 1999.

DeLong, James. *Southern California, A Book for the Million, Treating the Climate, Soils, Productions, General Resources, and Development of Semi-Tropical Southern California*. Lawrence, Kansas: Journal Company Steam Printing Establishment, 1877.

DeLyser, Dydia. *Ramona Memories: Tourism and the Shaping of Southern California*. Minneapolis: University of Minnesota Press, 2005.

Deverell, William, and Greg Hise, eds. *Land of Sunshine: An Environmental History of Metropolitan Los Angeles*. Pittsburgh: University of Pittsburgh Press, 2005.

Deverell, William. *Whitewashed Adobe: The Rise of Los Angeles and the Remaking of Its Mexican Past*. Berkeley: University of California Press, 2004.

Didion, Joan. "Where I Was From." Essay. In *We Tell Ourselves Stories in Order to Live: Collected Nonfiction*. New York: Knopf, 2006.

———. "On Morality." Essay. In *Slouching Towards Bethlehem*. New York: Farrar, Straus and Giroux, 1968.

Dumke, Glenn S. *The Boom of the Eighties in Southern California*. San Marino, California: Huntington Library, 1991.

Farmer, Jared. *Trees in Paradise: A California History*. New York: W.W. Norton & Company, 2013.

Farnsworth, R.W.C. *Southern California Paradise*. Oakland: Pacific Press, 1883.

Faulkner, William. *Uncle Willy and Other Stories*. London: Chatto & Windus, 1967.

Fogelson, Robert M. *The Fragmented Metropolis: Los Angeles 1850–1930*. Berkeley: University of California Press, 1993.

Foner, Philip S. "The AFL in the Progressive Era, 1910–1915." *History of the Labor Movement in the United States, Vol. 5*. New York: International Publishers, 1980.

Foster, John M. "Second Addendum Report: Archaeological and Historic Investigations at Campo De Cahuenga CA-LAN-1945H." Los Angeles: Los Angeles County Metropolitan Transportation Authority, 2000.

Frémont John Charles. *Memoirs of My Life*. Chicago: Belford, Clark and Co., 1887.

Fulton, William B. *The Reluctant Metropolis: The Politics of Urban Growth in Los Angeles*. Point Arena, California: Solano Press Books, 1997.

Gebhard, David, Robert Winter, and Robert Inman. *An Architectural Guidebook to Los Angeles: Fully Revised 6th Edition*. Santa Monica, California: Angel City Press, 2018.

Gold, Jonathan. *Counter Intelligence: Where to Eat in the Real Los Angeles*. Los Angeles: LA Weekly Books, 2000.

Greenstein, Paul, Nigey Lennon, and Lionel Rolfe. *Bread and Hyacinths: The Rise and Fall of Utopian Los Angeles*. Los Angeles: Classic Books, 1992.

Guzmán, Romeo, Carribean Fragoza, Alex Sayf Cummings, and Ryan Reft. *East of East: The Making of Greater El Monte*. New Brunswick, New Jersey: Rutgers University Press, 2020.

Hise, Greg, and William Deverell. *Eden by Design: the 1930 Olmsted-Bartholomew Plan for the Los Angeles Region*. Berkeley: University of California Press, 2000.

Hise, Greg. *Magnetic Los Angeles: Planning the Twentieth-Century Metropolis*. Baltimore: Johns Hopkins University Press, 1997.

An Illustrated History of Los Angeles County, California. Chicago: The Lewis Publishing Company, 1889.

Jackson, Helen Hunt. *Echoes in the City of the Angels*. Boston: Little, Brown, 1907.

———. *Glimpses of California and the Missions*. Boston: Little, Brown, 1907.

James, George Wharton. *Through Ramona's Country*. Chicago: Little, Brown, 1909.

Kress, George, and Walter Lindley. *A History of the Medical Profession of Southern California*. Los Angeles: Times-Mirror Printing House, 1910.

Kropp, Phoebe Schroeder. *California Vieja: Culture and Memory in a Modern American Place*. Berkeley: University of California Press, 2006.

Lipsitz, George. *Time Passages: Collective Memory and American Popular Culture*. Minneapolis: University of Minnesota Press, 1990.

Logan, Elizabeth A. "Urbane Bouquets: A Floricultural History of California, 1848 to 1915." Thesis, University of Southern California, 2013.

Lopez-Calvo, Ignacio, and Victor Valle, eds. *Latinx Writing Los Angeles: Nonfiction Dispatches from a Decolonial Rebellion*. Lincoln: University of Nebraska Press, 2018.

Los Angeles: A Guide to the City and Its Environs. New York: Hastings House Publishers, 1941.

Maltzan, Michael. *No More Play: Conversations on Urban Speculation in Los Angeles and Beyond*. Edited by Jessica Varner. Berlin: Hatje Cantz Verlag, 2011.

Massey, Doreen. *Place and Gender*. Minneapolis: University of Minnesota Press, 1994.

Matt, Susan J. *Homesickness: An American History*. Oxford: Oxford University Press, 2011.

McClung, William Alexander. *Landscapes of Desire: Anglo Mythologies of Los Angeles*. Berkeley: University of California Press, 2000.

McNamara, Kevin R., ed. *The Cambridge Companion to the Literature of Los Angeles*. Cambridge: Cambridge University Press, 2010.

McWilliams, Carey. *Southern California: An Island on the Land*. Santa Barbara: Gibbs Smith, 1973.

Monnet, Jérôme. "The Everyday Imagery of Space in Los Angeles." Essay. In *Looking for Los Angeles: Architecture, Film, Photography, and the Urban Landscape*, edited by Charles Salas. Los Angeles: Getty Research Institute, 2001.

Musicant, Marlyn, ed. *Los Angeles Union Station*. Los Angeles: Getty Research Institute, 2014.

Nicolaides, Becky Marianne. *My Blue Heaven: Life and Politics in the Working-Class Suburbs of Los Angeles, 1920-1965*. Chicago: The University of Chicago Press, 2002.

Nordhoff, Charles. *California for Health, Pleasure, and Residence*. New York: Harper & Brothers, 1873.

Norris, Frank. *The Octopus: A Story of California*. Garden City, New Jersey: Doubleday, 1901.

Pallasmaa, Juhani. *The Eyes of the Skin: Architecture and the Senses*. Chichester, New Jersey: Wiley, 2012.

Pearson, Chelsea Leah. "'Call Me a Californio': Translating Hemispheric Legacies in Helen Hunt Jackson, Don Antonio Coronel, and José Martí." Thesis, University of California, Santa Cruz, 2013.

Pitt, Leonard, and Dale Pitt. *Los Angeles A to Z: An Encyclopedia of City and County*. Berkeley: University of California Press, 1997.

Requa, Richard. *Architectural Details; Spain and the Mediterranean*. Los Angeles: The Monolith Portland Cement Company, 1926.

Robinson, Charles Mulford. "The City Beautiful: Suggestions." Essay. In *Report of the Municipal Art Commission for the City of Los Angeles, California*. Los Angeles: W.J. Porter, 1909.

Romo, Ricardo. *East Los Angeles: History of a Barrio*. Austin: University of Texas Press, 1983.

Río, David. *Beyond the Myth: New Perspectives on Western Texts*. Vitoria-Gasteiz, Spain: Portal Education, 2011.

Sanchez, George. *Becoming Mexican American: Ethnicity, Culture, and Identity in Chicano Los Angeles, 1900–1945*. Oxford: Oxford University Press, 1993.

Sitton, Tom, and William Deverell, eds. *Metropolis in the Making: Los Angeles in the 1920s*. Berkeley: University of California Press, 2001.

Starr, Kevin. *Coast of Dreams: California on the Edge*. New York: Random House, 2006.

Stewart, Kathleen. "Cultural Poesis: The Generativity of Emergent Things." Essay. In *The SAGE Handbook of Qualitative Research*. London: Sage Publications, 2005.

———. *Ordinary Affects*. Durham, North Carolina: Duke University Press, 2007.

Truman, Benjamin Cummings. *Semi-Tropical California: Its Climate, Healthfulness, Productiveness, and Scenery*. San Francisco: Bancroft & Company, 1874.

Ulin, David L. *Sidewalking: Coming to Terms with Los Angeles*. Berkeley: University of California Press, 2015.

———. *Writing Los Angeles: A Literary Anthology*. New York: Library of America, 2002.

Valle, Victor. *City of Industry: Genealogies of Power in Southern California*. New Brunswick, New Jersey: Rutgers University Press, 2009.

Wakida, Patricia, ed. *LAtitudes: An Angeleno's Atlas*. Berkeley: Heyday, 2015.

Warner, Charles Dudley. *Our Italy*. New York: Harper Brothers, 1902.

Watts, Jennifer A., ed. *Maynard L. Parker: Modern Photography and the American Dream*. New Haven, Connecticut: Yale University Press, 2012.

Weil, Simone. *Simone Weil: An Anthology*. Edited by Miles Siân. New York: Grove Press, 2000.

Weschler, Lawrence. Essay. In *Hand Eye Heart: Watercolors of the East Yorkshire Landscape, Feb 26–Apr 2, 2005*. Venice, California: L.A. Louver Gallery, 2005.

West, Nathanael. *The Day of the Locust*. London: Penguin Books, 2006.

Westwick, Peter J., ed. *Blue Sky Metropolis: The Aerospace Century in Southern California*. San Marino and Berkeley: Huntington Library and University of California Press, 2012.

Wilson, Karen S. *Jews in the Los Angeles Mosaic*. Berkeley: University of California Press, 2013.

Wit, Wim de, and Christopher James Alexander. *Overdrive: L.A. Constructs the Future, 1940–1990*. Los Angeles: Getty Research Institute, 2013.

ACKNOWLEDGMENTS

The patience, forbearance, and optimism of Paddy Calistro and Scott McAuley, publishers and co-founders of Angel City Press, made the publication of this collection possible. That they were willing to let me gather my footloose thoughts is another triumph of hope over experience. I am utterly in their debt. Executive Editor Terri Accomazzo and Marketing Director Jim Schneeweis have also earned my regard, as has graphic designer Amy Inouye who again has given my words a stylish presence.

Becoming Los Angeles began with an invitation in the fall of 2008 to write for KCET's website. In the ten years and hundreds of postings that followed, I was the beneficiary of generous support from Juan Devis, Zach Behrens, Daniel Medina, Carribean Fragoza, and many other KCET staff members. My editor most recently was Nathan Masters, producer of the KCET's *Lost LA* series. I'm grateful that KCETLink allowed me to observe Los Angeles in so many dimensions.

That the history of Los Angeles deserved close attention I learned from the life and work of the late Kevin Starr, who instigated some of these pieces. Professors William Deverell and Karin Huebner, both of USC, provided several occasions for speaking to their students about my suburban life. Those encounters challenged me to make the stories in this collection meaningful to another generation of Angelenos. Peter Westwick, editor of the anthology *Blue Sky Metropolis*, allowed me to reflect on the aerospace culture of my postwar suburb.

Some of those reflections began in 1995 with the book reviews and commentaries I wrote for the *Los Angeles Times*. I was invited there by Steve Wasserman, then the editor of the Book Review and now publisher and executive director of Heyday. Tom Curwen was Steve's deputy editor at the *Times*, a friend with whom I've discussed much of what this book attempts to do. Some of it was shaped by writing for Nicholas Goldberg, editor of the *Los Angeles Times* editorial pages, and for Susan Brenneman, deputy editor, and Sue Horton, Op-Ed and Sunday Opinion editor. Some of it came from conversations with Patt Morrison, *Times* columnist and Los Angeles aficionado; with Christopher Hawthorne, formerly the paper's architectural critic; and with Carolina Miranda, arts and culture writer. Professor Amy Wilentz of UC Irvine was another kind listener, as was Professor Susan Straight of UC Riverside.

My understanding of a critical sense of place began with conversations with Professor Neil Campbell of the University of Derby, Professor Martin Dines of Kingston University, London, and Jason Sexton, former editor of *Boom* magazine.

Research for these essays took me to the online archives of the *Los Angeles Times* and the files of the city's nineteenth-century newspapers. That era's booster tales, immigrant guides, and local histories came from the Internet Archive and the HathiTrust websites. The USC Digital Library offered dissertations on regional history.

Invitations to collaborate with the Huntington Library (through Jennifer Watts, former curator of Photography and Visual Culture), the Huntington-USC Institute on California and the West, the Los Angeles County Museum of Art, and the Getty Museum also helped deepen my understanding of the past and future city. Jane Pisano, past president of the Natural History Museum of Los Angeles County, welcomed me to visit the exhibition Becoming Los Angeles, which I saw in its early stages. Further encounters with the exhibition and discussions at the museum with William Estrada, cultural historian of nineteenth-century Los Angeles, helped focus this book's themes. The museum's similarly titled exhibition suggested the title of this book.

Diane Keaton, a smart connoisseur of architecture (as well as a memoirist), drew me into the romance and modernity of the Spanish Colonial Revival Style in writing the text for her photobook *California Romantica* (2006). That encounter colors several of the pieces here, as do the chapters and the introductions I've written for other books about Los Angeles. That I don't list all their editors and authors is not for lack of gratitude for the attention they gave my ideas.

A non-driving Angeleno can't range over a sprawling region without good friends with a car. Through the kindness of Randy Burger, Mary Alice and Liam McLoughlin, and Michael Ward, I have been a tourist and cultural anthropologist, a gawker and investigator, a lover and critic of the Los Angeles we share. For their many miles, many thanks.

ABOUT THE AUTHOR

Called a writer whose work is a "gorgeous distillation of architectural and so-cial history" by the *New York Times*, whose essays and memoirs, said the *Los Angeles Times*, "conjure the idiosyncratic splendor of Southern California life," D.J. Waldie is the author of the acclaimed *Holy Land: A Suburban Memoir* and other books that illuminate the ordinary and the everyday in lyrical prose, including *Where We Are Now* and *Real City*, from Angel City Press. In col-laboration with Diane Keaton, Waldie provided the text for two photographic explorations of home: *California Romantica*, dealing with homes in the Span-ish Colonial Revival Style of the early twentieth century, and *House*, examining post-modern interpretations of domesticity. *California Romantica* became a *Los Angeles Times* nonfiction bestseller in 2007. D.J. Waldie's narratives about suburban life have appeared in *BUZZ*, *The Kenyon Review*, *The Massachusetts Review*, *The Georgetown Review*, *Salon*, *dwell*, *Los Angeles Magazine*, *Spiritus*, *Gulf Coast*, *Urbanisme*, *Bauwelt*, and other publications. His book reviews and commentary have appeared in the *Los Angeles Times*, the *Wall Street Journal*, and the *New York Times*. He lives in the home where he was born in Lakewood, California, where he eventually became its deputy city manager.

Becoming Los Angeles: Myth, Memory, and a Sense of Place
By D.J. Waldie

Design by Amy Inouye, Future Studio

10 9 8 7 6 5 4 3 2 1

ISBN-13 978-1-62640-079-5 (print edition)
ISBN-13 978-1-62640-080-1 (e-pub edition)

The majority of the pieces in the present collection first appeared in a considerably different form on the KCET website between 2008 and 2018. They appear here courtesy of KCETLink. Grateful acknowledgment for their permission also is made to the publications where other portions of *Becoming Los Angeles* first appeared: "The Greatest Gift" and "La Virgen," *Los Angeles Times*; "Shelter. Fallout," (originally "The Cold War Lives on Inside Us All") *Salon*; "Who Are We?," *LMU* magazine; "Robert Winter: Revivalist," *Alta: The Journal of Alta California*; "Time and Again at Union Station" in *Union Station: 75 Years in the Heart of LA*; "The Death of Riley" (originally "Lost in Aerospace") in *Blue Sky Metropolis*; "A Traveler Comes to a Bridge," text for the art exhibition *Positively 4th Street*; and "Everything Visible" (originally "À propos du photographe John Humble—Tout visible"), *Urbanisme* no. 361.

The cover of *Becoming Los Angeles* was photographed by Ludwig Favre, who specializes in capturing the essence of major cities and landscapes of America; he is based in Paris.

Library of Congress Cataloging-in-Publication Data is available.

 Published by Angel City Press
www.angelcitypress.com

Printed in Canada